The Minotaur: A Kubrick Odyssey

by

S. William Snider

Mysterion
West Virginia

The Minotaur: A Kubrick Odyssey

Cover Art and Design by: Elma Maria

Edited by: Brennan Utley

Mysterion

West Virginia

recluseofbabylonia@hotmail.com

https://www.patreon.com/thefarmpodcastII

For "Annie," Ed & AW --Always

For The Lark, "Drag," Big T & all the storage box kids who were there at the beginning

For Chris Knowles and Hank Albarelli for believing in me

For Jasun Horsley and all his inspirations and challenges

And for Stanley Kubrick and the dreams he seeded

Contents

Introduction:

Where Did the Money Come From?

Stanley Kubrick is my all time favorite director by a pretty wide margin. I've relentlessly studied his films since I was a teenager. When I began my journey into conspirology, he was an obvious subject. Even the most superficial viewer leaves a Kubrick film sensing there's more than meets the eye.

For my part, I consider the revelations I experienced upon rewatching *Dr. Strangelove: Or How I Learned to Stop Worrying and Love the Bomb* in the 2010s, after intensive study of the John F. Kennedy (JFK) assassination, a pivotal point in my development as both a parapolitical researcher and general human being. What I mean by that is *Dr. Strangelove* is far closer to a documentary than few dare imagine. Several of the most outrageous lines uttered in the film's War Room are uncomfortably close to arguments the Joint Chiefs of Staff made in favor of a preemptive nuclear strike on the Soviets to JFK.

On the one hand, I felt beside myself at picking up on a thread all but ignored by incalculable "Cryptokubrologists" applying a conspiratorial reading to his work. On the other hand, words are scarcely adequate to express the horror I felt at realizing this "nightmare comedy" was one of the most accurate depictions of the national security state ever captured on celluloid. And as an added bonus, it provided me with a proverbial Rosetta Stone into Kubrick's murky relationship with such circles.

But truth be told, the moon landing allegations never interested me. It's not that I'm opposed to throwing shade on a personal hero of mine. And indeed, we're going to explore plenty of skeletons in Mr. Kubrick's closet throughout this work.

But I've always been bothered by the moon landing narrative. And this goes beyond the uncomfortable fact that it started as a prank in the Usenet during the mid-1990s before taking on a life of its own during the following decade in conspiracy circles.[1] This narrative

---

[1] Supposedly the earliest reference to Kubrick filming the Apollo footage appeared in a Usenet group called "alt.humor.best-of-usenet," but I was unable to locate the original. The earliest reference I can find to Kubrick and the Apollo landing on Usenet traces to 1996: Anon. (1995). Another Masterpiece By Stanley Kubrick. alt.humor.best-of-usenet. https://06428646409318951020.googlegroups.com/attach/ec42c5ee2017d9ef/WHO?part=2&view=1&vt=ANaJVrHFI7kHjPT9YnvZrfH0OZ7XHD0twoEU6lhTAQIOr1CLPPmYK8XMOCqzX1RYexYLT0JPtvVvPmzIdrU1fuSN5AwV5l5W7YWF8eVZ6QZG5aHGAhvV-HM. These claims were later repeated almost verbatim by early advocates like Clyde Lewis during the following decade. See Lewis, C. (2007). Good luck, mr. Gorsky!. Ground Zero. https://web.archive.org/web/20190911042654/http://archives.groundzeromedia.org/dis/gorsky/gorsky.html. The first mainstream rumblings of Kubrick's involvement appeared in the 2002 French mockumentary *The Dark Side of the Moon*. See Jasun Horsley, *Kubrickon* (London: Aeon Books, 2023), 105. Another early proponent of Kubrick's role in faking the Apollo footage is American conspiracy filmmaker Bart Winfield Sibrel. Emilio D'Alessandro, Kubrick's longtime driver and assistant, recounts how Sibrel sent Kubrick a cardboard kaleidoscope for his sixty-fourth birthday. This spurred the director to look more deeply into Sibrel, where upon he realized his admirer had made several documentaries fingering Kubrick for the moon landing hoax. See Emilio D'Alessandro with Filippo Ulivieri, *Stanley and Me: Thirty Years at His Side* (New York: Arcade Publishing, 2020), 234-235. It's a good story, but impossible. Sibrel's first Apollo documentary, *A Funny Thing Happened on the Way to*

was a rebranding of earlier NASA conspiracy theories linking Kubrick to the Apollo mission. These tropes were first popularized during the 1970s by former Navy man and Rockwell employee Bill Kaysing and radio host Mae Brussell. Kaysing wrote the first full length book, *We Never Went to the Moon: America's Thirty Billion Dollar Swindle* (1976), to deal with the subject. Here, he claims that *2001: A Space Odyssey* was used as cover to develop the special effects necessary for the fake moon landing.[2] The bulk of the evidence presented in this opus consists of listing all of the organizations Kubrick consulted with for the film.

The list is certainly impressive, featuring several branches of NASA and the Air Force and many others totaling four full pages. But this was par the course for Kubrick. The research he did for projects was staggering, and contributed to the increasing lag time between films as the years rolled on. And he always consulted with individuals and institutions concerned with subject matter appearing in his films. This shall be explored further throughout this work.

It's important to note Kaysing does not accuse Kubrick of actually faking the moon landing. Rather, he implies Kubrick developed special effects later used at a secretive base in the Nevada desert for the footage that hoodwinked much of the planet. It took a few more years for Cryptokubrologists to place Kubrick in the director's chair.

Kaysing probably got the idea of the Nevada base from the James Bond film *Diamonds Are Forever* (1971), which he cites as evidence for his thesis.[3] In that picture, Bond (Sean Connery) gallops through a highly classified US base clearly modeled on Nevada's Area 51. As Bond makes his way through a series of incredible sets, he stumbles upon a soundstage made up like the surface of the moon. There, a sound crew is in the midst of filming a pair of performers dressed as astronauts doing a moonwalk. Bond commandeers a land rover after ruining the shot.

Where did the filmmakers get such a notion?

Kubrick, of course! *Diamonds* set designer Ken Adams had previously worked with Kubrick on *Strangelove*, and was the director's first choice for production design on *2001*. Adams passed, but later worked with Kubrick on *Barry Lyndon*. And Kubrick used cameras developed by NASA on *Lyndon*, completing the circle. Or so Cryptokubrologists reason.

While Area 51 did not become a pop culture staple until the late 1980s, it was known that the national security state did experiments in the California desert for some time. As the

---

the Moon, didn't drop until 2001. Kubrick famously died in 1999 while editing *Eyes Wide Shut*. Sibrel surely didn't wake up one day with the realization that Kubrick faked the moon landing, but developed the premise over time. And possibly, online. Kubrick was supposedly tech savvy to the end, and may have stumbled upon some of Sibrel's pre-documentary musings. But it's an interesting mistake for D'Alessandro to make as it adds credence to the moon landing allegations.

[2] William Kaysing, *We Never Went to the Moon: America's Thirty Billion Dollar Swindle* (Mount Pleasant, WV: New Saucerian Press, 2017),75-86, etc.

[3] William Kaysing, *We Never Went to the Moon: America's Thirty Billion Dollar Swindle*, 62.

Astronauts of Apollo 11 also did their training in the Nevada desert, the linkage was easy. The moon landing was met with suspicion in certain circles from the very beginning. I suspect the filmmakers behind *Diamonds* were having a bit of fun with this notion, but many of the same circles took them deadly seriously.[4]

Later, Kaysing tried to bolster his case on Mae Brussell's show via *2001*'s expanding budget. He argued that the film's budget nearly doubling during production was evidence the government was covertly funding Kubrick.[5] But going over budget was a staple of Kubrick's filmmaking process. Nor was *2001* the most dramatic instance of this. The budget of *Barry Lyndon* nearly quadrupled. While this was surely due to the NASA cameras, it must be said that the MGM CEO being sacked over *2001* and Kubrick's battle with the shareholders during postproduction makes Kaysing's allegations a little harder to square. We'll look at *2001*'s behind-the-scenes battles below. For now, it's important to emphasize Brussell's patronage of Kaysing. She first plugged his book in 1977.

The more I've looked at Kubrick's life, the more I'm inclined to stick with my intuition: that the moon landing claims constitutes a sleight of hand.

To be sure, they make for a compelling explanation of Kubrick's career. Only a handful of directors, namely George Lucas, Steven Spielberg and James Cameron, have enjoyed the kind of power that Kubrick wielded over the course of most of his career. He had the ability to make films totally outside Hollywood. Kubrick owned his own cameras and other crucial equipment; the costumes and props, fleets of vehicles, and nearly acquired his own soundstage at one point.

Only Lucas, Spielberg and Cameron have enjoyed this kind of independence.[6] But while *Spartacus*, *Dr. Strangelove*, *A Clockwork Orange* and *The Shining* were all hits, only *2001* was an epic moneymaker. Adjusted for inflation, it's still one of the most successful movies ever made. But Kubrick's canon never generated anywhere near the profits of the *Star Wars*, *Indiana Jones*, or *Avatar* franchises, or stand alone films like *E.T.*

Kubrick never had to justify his independence via the box office in a way his peers did. As Hollywood is not an industry known for indulging artist aspiration, this has fueled speculation as to how Kubrick managed such independence. In this context, the moon landing hoax is a

---

[4] *Diamonds Are Forever* enjoys a special place among conspiracy theories. The so-called Gemstone File, which fingers shipping magnate Aristotle Onassis for the assassination of JFK and the kidnapping of Howard Hughes along with a role in the "secret space program," relies heavily on *Diamonds.* See Kenn Thomas & David Hatcher Childress, *Inside the Gemstone File: Howard Hughes, Onassis & JFK* (Kempton, IL: Adventures Unlimited Press, 1999), 69-87, etc.

[5] Interview with Bill Kaysing, World Watchers International, KLRB, January 18, 1981, https://www.youtube.com/watch?v=zUi0krwMKCs (accessed March 22, 2024).

[6] Kubrick also did much to encourage Spielberg and Lucas, longtime frenemies, to embrace his methods. See Emilio D'Alessandro with Filippo Ulivieri, *Stanley and Me: Thirty Years at His Side*, 226-227.

comfortable explanation: Kubrick faked it and they had to let him make any movie he wanted for the rest of his career.

Except that he wasn't always able to make the movies he wanted.

Even a precursory glance at Kubrick's career cast doubt on this perception. He literally invested years in a project centered around Napoleon's life, but was never able to get it out of pre-production.[7] Kubrick later planned a Holocaust epic during the '90s that he was forced to abandon after Spielberg dropped *Schindler's List*.[8]

On closer inspection, Kubrick's total independence becomes even more dubious of a proposition. Consider his greatest box office triumph, *2001: A Space Odyssey*. In popular imagination, this is the first film that he had total control over, without either a producer like James B. Harris or an A-list star like Peter Sellers to challenge his authority. MGM head Robert O'Brien gave Kubrick an almost blank check to make *2001*, but not totally blank. Kubrick's *2001* contract stipulated that the "then-president" of MGM would have the right to request changes to the film. But if Kubrick disagreed, his version would be screened against the studio's preference to test audiences. Their reaction would be the deciding factor. MGM also retained a say over choice of actors, but with an annex of casting suggestions from Kubrick the studio had approved.[9]

O'Brien's decision proved to be highly controversial within the studio. The reason being is that the cost of the film, a then-staggering $11 million, put the long term existence of the studio at risk. This was not the budget O'Brien agreed to originally in 1965, which was $4 million. But even that was a hefty amount. This initial investment, combined with the ongoing delays and mounting budget, created a perfect storm in which the company's long term viability was dependent on the film becoming a major commercial success.[10]

---

[7] Kubrick's attempted Napoleon biopic is the stuff of legend. Probably the most precise account can be found in James Fenwick, *Stanley Kubrick Produces* (New Brunswick, NJ: Rutgers University Press, 2021), 157-161. A more in depth account can be found in Gene D. Phillips, "The Epic That Never Was: Stanley Kubrick's 'Napoleon,' " in *The Stanley Kubrick Archives*, ed. Alison Castle (Cologne: Taschen, 2008), 634-651; and Vincent LoBrutto, *Stanley Kubrick: A Biography* (New York: Donald I Fine Books, 1997), 321-333. As recently as 2023, Steven Spielberg was attempting to finally realize Kubrick's *Napoleon* film as a miniseries on HBO. See White, P. (2023, February 22). Steven Spielberg "mounting a big production" for Stanley Kubrick's 'napoleon'; project is set as seven-part limited series for HBO. Deadline. https://deadline.com/2023/02/steven-spielberg-stanley-kubricks-napoleon-7-part-series-hbo-1235266372/. Previously, Spielberg brought another long gestating Kubrick project, *A.I. Artificial Intelligence*, to fruition after Kubrick failed to do so in his lifetime. 2023 also witnessed the triumph of Ridley Scott's own *Napoleon* epic, which bears some similarities to what Kubrick had planned.

[8] For more in Kubrick's aborted *Aryan Papers* project, see James Fenwick, *Stanley Kubrick Produces*, 183-190; Jan Harlan, "From *Wartime Lies* to 'Aryan Papers' " in , *The Stanley Kubrick Archives* ed. Alison Castle, 664-667; and Vincent LoBrutto, *Stanley Kubrick: A Biography*, 498-499.

[9] Michael Benson, *Space Odyssey: Stanley Kubrick, Arthur C. Clarke, and the Making of a Masterpiece* (New York: Simon & Schuster Paperbacks, 2018), 89-90; James Fenwick, *Stanley Kubrick Produces*, 138. Fenwick notes that Kubrick attempted to hire Sterling Hayden, an actor he'd previously worked with on *The Killing* and *Dr. Strangelove*, for *2001* but MGM vetoed the move.

In 1965, Chicago real estate tycoon Paul Levin became a majority stakeholder in MGM. This led to a power struggle over MGM's leadership in the midst of *2001*'s production during the following year. By 1967, Levin was actively trying to oust O'Brien as MGM's CEO.[11] Kubrick took out a full page advertisement in *The New York Times*, *The Wall Street Journal*, and the trade publication *Variety* to support O'Brien. And he persuaded 63 other filmmakers (including director John Frankenheimer, whom you'll be reading much more about) to sign it. In 1968, shortly before *2001*'s release, Kubrick bought the equivalent of $1.5 million of MGM shares as a show of support for O'Brien and his film. Levin retaliated by sending the Securities and Exchange Committee after Kubrick over insider trading. Nothing came of it, but it hindered Kubrick's efforts to support O'Brien.[12]

It was all for naught. Despite *2001* box office triumph, O'Brien was ousted as the CEO in January 1969.[13] MGM promptly passed on Kubrick's white whale, his *Napoleon* biopic, leaving the director out in the wilderness. Despite *Spartacus*, *Lolita*, and *Dr. Strangelove* being among the most financially successful films of the decade and *2001* becoming a full-blown cultural phenomena. It was one of the five most successful MGM films then released by the early 1970s, along with *Gone With the Wind*, *Lawrence of Arabia*, *The Wizard of Oz*, and *Dr. Zhivago*. It was still in release circa 1972, nearly four years after it dropped. By that point, it grossed $27 million domestically, qualifying as the seventeenth most successful movie ever made at that time.[14] It was re-released five times during the decade. By 1974, it made nearly $40 million worldwide (over $250 million in 2024 dollars).[15]

In Cryptokubrology, it was either during the production of *2001* or the year following its 1968 release when the director is believed to have filmed the fake moon landing. If the former was the case, surely MGM, the public funding conduit, would have been in the loop. Yet the company's CEO was sacked as a result of the film while Kubrick fought a shareholders revolt resulting in a SEC filing against the director. Would such intrigues have been allowed to play out against a project that surely would have been veiled in the greatest levels of secrecy? And if Kubrick shot the footage afterwards, by which time *2001* was a box office success, would he have struggled to find funding throughout the rest of the 1960s?

Further, Kubrick's activities during the making of *2001* have been well documented by numerous researchers in the decades since the film's release. In *2001 Between Kubrick and Clarke: The Genesis, Making and Authorship of a Masterpiece*, Filippo Ulivieri painstakingly

---

[10] James Fenwick, *Stanley Kubrick Produces*, 151; John Baxter, *Stanley Kubrick* (New York: Carroll & Graf Publishers, Inc., 1997), 212; Vincent LoBrutto, *Stanley Kubrick: A Biography*, 269, 271.

[11] James Fenwick, *Stanley Kubrick Produces*, 157; Michael Benson, *Space Odyssey: Stanley Kubrick, Arthur C. Clarke, and the Making of a Masterpiece*, 390.

[12] James Fenwick, *Stanley Kubrick Produces*, 157.

[13] John Baxter, *Stanley Kubrick*, 239; James Fenwick, *Stanley Kubrick Produces*, 157.

[14] Filippo Ulivieri and Simone Odino, *2001 Between Kubrick and Clarke: The Genesis, Making and Authorship of a Masterpiece* (self-published, 2019), 122.

[15] Vincent LoBrutto, *Stanley Kubrick: A Biography*, 316-317.

chronicles Kubrick's activities throughout the 1964-1968 period, at times offering a day by day synopsis of what the director was doing.[16] It probably goes without saying, but no such gap appears in Kubrick's life during this time in which he could have engaged in something as ambitious as faking the moon landing.

In fairness to the moon hoax proponents, Kubrick's *2001* co-writer Arthur C. Clarke met with NASA officials during 1965, possibly leading to a team of NASA scientists visiting the *2001* set in the fall of that year. They were impressed enough to dub Kubrick's offices "NASA East." *2001* had become "a speculative space program," enabling NASA "to test their design ideas in the visual medium of cinema...".[17] Why exactly NASA would want to gauge how their designs appeared cinematically is a mystery, but hardly evidence of Kubrick conspiring with them. It does raise a possibility rarely aired, however: that Kubrick suspected NASA had stolen his *2001* work to fake the moon landing. In saying that, I'm not suggesting the moon landing was faked, only that Kubrick possibly *believed* this to be the case. There is certainly more merit to this possibility than Kubrick's direct involvement in such a hoax.

Kubrick's post-*2001* activities are almost as well-documented, leaving little possibility of such an elaborate hoax. He was deeply immersed in pre-production on his *Napoleon* epic mere weeks after finishing *2001* till September 1969, when MGM formally dropped the project. Kubrick employed Felix Markham, Britain's leading Napoleon expert, and 20 Oxford graduate students to assist with research by June 1968. Over 500 books were consulted in addition to the archival research. Kubrick began scouting locations by November 1968 with an eye towards starting principal photography during the winter of 1969. Overtures were made to the Romanian Army to provide the production with the thousands of extras it would require for the battle sequences. All the while, Kubrick hashed out a screenplay by himself that was completed by September 1969. It weighed in at over 150 pages.[18] Amidst this work load, would he have had the time to fake the Apollo landing?

And assuming he did, surely he would have been rewarded with his passion project. But it wasn't until he shelved *Napoleon* that Warner Brothers offered him a three picture deal in 1970.[19] And the first movie he was set to make for the company was very much a reflection of industry trends.

---

[16] Filippo Ulivieri and Simone Odino, *2001 Between Kubrick and Clarke: The Genesis, Making and Authorship of a Masterpiece*, 47-128.

[17] Filippo Ulivieri and Simone Odino, *2001 Between Kubrick and Clarke: The Genesis, Making and Authorship of a Masterpiece*, 86.

[18] Gene D. Phillips, "The Epic That Never Was: Stanley Kubrick's Napoleon" in , ed. Alison Castle, 635-638, 644-645, 649; John Baxter, *Stanley Kubrick*, 236-240; Vincent LoBrutto, *Stanley Kubrick: A Biography*, 323-327; Pearce, L. (2023, February 21). Steven Spielberg confirms plans to adapt Stanley Kubrick's unmade Napoleon script. The Film Stage - Your Spotlight On Cinema. https://thefilmstage.com/steven-spielberg-confirms-plans-to-adapt-stanley-kubricks-unmade-napoleon-script/#:~:text=After%20Kubrick%20passed%2C%20Baz%20Luhrmann,details%20Kubrick's%20precise%20production%20plans..

In 1969, *Easy Rider* was released and promptly changed the landscape in Hollywood. Budgeted at less than $500,000, the movie made well over $60 million in its first run.[20] Adjusted for inflation, this is still one of the most successful movies ever made. What producer Bert Schneider did was take a genre picture—in this case, the biker film—and add nudity, drugs and profanity, and a little counterculture gloss, all now possible because of easing censorship.[21]

The youth market was floored. Now, every studio wanted their own *Easy Rider*: a low budget film, typically working in an established genre, that could be given a counterculture makeover and bring in the 18-25 demographic.[22]

This is the context you have to see *A Clockwork Orange* in. Like *Easy Rider*, it's a variation on the exploitation film. With *Rider*, it was the biker subgenre being mined. With *Orange*, it was the juvenile delinquent film. Kubrick pondered making an exploitation film throughout the 1960s. *Strangelove* scribe Terry Southern's *Blue Movie* novel came out of discussion he had had with Kubrick about making a studio softcore porn film during the making of *Dr. Strangelove*.[23] And certainly, Kubrick managed that partly with *Orange*.

Orange was the lowest budgeted film Kubrick had made since *Lolita*. Adjusted for inflation, it had a budget roughly on par with what he had for *Paths of Glory*.[24] Further, much of the budget went into securing the rights to the Anthony Burgess novel the film is based upon and paying star Malcolm McDowell. Kubrick probably didn't hire Burgess as a screenwriter for this adaptation, or anyone for that matter, because he couldn't afford a writing partner. Much of the movie was shot on location with only a minimum amount of sets built. What's more, this is one of the only, and certainly the last, film Kubrick brought in on budget.[25] Basically, *Orange* is the most un-Kubrick like film in terms of production. Even the direction is much more frantic than any of his other films, with its staccato jump cuts edited precisely to the soundtrack. No doubt this was another outreach to the youth market.

---

[19] James Fenwick, *Stanley Kubrick Produces*, 159.

[20] Fenwick, *Stanley Kubrick Produces*, 158.

[21] For more on the wide-ranging influence of *Easy Rider*, see Peter Biskind, *Easy Riders, Raging Bulls: How the Sex-Drugs-and-Rock 'N' Roll Generation Saved Hollywood* (New York: Simon & Schuster Paperbacks, 1998).

[22] Fenwick, *Stanley Kubrick Produces*, 158-159

[23] John Baxter, *Stanley Kubrick*, 194-195; Fenwick, *Stanley Kubrick Produces*, 194.

[24] *Orange* had a budget of $2 million in 1970. *Paths* had one of $1 million in 1957 while *Lolita* was funded to the tune of $1.75 million in 1959. in today's dollars, *Orange* and *Paths* were a little over $15 and $20 million, respectively. *Lolita* would be about $17 million. Suffice to say, this was quite a step back for Kubrick after making *2001*, which had a budget well over $100 million in today's dollars.

[25] Fenwick, 160-161, 165-166; Baxter, 246-247. Kubrick used a small crew for *Orange* and even considered shooting it black and white to save on costs. No doubt his desire to keep costs down was driven by a clause in his contract promising "severe penalties" if he went over budget. Kubrick made a game effort to bring it on time as well, but the shooting went over 60 days past schedule. This was partly due to an injury McDowell sustained during shooting, however.

Pound for pound, *Orange* is probably Kubrick's most successful film in terms of box office. Don't get me wrong, it made a little less than half of what *2001* did. But, *2001* also cost nearly five or six times as much. To say nothing of the massive and expensive marketing campaign *2001* required. *Orange* benefitted as much from word of mouth. Further, it was banned for decades in the UK, which likely would have been its most lucrative market.[26]

For these reasons, *A Clockwork Orange* was more the movie Kubrick made his reputation on within the industry than *2001*. Kubrick himself even acknowledged that he had problems procuring money for his films consistently until *A Clockwork Orange*.[27]He was on his best behavior for his first picture with Warner Brothers and even then, he couldn't get them to let him follow *Orange* up with his Napoleon film. Warner really wanted him to make *The Exorcist*, but Kubrick passed.[28]

Barry Lyndon was the compromise they arrived at. Kubrick would get to make a period piece while Warner would theoretically be exposed to less financial risk than with *Napoleon*. At least, that was the studio's rationale. But the film ended up going massively over budget. Originally set at $2.5 million, it ballooned to over $11 million by the time the film was completed. To say nothing of the ad campaign. And it was all for naught. The film is still acknowledged as the biggest flop of Kubrick's career.[29] Throwing salt in the wound was that *The Exorcist*, the film Warner really wanted Kubrick to direct, had become one of the studio's most successful films ever while Kubrick was burning through millions to film by candlelight.

Ah yes, those spectacular scenes filmed by candlelight. When Cryptokubrologists consider *Barry Lyndon*, they exclusively focus on the camera lenses the director used to make those shots possible. They were developed by NASA for the Apollo program, you see. From this, a narrative emerges constituting proof of Kubrick's involvement in faking the moon landing: NASA later did a quid pro quo by giving the director these lenses to realize his dream of filming by candlelight.

Except NASA had nothing to do with Kubrick acquiring the camera lenses.

It's true that they were developed for NASA to be used on Apollo launches by a German company. But NASA had not purchased all of these lenses and a few remained with their developer, Zeiss Company, during the mid-1970s. Kubrick procured the lenses directly from Zeiss.[30] The only real mystery is how he found out about them. But Kubrick religiously

---

[26] LoBrutto notes (*Stanley Kubrick: A Biography*, 449) that *Orange* had earned $40 million worldwide by 1978. In today's dollars, that's nearly $200 million. it had a budget of $2 million, a little over $10 million in 2024.

[27] Filippo Ulivieri and Simone Odino, *2001 Between Kubrick and Clarke*, 16.

[28] Baxter, 272-273;

[29] Fenwick, 169-172; LoBrutto, 384; Baxter, 280, 295.

[30] LoBrutto, 378; Baxter, 283; Rodney Hill, "Barry Lyndon" in *The Stanley Kubrick Archives*, ed. Alison Castle, 477.

tracked developments in camera technology and had numerous contacts throughout the industry. He hardly would have needed NASA to find them.

The great irony here is that the production of *Barry Lyndon*, which was stopped midway through due to threats received by Kubrick, provides some of the best evidence of the director's spooky side. And to the best of my knowledge, none of the great works of Cryptokubrologists have even addressed these implications. But in Chapter 3, this work will. For now, let us return to the director's career trajectory.

Kubrick's position with Warner was precarious after *Lyndon* tanked so spectacularly and with only one final film left in his three film deal. While no one will ever acknowledge it in the Kubrick camp, the director badly needed a hit at this point to ensure the same kind of independence when he signed his next contract.

I propose that Warner Brothers, being aware of this, pushed Kubrick to adapt *The Shining*. The studio believed Kubrick adapting a horror novel would be sound business when they offered him *The Exorcist*.[31] He was given a copy of *The Shining* before it was even released by the studio. James Fenwick suggests that this may have been an attempt by Warner to influence the selection of Kubrick's next film.[32] Certainly this is the only film the director made for Warner Brothers that originated with the studio. The formal announcement of Kubrick adaptation came shortly after the book became another bestseller for Stephen King.

It's often remarked that the film's protagonist, the alcoholic Jack Torrance (Jack Nicholson), resembles Kubrick in the film.[33] It's my belief that this is partly because the Jack Torrance character came to reflect Kubrick's own frustrations with adapting King. Consider Nicholson's rant to Shelly Duvall about the importance of a contract: "Have you ever had any single moment's thought about my responsibilities? To my employers. Has it ever occurred to you that I have agreed to look after the Overlook until May the first. Does it matter to you at all that the owners have put their complete confidence and trust in me. That I have signed an agreement, a contract, in which I have accepted that responsibility?"

And who can forget the infamous "All work and no play makes Jack a dull boy." This is Kubrick's reflection on making the film. Jack Torrance wants to write the great American novel. He believes that becoming the caretaker of the Overlook will enable him to do so by

---

[31] After *Lyndon* tanked, Warner first attempted to get Kubrick to direct *The Exorcist II: Heretic*. In fairness, Kubrick toyed with the idea of making a horror movie since the mid-1960s. See Baxter, 302; Rodney Hill, "The Shining" in *The Stanley Kubrick Archives*, ed. Alison Castle, 520. One suspects making a horror film by the late 1970s wasn't so much the issue for Kubrick as the source material Warner proposed.

[32] Fenwick, 172-173.

[33] Kubrick's friend, Andrew Walker, found the resemblance between Kubrick and Nicholson in the film uncanny, believing the director at least subconsciously found parallels between making the film and Jack Torrance's breakdown. See Alexander Walker, *Stanley Kubrick, Director: A Visual Analysis* 2nd ed. (New York: W.W. Norton & Company, 1999), 271-274..

providing an environment conducive to writing, but the job contributes to his mental breakdown, making him incapable of working on his novel.

In Kubrick's case, it's his *Napoleon* film. He signs a contract with Warner Brothers hoping that it will enable him to make the film as a reward for his good work. Instead, they keep pushing him to make a horror movie, and when they finally corner him, it's a second rate horror novel (from Kubrick's perspective), at that.

Kubrick was generally careful to say all the right things about King and *The Shining*, but even when praising the author, Kubrick made some curious statements. In one instance, he noted: "I should say that King's greatest ingenuity lies in the construction of the story. He does not seem to be very interested in writing itself. They say he wrote, read over, re-wrote maybe once and sent everything to the editor. What seems to interest him is invention and I think that is his forte."[34] Elsewhere, Kubrick stated: "It is in the pruning down phase that the undoing of great novels usually occurs because so much of what is good about them has to do with the fineness of the writing, the insight of the author and often the density of the story. But *The Shining* was a different matter. Its virtues lay almost entirely in the plot, and it didn't prove to be very much of a problem to adapt it into the screenplay form."[35]

King had already written a screenplay for *The Shining*, but Kubrick never bothered to read it.[36] Kubrick had no interest in collaborating with King, instead enlisting American novelist and professor Diana Johnson to adapt the novel with him.[37] King occasionally fielded questions from Kubrick and was granted a single day's visit to the set.[38]

This was in stark contrast to Kubrick's prior and future adaptations. Since *Dr. Strangelove*, Kubrick had worked with the novelist in some capacity for the screenplay with four exceptions. One was *The Shining*. The other three were *A Clockwork Orange*, *Barry Lyndon* and *Eyes Wide Shut*. In the case of the latter two, collaboration was not possible as the author of the source material had already passed into the great beyond.

Some have likened Kubrick's working relationship with King to the one he had with Anthony Burgess.[39] In both cases, the author worked as a kind of springboard for Kubrick to bounce ideas off of while he adapted their novel. But, as noted above, Kubrick's decision to not enlist Burgess in translating *Orange* to the screen probably had more to do with financial constraints than disdain for collaboration. Kubrick later flirted with the idea of using Burgess as a collaborator in both his *Napoleon* project and what became *Eyes Wide Shut*.[40]

---

[34] LoBrutto, 411.

[35] LoBrutto, 413.

[36] LoBrutto, 412.

[37] Baxter, 307;

[38] LoBrutto, 414-415.

[39] LoBrutto, 414.

[40] LoBrutto, 330; Robert P. Kolker and Nathan Abrams, *Eyes Wide Shut: Stanley Kubrick and the Making of His Final Film* (New York: Oxford University Press, 2019), 32.

Kubrick never had any desire to collaborate with King. Johnson suggested that Kubrick was attracted to *The Shining* because of its "psychological underpinnings" relating to the "archetypal enactment."[41] Kubrick viewed *The Shining* as the bare bones of a story that he could apply various themes he wished to explore onto.

In many ways, *The Shining* is even more ambiguous than *2001*, opening it up to a wide variety of interpretations, and from early on, it was viewed as a kind of companion piece to the space opera. Among the first to liken the two was Thomas Allen Nelson in his 1982 work *Kubrick: Inside an Artist's Maze*. Nelson was particularly smitten by the numerology of *The Shining*. He observed: "Danny wears a jersey numbered 42, and he briefly watches with Wendy the Robert Mulligan film, *Summer of '42*. Forty-two is 21 doubled (1921, 21 pictures on the gold corridor wall). The number 12 is a mirror image for 21, the radio call number for the Overlook is KDK 12, and the two screen titles for part three ("8 am" and "4 pm") add up to 12, which means the film that the film duplicates and reverses the numbering of *2001* if you omit the zeroes. In *2001*, we learn HAL's birthday (the day he became operational in Urbana, Illinois) is 12 January 1992, which not only reverses the numerical title of the film (12) but, if added together, the year's number (1 + 9 + 9 + 2) equal 21. Kubrick changed Room 217 in the novel to 237 in the film (one published report explains it as a "legal" necessity). The numbers 237 added together equal 12. Numerically speaking, *The Shining* is *2001* in reverse gear. Double, double, toil and trouble."[42] Shockingly, Nelson forgot to mention that *The Shining* was released 12 years after *2001*, as well.

If a staid English professor and film critic like Nelson was drawing such conclusions from *The Shining* in those pre-internet days, we should hardly be surprised by where conspiracy theorists took Cryptokubrologists. But in my estimation, it is problematic at best to rely on interpreting Kubrick's films as a window into his real world activities.

It is almost exclusively through endless viewings of Kubrick's films that the moon landing allegations rest. Circumstantial evidence from the man's real world activities is harder to come by. This is why I've opted to dwell at length here on the reality of the "total control" Kubrick exercised over his career. *2001* did not grant Kubrick carte blanche in choosing his projects. They were driven by commercial considerations and, in the case of *The Shining*, may even have been imposed on the director for past miscalculations.

Contrary to popular belief, the box office results of *The Shining* were mixed, with the film barely breaking even upon release.[43] It was enough to get Kubrick a new three picture deal with Warner, but not enough to ensure the kind of independence he was believed to have.

---

[41] Rodney Hill, "The Shining" in *The Stanley Kubrick Archives*, ed. Alison Castle, 520.

[42] Thomas Allen Nelson, *Kubrick: Inside a Film Artist's Maze* (Bloomington: Indiana University Press, 1982), 230n.

[43] Fenwick, *Stanley Kubrick Produces*, 169-170. *The Shining* grossed $31 million on its initial run. With a budget of $18 million and an ad campaign that cost an additional $12 million, this didn't leave Warner much return on their investment.

While war long fascinated Kubrick, when he pitched *Full Metal Jacket* to Warner Brothers, it was framed as a more conventional action film. This came during an era in which Vietnam-centric action films such as the *First Blood* and *Missing in Action* films were doing strong business at the box office. *Full Metal Jacket*'s Animal Mother (Adam Baldwin) character was inspired by the onscreen personas of Arnold Schwarzenegger and Sylvester Stallone.[44] While Kubrick no doubt meant Mother as a parody of 1980s action heroes, he was also subtle enough for this to be lost on many viewers in Reagan's America.

Besides *Barry Lyndon*, the only other post-*2001* movie Kubrick made that truly constituted a passion piece was his final film, *Eyes Wide Shut*. This is not consistent with the kind of clout an individual who faked the Apollo 11 landing would have.

***

And yet, there are too many enigmas in Kubrick's life to forgo parapolitical musings. At the forefront is a question that has never been satisfactorily answered: where did the money come from?

Kubrick's early forays into direction lost money upon initial release. *Fear and Desire* and *Killer's Kiss* both lost money, leaving Kubrick with met losses.[45] For *The Killing*, Kubrick agreed to direct it for no salary and lived off loans from his partner, producer James B. Harris.[46] That film lost money during its initial run, as did the follow-up, *Paths of Glory*.[47] Kubrick was well paid for *Spartacus* to the tune of $5k a week, but much of that money went towards his next film, *Lolita*. Both films were a success, especially the latter, but the profits from *Lolita* primarily went towards Kubrick extracting himself from a contract he signed with actor Kirk Douglas' production company.[48]

The director does not seem to have actually made any money off of his films until *Dr. Strangelove*. And yet Kubrick was able to maintain two separate residences in New York City by 1962, including an apartment in Central Park West.[49] That apartment was apparently the basis for the plush dwelling of Bill and Alice Harford in *Eyes Wide Shut*.[50] Kubrick's final US residence, which he rented even before *2001* dropped, was described as a "Gatsby-like mansion" on Long Island.[51] When Kubrick relocated to England permanently after 1968, he purchased a large house in Abbot's Mead. He even retained his apartment in Central Park

---

44 Fenwick, 191-192. Supposedly, Arnold was even offered the part, but opted for *Commando* instead. Therein, he played exactly the type of character Kubrick sought to parody with Animal Mother.
45 Fenwick 31-32, 54-55.
46 LoBrutto, 115.
47 Fenwick, 95-97.
48 Fenwick, 101-102, 115-116.
49 LoBrutto, 224; Baxter, 165.
50 Robert P. Kolker and Nathan Abrams, *Eyes Wide Shut: Stanley Kubrick and the Making of His Final Film*, 80.
51 LoBrutto, 321; Baxter, 229.

West for a time.[52] In 1978, Kubrick acquired a country manor in Hertfordshire, where he remained until his death.[53]

During the 1990s, he attempted to acquire a small airport in Leavesden with an eye towards converting it into his own private studio. But he was beaten to the punch by George Lucas, who shared Kubrick's vision for the place. Lucas ended up shooting *Phantom Menace* there.[54] It's hardly surprising George Lucas, who produced the first six *Star Wars* films and the original *Indiana Jones* trilogy, could afford such digs. But if Lucas was following Kubrick's lead in acquiring the space and materials needed to make films independent of the studios, how was Kubrick able to set such a precedent on the windfalls of *2001* and *A Clockwork Orange*?

Kubrick embraced some unorthodox approaches to supplementing his income over the years. While putting together *Fear and Desire*, Kubrick famously supported himself off winnings from chess matches.[55] In the aftermath of *Paths of Glory*, Kubrick paid the bills for a time from winnings he acquired at high stakes poker games in LA.[56]

Another clue comes from the culture around Hertfordshire: it was known as the stockbroker belt. Kubrick was a longtime private investor. Hertfordshire was described as an environment in which the business savvy Kubrick could "flourish."[57] Kubrick got into stock speculation at the same time as the high stakes poker games in LA. He was known to arrive at his broker's office as early as 6:30 AM to snap up profits on shifts between the British and US exchanges. At some point, Kubrick became a gold bug. It was rumored much of his personal future resided in Switzerland in the form of gold. His brother-in-law Jan Harlan was fully occupied throughout Kubrick's life as his resident financial advisor.[58]

But, would this have been enough to explain how he was able to afford his lifestyle? Country manors aren't cheap and Kubrick gradually transformed his residence into a de facto studio. He owned virtually all the extensive equipment he used on his films in addition to fleets of cars, props housed across the world, and so on. Kubrick's set up wasn't quite what George Lucas had with Skywalker Ranch or Steven Spielberg's Dreamworks, but it was close.

***

The conspiratorial musings on Kubrick, which are legion, are as cringe as they are numerous. Despite the unprecedented amount of analysis Kubrick's films have inspired, the best most Cryptokubrologists can muster are the NASA-designed cameras in *Barry Lyndon*; Danny Lloyd's NASA shirt in *The Shining*; and the famous sequence from the James Bond movie

---

52 Baxter, 195-196; LoBrutto, 341.

53 Emilio D'Alessandro with Filippo Ulivieri, *Stanley Kubrick and Me*, 132.

54 D'Alessandro with Ulivieri, 216-217.

55 LoBrutto, 78; Benson, *Space Odyssey*, 184.

56 Benson, 78-79; Baxter. 149.

57 LoBrutto, 335.

58 Baxter, 149.

Diamonds are Forever in which the British spy wanders through a thinly fictionalized version of Area 51, encountering a soundstage made to look like the surface of the moon. Adding insult to injury is the obsession Cryptokubrologists have with linking Kubrick to the moon landing at the expense of virtually every other suspect and/or intriguing aspects of his life.

Speaking as a Cryptokubrologist, it's *embarrassing* to be associated with this "research."

The only parapolitical exploration of Kubrick's life worth reading is Jasun Horsley's *Kubrickon*. Granted, I'm biased in this case as Jasun's excellent work is partially based on my research at a few points.[59] But even without my input, it's still the most thorough and well balanced examination of Kubrick's "deep" side presently available.

It's also what partly inspired me to embark upon my own Kubrick book. Jasun is not a fan of Mr. Kubrick. This no doubt contributes to Jasun's even-keeled take on the director. But as a passionate Kubrick fan, it didn't seem right that the only compelling conspiratorial work should be by a detractor while virtually *everything* else by self-identified fans is drivel.

That was a factor behind my decision to embark upon this project. Kubrick deserves better than one serious parapolitical analysis of his life. While I doubt the combined vision of *Kubrickon* and this work will silence the peanut gallery, they'll hopefully provide inspiration for more serious research going forward.

As such, this should hardly be regarded as a definitive work. Indeed, it would be foolhardy to believe anything definitive concerning Kubrick is possible. But even getting into that ballpark would require intense archival research that is beyond your humble author's budget. I've had to rely almost exclusively on secondary sources. I've tried to compensate for this deficiency by consulting virtually all major works on Kubrick published at the time of this writing.[60] But obviously, there's only so far one can go without primary sources.

---

[59] See, for instance, Horsley, *Kubrickon*, 89-92, 165 (n 54), etc.

[60] Among the works sourced include Horsley, *Kubrickon*; Vincent LoBrutto, *Stanley Kubrick: A Biography*; James Fenwick, *Stanley Kubrick Produces*; Emilio D'Alessandro with Filippo Ulivieri, *Stanley and Me: Thirty Years at His Side*; Alison Castle (ed.), *The Stanley Kubrick Archives*; John Baxter, *Stanley Kubrick: A Biography*; Nathan Abrams, *Stanley Kubrick: New York Jewish Intellectual* (New Brunswick, New Jersey: Rutgers University Press, 2018); Robert P. Kolker and Nathan Abrams, *Kubrick: An Odyssey* (New York: Pegasus, 2024); Norman Kagan, *The Cinema of Stanley Kubrick* 2nd ed. (New York: The Continuum Publishing Company, 1995); Thomas Allen Nelson, *Kubrick: Inside a Film Artist's Maze*; Alexander Walker, *Stanley Kubrick, Director: A Visual Analysis* 2nd ed; Michael Herr, *Kubrick* (New York: Grove Press, 2000); Frederick Raphael, *Eyes Wide Open: A Memoir of Stanley Kubrick* (New York: Ballantine Books, 1999);Michael Benson, *Space Odyssey: Stanley Kubrick, Arthur C. Clarke, and the Making of a Masterpiece*; George Case, *Calling Dr. Strangelove: The Anatomy of the Kubrick Masterpiece* (Jefferson, North Carolina: McFarland & Company, Inc., 2014); Mick Broderick, *Reconstructing Strangelove: Inside Stanley Kubrick's 'Nightmare Comedy'*(London: Wallflower Press, 2017); Joe R. Frinzi, *Kubrick's Monolith: The Art and Mystery of* 2001: A Space Odyssey (Jefferson, North Carolina: McFarland & Company, 2017); Filippo Ulivieri and Simone Odino, *2001 Between Kubrick and Clarke: The Genesis, Making and Authorship of a Masterpiece*; and Robert P. Kolker and Nathan Abrams, *Eyes Wide Shut: Stanley Kubrick and the Making of His Final Film*.

Besides pushing back at the poor Cryptokubrologists, my hope for this work is to persuade the reader that a parapolitical analysis of Kubrick *is* warranted. The endless conspiratorial masturbation over the moon landing hoax easily discourages any kind of speculative analysis by serious researchers. If I do my job right here, the notion that Kubrick played a significant if little acknowledged role in Cold War intrigues will be given serious consideration, and ideally, enable someone with the resources to begin the kind of deep dive this subject so justly deserves.

Make no mistake about it: Kubrick was a player in the proverbial game of thrones. He knew it and those around him knew. Collaborator Michael Herr made a comment about Kubrick in this regard echoed by many others: Kubrick "played the game pretty well, although perhaps not as well as he thought."[61]

What did Herr mean by this enigmatic statement? This is my stab at explaining it. So, let's start our exploration at the most logical of places: the early years.

---

[61] Michael Herr, *Kubrick*, 95.

Chapter One:

A *Realist* Surrealist is Born

New York Stories

Stanley Kubrick was born July 26, 1928 in Manhattan. Both sides of his family immigrated to the United States at the turn of the twentieth century. Both hailed from the Galicia region of the Austro-Hungarian Empire before settling in the Bronx.[62] And like many Eastern European immigrants from this era, both were Jewish.

Kubrick's status as a Jew has been a subject of much debate. Frederick Raphael, who co-wrote *Eyes Wide Shut* with the director and later wrote of these experiences in *Eyes Wide Open*, depicts Kubrick as pathologically obsessed with the Gentile mind. He recounts Kubrick's instance upon none of the characters in *Eyes* having Jewish names and his ruminations on what non-Jews thought of them.[63]

"Coulpa Jews, what do we know what these people talk about when they're by themselves?" Kubrick asked the scribe at one point. When Raphael insists Kubrick must have some idea from overhearing conversations at restaurants and theaters, the director responded: "Maybe, but I'll tell you something: they always know you're there."[64]

Raphael believed that Kubrick's cinematic overture can only be understood through his Jewish heritage, especially the recurring sense of paranoia. Raphael was of the opinion that this reflected Kubrick's lingering doubts about non-Jews in the aftermath of the Holocaust. The scribe believed the director was so conscious of his Jewish heritage that he deliberately avoided making any of the characters in his films explicitly Jewish.[65]

Raphael's Kubrick is a highly contradictory creature. The writer delights in pointing out Kubrick never confronted anti-Semitism directly in his films despite all the other unsettling topics he covered. He has Kubrick proclaim that's never truly been a film about the Holocaust circa 1995. When Raphael brings up *Schindler's List*, Kubrick demised it, then elaborates that the Holocaust was about six million Jewish deaths while the film is about 600 Jews who survive. [66]

Raphael later reflects that "Jewishness is not something that unites us; on the contrary, it will license him to deal consciencelessly with me. Jews are often real Jews only with each other. Gentiles never suspect this. They accuse us of having a secret and common agenda: the only secret is that we practice on each other enmities, treacheries, and ruthlessness which we

---

[62] John Baxter, *Stanley Kubrick: A Biography*, 15-17; Vincent Lobrutto, *Stanley Kubrick: A Biography*, 6-7.

[63] Raphael's assessment was not entirely accurate. Kubrick had feature explicitly Jewish characters in his films at times (i.e. Lt. Goldberg in *Dr. Strangelove* and David the Jew in *Spartacus*). But it's undeniable that he often rewrote Jewish characters in his source material as Gentiles. See Robert P. Kolker and Nathan Abrams, *Eyes Wide Shut: Stanley Kubrick and the Making of His Final Film*, 48.

[64] Frederick Raphael, *Eyes Wide Open: A Memoir of Stanley Kubrick*, 105-106.

[65] Raphael, *Eyes Wide Open*, 108.

[66]Raphael, *Eyes Wide Open*, 107.

might not dare to indulge in other directions." This came on the heels of Kubrick informing Raphael that Hitler was "right about almost everything."[67]

Suffice to say, Raphael concluded that Kubrick was a self-hating Jew. Kubrick feared and idolized Gentiles in equal measure. While keenly aware of his own Jewishness, he did all he could to distance his work from it. To Raphael, film was a means for Kubrick to transcend his Jewishness and assume the "alien" identities of his characters.

Many Kubrick collaborators and intimates took issue with Raphael's depiction. Steven Spielberg "didn't recognize the voice of Stanley" in the scribe's account. Louis Blau, a long time legal counsel to Kubrick, stated: "Raphael's remarks about (Kubrick's) anti-Semitism and the holocaust are beyond contempt."[68]

I note these allegations here, at the onset of our journey, to highlight something alleged about Kubrick. Perhaps Matthew Modine, Pvt. Joker in *Full Metal Jacket*, was most blunt in the introduction to *Stanley Kubrick and Me*. He notes that "Kubrick was a bit of a chameleon. Perhaps a large part of his genius was his clever ability to become a different person to whomever it was he was dealing with."[69]

Thus, Raphael's depiction of Kubrick, while fascinating, probably reflects more on what Kubrick thought of Raphael than the director himself. Kubrick likely suspected Raphael was sensitive about his Jewishness and opted to goad him about it.[70] This is an aspect of Kubrick we'll reflect on time again throughout this work, so do keep it in mind.

But, to return to the Kubrick family. Jacques "Jack" Kubrick, Stanley's father, is a curious figure. He was a homeopathic doctor who graduated from the New York Homeopathic Medical College in 1927, the year before Stanley was born.[71] This institution still exists as the New York Medical College. The fact that Kubrick's dad was a long practicing homeopath is little remarked upon. Homeopathy is one of the oldest types of alternative medicines, having been developed in Germany towards the end of the eighteenth century. It was based on the principle that "like cures like," thus medicines and treatments mimicked the symptoms of the disease they combated.

Homeopathy was extremely popular in the US during the nineteenth century. But by the early 20th, it was largely dismissed as pseudoscience. And yet Kubrick's father appears to have had little trouble making a living as a homeopathic physician. Growing up against a

---

[67] Raphael, *Eyes Wide Open*, 152-153.

[68] Archerd, A. (1999, June 18). Kubrick "memoir" shocks Spielberg. Variety. https://variety.com/1999/voices/columns/kubrick-memoir-shocks-spielberg-1117503222/.

[69] Matthew Modine, "Foreword," in *Stanley Kubrick and Me: Thirty Years at His Side* by Emilio D'Alessandro with Filippo Ulivieri, vii.

[70] For an in-depth discussion of Kubrick's Jewishness, see Nathan Abram, *Stanley Kubrick: New York Jewish Intellectual*.

[71] Vincent Lobrutto, *Stanley Kubrick: A Biography*, 7; John Baxter, *Stanley Kubrick: A Biography* , 16.

backdrop of holistic medicine probably contributed to Kubrick's cynical view towards the medical profession.[72]

Kubrick's uncle from his mother's side of the family is also worth noting. This would be Martin Perveler. Also hailing from the Bronx, Perveler relocated to California at some point during his 20s. In 1938, he became a licensed pharmacist in California and established a series of successful pharmacies throughout the Burbank-Pasadena-San Gabriel area. He got married in 1939 and became a millionaire not long afterwards.[73]

Kubrick lived with his uncle in Pasadena during 1940 and 1941, where he briefly attended school.[74] This was his first exposure to Hollywood. Then, as now, Pasadena was a very exclusive, aristocratic community, which should demonstrate the prominence Kubrick's uncle had achieved by this point. The time frame is also interesting.

The period from roughly 1937 to 1942 marked the height of rocket scientist Jack Parsons' involvement with the Suicide Squad and his embrace of Thelema.[75] Some of this stuff received press from the local papers. Given Kubrick's later interests, it would be interesting to know if he followed any of these developments during his time in Pasadena. It would also be interesting to know if his millionaire uncle had any links to these characters. Perveler was instrumental in launching Kubrick's career. He later contributed much of the funding for *Fear and Desire*, Kubrick's first feature film.[76]

The Perveler side of Kubrick's family may have influenced him in other ways later in life. Joseph Perveler, another of Kubrick's uncles, had a son named Paul. Kubrick knew Paul S. Perveler during his youth. They attended Camp Winneshewauka, a summer camp in Vermont, during 1944.[77] Paul was born on April Fool's Day 1937.[78] As Kubrick was nearly a decade older, it's debatable how close he was with Paul.

---

[72] For more on Kubrick's distrust of doctors, see Lobrotto, 328; and Kolker and Abrams, 66-67. Conversely, Kubrick largely subsisted on "industrial, carefully controlled products with the expiration date and the address of the factory clearly printed on the package." He was especially passionate about microwaves and frozen food. See D'Alessandro with Ulivieri, *Stanley Kubrick and Me*, 165.

[73] Lobrutto, 9.

[74] Lobrutto, 9; Baxter, *Stanley Kubrick: A Biography*, 20; James Fenwick, *Stanley Kubrick Produces*, 13. Fenwick claims it was actually Burbank that Perveler was living in when Kubrick was living with him. Lobrutto states Perveler was in Pasadena, where Kubrick attended school. Baxter doesn't give Perveler's location, but also notes Kubrick attended school in Pasadena.

[75] Jack Whiteside Parsons (1914-1952) invented the first rocket engine to use castable, composite rocket propellant. A variation on this formula was later used to develop the rocket fuel that took humanity into space. Parsons was a co-founder of the California Institute of Technology's Jet Propulsion Laboratory (JPL, which some believe was a sly play on "Jack Parsons Laboratory"). He was also an enthusiastic practitioner of Thelema, the magick system popularized by British occultist Aleister Crowley. For more on Parsons' remarkable life, see George Pendle, *Strange Angel: The Otherworldly Life of Rocket Scientist Jack Parsons* (Orlando: A Harvest Book, 2005).

[76] LoBrutto, 78-79; Baxter, 49; Fenwick, 28.

[77] Robert P Kolker and Nathan Abrams, *Kubrick: An Odyssey*, 22.

[78] Vincent Bugliosi with Ken Hurwitz, *Till Death Us Do Part: A True Murder Mystery* (New York: W.W.

But the two relations did share some characteristics. Most notably, Perveler was self-conscious of his Jewishness as well. While Kubrick downplayed Jewish characters and themes in his films, Perveler often passed himself off as another ethnicity, usually Italian.[79] Perveler's discomfort with being Jewish may have bordered on the self-loathing Kubrick has been accused of.

On the other hand, both men were strikingly different. In contrast to Kubrick the intellectual, Perveler was a physical specimen. Paul had the build of the 1930s Jewish prizefighters Kubrick so admired. Perveler claimed to bench 225 pounds and had additional alpha male bonafides besides his physique. Paul was drafted into the Army in 1958 and did basic training at Fort Ord, California followed by additional training at Fort Hood. He ended up in the Army's 2nd Tank Corp. His military career was checkered, Perveler being twice promoted to sergeant before being busted back to private. Much of his active duty was spent in West Germany. Perveler returned to the States in 1960 after 18 months in the Army.[80]

Less than two years later, Perveler went into law enforcement. During 1962 and 1963, Paul worked as a police officer for the Los Angeles Police Department (LAPD) in Hollywood and West LA. He was forced to resign towards the end of 1963 after helping arrange an abortion for a fellow officer.[81] At the time, abortion was illegal, but Perveler avoided any criminal charges. From there, he worked as a private detective and an insurance claims investigator before opening up his own bar towards the end of the decade.

Perveler would be convicted of murder in 1969. His crimes eerily paralleled the 1944 Billy Wilder-directed noir classic *Double Indemnity*. He murdered both his wife and his mistresses' husband after taking substantial insurance claims out on both. Perveler also attempted to kill his first wife multiple times and possibly his parents. Perveler gave them a Mexican vacation as an anniversary gift. Somewhere between Tijuana and Ensenada, Joseph was shot in the face by an unknown assailant, but survived.[82]

Perveler was originally sentenced to death, but it was changed to a life sentence after California struck down its capital punishment law in 1972. Perveler was Kubrick's first cousin, a fact that was not widely known until the 2010s. A true crime book and film were made about the killer, both dubbed *Till Death Us Do Part*. The 1992 TV movie co-starred Arliss Howard, who had previously had a lead role in *Full Metal Jacket*.[83] Perveler's crime spree occurred during an interesting time in Kubrick's life, which is explored in Chapter 2.

Norton & Company Inc., 1978), 37.

[79] Vincent Bugliosi with Ken Hurwitz, *Till Death Us Do Part: A True Murder Mystery*, 38, 48.

[80] Vincent Bugliosi with Ken Hurwitz, *Till Death Us Do Part: A True Murder Mystery*, 40-41.

[81] Vincent Bugliosi with Ken Hurwitz, *Till Death Us Do Part: A True Murder Mystery*, 48-49.

[82] Vincent Bugliosi with Ken Hurwitz, *Till Death Us Do Part: A True Murder Mystery*, 71.

[83] Robert P Kolker and Nathan Abrams, *Kubrick: An Odyssey*, 309-310.

For now, it's worth contemplating Kubrick's possible interest in his cousin. While superficially they seem quite different, Kubrick may have been fascinated by Perveler. He exemplified the kind of rugged, "macho" image of Jews Kubrick toyed with during the late 1950s and early 1960s. In both *Paths of Glory* and *Spartacus*, Kubrick showcased the muscular builds of Kirk Douglas and Tony Curtis. Both actors were Jews whose on-screen personas defied then-popular stereotypes of Jews as mild and meek. [84] Paul Perveler, a military veteran and former cop with the build of prizefighter, was in many ways a real life personification of the hyper-masculine Jewish persona Kubrick was cinematically fixated upon. In this context, Kubrick's interest in his cousin becomes more plausible.

***

Kubrick was too young to be drafted for WWII. But when the Korean War broke out in 1950, he was eligible. Kubrick claimed the Army rejected him on the basis that he was "unfit" for service. A high school friend claimed that he was turned down over "some oddball thing" with new recruits.[85] In actuality, Kubrick was granted a student deferment.[86] How he managed this is unknown as Kubrick only attended sporadic college classes.

Greenwich Village's postwar hipster scene greatly influenced Kubrick while he was working for *Look*. At the forefront was the German dada artist and City College of New York (CCNY) professor Hans Richter. Kubrick may have first encountered Richter while taking evening classes at CCNY. This led to Kubrick making a brief appearance in Richter's experimental 1947 film *Dreams That Money Can Buy* along with Toba Metz and Ruth Sobotka, his first and second wives.[87]

There are some very unsettling implications to this. *Dreams That Money Can Buy* was a collaboration between Richter and various Dadaist and surrealist artists, each contributing different dream sequences to the work. Other participants included Max Ernst, Marcel Duchamp and Man Ray.

During this time, the latter maintained a peculiar friendship with a prominent Los Angeles-based doctor and onetime LA "venereal czar" named George Hodel. Man Ray and Hodel were a part of Los Angeles' thriving surrealist scene in the aftermath of World War II. They intermingled with such figures as artists William Copley and Beatrice Wood, the wealthy art collectors Walter and Louise Arensberg, novelist Henry Miller, poet Kenneth Rexroth, actors Edward G. Robinson and Vincent Price, and directors Albert Lewin and John Huston.[88]

---

[84] Nick Abrams, *Stanley Kubrick: New York Jewish Intellectual*, 24, 47-49, etc.

[85] Nathan Abrams, *Stanley Kubrick: New York Jewish Intellectual*, 31, 33, 47.

[86] Robert P Kolker and Nathan Abrams, *Kubrick: An Odyssey*, 51.

[87] Fenwick, 28; Robert P Kolker and Nathan Abrams, *Kubrick: An Odyssey*, 30-31; Kolker and Abrams, *Eyes Wide Shut: Stanley Kubrick and the Making of His Final Film*, 14. There's actually no record of Kubrick attending CCNY, but he may have sat in on several of Richter's lectures as a guest.

[88] For an overview of LA's surrealist scene and Hodel's links to it, see Mark Nelson and Sarah Hudson Bayliss, *Exquisite Corpse: Surrealism and the Black Dahlia Murder* (New York: Bulfinch Press, 2006).

Before he directed such classics as *The Maltese Falcon* and *Treasure of the Sierra Madre*, Huston knew Hodel when they were teenagers. Their paths continued to cross for years afterwards. In 1926, Huston married a woman named Dorothy Jeanne Harvey. They divorced during 1933 but remained close. In 1940, Dorothy married George Hodel and had several kids with him. Huston was a regular at the Hodel residence for years after.[89] Kubrick was influenced by Huston and *The Killing* largely derives from Huston's *The Asphalt Jungle* (1950) down to star Sterling Hayden.[90]

But, to return to the doctor. By 1950, Hodel was at the center of scandal after being charged with incest after allegedly raping his teenage daughter, Tamar. Even more ominous, compelling evidence has come to light in the twenty-first century that Hodel was involved in the murder of Elizabeth Short, more commonly known as the Black Dahlia. The murder occurred in early 1947. Man Ray may have had some knowledge of Hodel's involvement.[91]

Life magazine used images from *Dreams Money Can Buy* in its December 1946 issue, released six weeks before Short's murder. A recurring theme in the film is a photograph of Man Ray's eyes. This image was taken from an enlarged and cropped version of Man Ray's 1946 work "Self-Portrait." Man Ray gave George Hodel a version of this "Self-Portrait" in 1946 as a gift.[92] During the time, Man Ray was one of Hodel's closest associates in LA's surrealist circles, along with legendary director John Huston. Hodel and Huston had known one another for decades.[93]

---

[89] Mark Nelson and Sarah Hudson Bayliss, *Exquisite Corpse: Surrealism and the Black Dahlia Murder*, 157; Steve Hodel, *Black Dahlia Avenger A Genius for Murder: A True Story* 2nd Ed. (New York: Arcade Publishing, 2015), 60-64.

[90] Baxter, *Stanley Kubrick: A Biography*, 74-75.

[91] The Hodel allegations are highly controversial and largely driven by former LAPD officer Steve Hodel, George's son. Steve Hodel began making these during the early '00s and as time marched on, they became increasingly incredible. Not only does Steve Hodel finger his father for Short's murder, but numerous other unsolved LA killings during that era; the Chicago "Lipstick" killings; the Philippines "Torso murder;" and even the Zodiac killings. Steve sees his father as nothing less than a real life Hannibal Lecter, a criminal mastermind that outwitted authorities to his dying breath. Suffice to say, the further the younger Hodel strayed from the Elizabeth Short murder, the more improbable his claims became. But much of the evidence he presents for George Hodel's involvement in the Short murder, including transcripts from when the LA District Attorney's Office bugged Hodel's residence and recorded him all but confessing to the crime, is compelling. See Steve Hodel, *Black Dahlia Avenger A Genius for Murder: A True Story*; Steve Hodel, *Black Dahlia Avenger II: Presenting the Follow-Up Investigation and Further Evidence Linking Dr. George Hill Hodel to Los Angeles's Black Dahlia and Other 1940s Lone Woman Murders* 2nd Ed.(Los Angeles: Thoughtprint Press, 2014)); Steve Hodel with Ralph Pezzullo, *Most Evil: Avenger, Zodiac, and the Further Serial Murders of Dr. George Hill Hodel* (New York: Berkley Books, 2009); Steve Hodel, *Most Evil II: Presenting the Follow-Up Investigation and Decryption of the 1970s Zodiac Cipher in Which the San Francisco Serial Killer Reveals His True Identity* (Los Angeles: A Rare Bird Book, 2015). For more on George Hodel's relationship with Man Ray, see Mark Nelson and Sarah Hudson Bayliss, *Exquisite Corpse: Surrealism and the Black Dahlia Murder*.

[92] Mark Nelson and Sarah Hudson Bayliss, *Exquisite Corpse: Surrealism and the Black Dahlia Murder*, 92-93.

[93] For more on LA's surrealist scene, see Nelson and Bayliss, *Exquisite Corpse: Surrealism and the Black*

It's unknown if Hodel ever saw *Dreams*, but it's highly probable given his passion for surrealism. In addition to Man Ray, Hodel admired several other artists featured in the movie. Hodel was also a fan of the film's composer, Josh White. Tamar Hodel arguably became even more obsessed with White. She developed a infatuation with him during her father's incest trial and later became romantically involved with the musician.[94]

But there's an even more direct connection to Kubrick. Man Ray's section in *Dreams Money Can Buy* was called "Ruth, Roses, and Revolvers." One performer in this sequence was a woman named Ruth in real life --Ruth Sobotka. Yes, Stanley Kubrick's second wife. What's more, Kubrick and his soon-to-be first wife Toba Metz appear as extras in Man Ray's section.[95]

This raises the distinct possibility Kubrick met Man Ray. He has acknowledged the artist as an influence,[96] but it may have been greater than previously believed. The first production company Kubrick founded was called Minotaur. This is often viewed as a reference to the Jungian conception of the maze and the Minotaur. And it may partially be. But "Minotaur" is also the name of one of Man Ray's most celebrated works, consisting of the image of a naked woman's upper torso. It has been suggested that this piece partially inspired the mutilations George Hodel allegedly committed upon Elizabeth Short.[97] As for Kubrick, it has been suggested the famous "crazy Kubrick stare" was influenced by Man Ray's "Self Portrait." The same one so admired by Hodel.

I've opted to dwell on these figures because we'll be encountering George Hodel and his family time and time again throughout this work. Hence, Kubrick's ties to these circles are far more significant than anyone has realized.

What's more, the importance of surrealism in Kubrick's films cannot be overstated. In my estimation. Kubrick already had an interest in this art form prior to his relationship with Ruth Sobotka. His fascination surely increased after their marriage and may have been a contributing factor to it. Ruth was a staple of NYC's vibrant Dada and surrealist circles since the late 1940s.[98]

Dahlia Murder. For more on Hodel's relationship with John Huston, see Steve Hodel, *Black Dahlia Avenger*.

[94] Nelson and Bayliss, *Exquisite Corpse*, 93-94, 159.

[95] Kolker and Abrams, *Eyes Wide Shut: Stanley Kubrick and the Making of His Final Film*, 28; Robert P Kolker and Nathan Abrams, *Kubrick: An Odyssey*, 30-31; Fenwick, *Stanley Kubrick Produces*, 28.

[96] Robert P Kolker and Nathan Abrams, *Kubrick: An Odyssey*, 31; Stanley Kubrick Didactics. Los Angeles County Museum of Art. (2010, December 19). https://www.lacma.org/sites/default/files/Stanley%20Kubrick%20didactics%2010.19.12.pdf; Rodzvilla, J. (2014, October 23). Artifacts from cinematic heaven and hell: The Kubrick cult moves to tiff. Independent Magazine. https://independent-magazine.org/2014/10/23/stanley-kubrick_exhibit_lacma_neil-kendricks/.

[97] Steve Hodel, *Black Dahlia Avenger*, 212-213; Nelson and Bayliss, *Exquisite Corpse*, 65-79.

[98] Kolker and Abrams, *Eyes Wide Shut: Stanley Kubrick and the Making of His Final Film*, 14.

Dadaism and surrealism haunted Kubrick's work for the rest of his life. In the preproduction of *2001*, Kubrick looked to Dadaist and surrealist art for inspiration in visualizing extraterrestrial landscapes.[99] In *Stanley Kubrick, Director*, longtime *Evening Standard* film critic Alexander Walker made an interesting observation about Kubrick's creative process. And he would have been in a position to know. He was one of the only critics Kubrick had a personal relationship with. They had been friends since the late 1950s and Walker unofficially consulted on several scripts for Kubrick.

Of the writing process for *The Shining*, Walker noted: "...They [Diana Johnson and Kubrick] worked on the script separately, as was his custom with collaborators. Each broke down the story, extracting the plot essentials, questioning the characters' motivations. Then scripts were exchanged...This process can be viewed as rather like the party game played with paper and pencil and known as... 'Exquisite corpses.'" The contributors to a composite portrait make their own creative additions at each "blind" fold in a sheet of paper, which, unfolded, reveals an entity that's unexpected but often more suggestive than any conscious, consensual creative effort."[100]

While there was a parlor game predating it, what is now known as "exquisite corpse" was a creative technique that functioned as a game among surrealists. It was developed by the movement's figurehead, Andre Breton, along with Simone Kahn, his first wife, and poet Jacques Prevert. The first version used only words, but drawings soon became the norm. Kahn described the exquisite corpse as "a system, a method of research" to surrealism and "even, perhaps, a drug." The process has been likened to automatic writing. In both cases, words and images flowed directly from the unconscious without forethought.[101]

Kubrick developed his version of this process. He and his writing partner frequently wrote separate scripts and then exchanged them. From there, Kubrick crafted a new script or scene with the most compelling part of either. And frequently, he brought in other writers, almost always without telling his writing partner, to do their own version of a scene. This was his version of the exquisite corpse. And it probably was not the only influence surrealism had on his creative process.

As far as cinema was concerned, Kubrick viewed it as an almost entirely derivative art form. The acting and dialogue came from the theater, the images from photography, the score from classical music, etc. To Kubrick's mind, the one truly original aspect of filmmaking was editing. It enabled the director to envision a film in a variety of ways before deciding on the finished product.[102] I suspect this is the actual reason Kubrick did 70-80 takes of a scene. In

---

[99] Michael Benson, *Space Odyssey: Stanley Kubrick, Arthur C. Clarke, and the Making of a Masterpiece*, 107-108.

[100] Alexander Walker, *Stanley Kubrick, Director: A Visual Analysis*, 281.

[101] Nelson and Bayliss, 96-97.

[102] Alexander Walker, *Stanley Kubrick, Director*, 42; Kolker and Abrams, 113; Joe R. Frinzi, *Kubrick's Monolith: The Art and Mystery of* 2001: A Space Odyssey, 42-44.

many cases, he simply did not know what he was looking for and frequently wouldn't know until he began editing. There, he could construct a scene in a variety of ways until he found something that worked.

My suspicion is that Kubrick applied something akin to the cut-up technique while editing. In other aspects of filmmaking, there is evidence of this. Bryan Loftus, who provided special photographic effects to *2001*, was pushed by Kubrick to produce random color palettes for his planetary landscapes. In response, Loftus mounted spinners and roulette wheel-style diagrams on three Kodak film boxes. He would then randomly select from them for a new shot. His approach was likened to the cut-up method and delighted Kubrick. "We've taken the human element out of it!" the director exclaimed.[103]

The cut-up technique is itself a variation on the exquisite corpse. It was popularized by William S. Burroughs, whom Kubrick was a fan of.[104] He may have known Burroughs. While writing *2001*, Arthur C. Clarke resided at NYC's Chelsea Hotel, where Kubrick frequently visited him. Burroughs was a resident of the hotel at the same time Clarke and Kubrick were putting together *2001*. And Clarke certainly encountered Burroughs while he resided there.[105] As such, I would be shocked if Kubrick was not aware of the cut-up technique.

But beyond this, its use provides the most compelling explanation for certain befuddling aspects of Kubrick's films. Take the continuity errors in *The Shining*, for instance.[106] Kubrick invested months editing his films, making it improbable that he was not aware of these errors. And yet they were left in. It is my contention that Kubrick went with a cut he believed was more likely to affect viewers on a subconscious level. This is very indicative of the cut-up technique.

Another probable influence from the Greenwich Villages days was Paul Krassner and his publication, *The Realist*. Krassner's scathing political and cultural satire made him a counterculture icon by the late 1960s. He was a close friend of Lenny Bruce, Dick Gregory, and other boundary-breaking stand-up comedians, a part of Ken Kesey's Merry Pranksters, and a founding member of the Yippie movement. Later, he befriended conspiracy radio titan Mae Brussel and offered up some of the earliest alternative takes on the JFK assassination and the Manson killings.[107]

---

[103] Michael Benson, *Space Odyssey: Stanley Kubrick, Arthur C. Clarke and the Making of a Masterpiece*, 328.

[104] Michael Herr, *Kubrick*, 13.

[105] Michael Benson, *Space Odyssey*, 41, 79; LoBrutto. *Stanley Kubrick: A Biography*, 264.

[106] For a good examination of said errors, see Tyler, A. (2022, May 7). The shining's continuity error trick that made Kubrick's movie even better. ScreenRant. https://screenrant.com/shining-movie-stanley-kubrick-continuity-mistakes-deliberate-good/.

[107] There's no better place to find a rundown of Krassner's extraordinary life than his autobiography, *Confessions of a Raving, Unconfined Nut: Misadventures in the Counterculture* 2nd. Ed. (Berkeley, CA: Soft Skull Press, 2012). But I advise taking a grain or two of salt with this work.

Kubrick first encountered *The Realist* shortly after its launch in 1958. He remained a reader until at least the mid-1960s.[108] *The Realist* was always an underground publication, but especially in its early years. Kubrick would have been among only a few hundred early readers. It was an elastic mix that also included Bruce, arch Discordian Robert Anton Wilson, the American Humanist Association's Edwin Wilson, and various members of the Libertarian League and the Fortean Society.[109] The style of satire and black comedy that proliferated in *The Realist* has been cited as an influence on the humor displayed in Kubrick's films, most notably *Dr. Strangelove*.[110] *Dr. Strangelove* co-writer Terry Southern was a contributor to *The Realist* and a friend of Krassner. It's possible Krassner had an even deeper influence on Kubrick, as shall be explored in chapter 2.

For now, it's worth noting that Krassner was the original patron of Mae Brussell and an occasional guest on her show. Other figures within *The Realist* milieu like Lenny Bruce also appeared during the 1970s. Whether Kubrick was aware of Mae Brussell or ever listened to her show is unknown. But if he did follow it in some way, he may have encountered Bill Kaysing's *2001* allegations there. Brussell first mentioned Kaysing's *2001* musings during a radio show in 1977.[111]

Previously, I mentioned the possibility that Kubrick believed his *2001* work was co-opted for the moon landing. Now, I'd like to raise another little considered possibility: Kubrick was aware of Kaysing's allegations and decided to have fun with it. Much of the cinematic "evidence" for Kubrick faking the moon landing resides in *The Shining*, a film Kubrick began working on around the time Brussell first discussed Kaysing.

Kubrick was very image conscious. He cultivated a perception of himself as an alchemist who's films were so important they transcended the medium. Playing into Kaysing's claims would only perpetuate this image. And it may have provided Kubrick with a good laugh in the process. If his sense of humor was informed by *The Realist*, pranking this milieu in such a fashion would have tugged at Paul Krassner's heartstrings. And if Krassner had some inclination of Kubrick's admiration, how could he have resisted getting in on the fun?

Spooks and Pedophiles

Kubrick made some spooky contacts early in his career. It all started with Alexander Singer, who was a high school classmate of Kubrick's at William Howard Taft. Singer seems to be

---

[108] Mick Broderick, *Reconstructing Strangelove: Inside Stanley Kubrick's 'Nightmare Comedy'*, 6; Nathan Abrams, *Stanley Kubrick: New York Jewish Intellectual*, 8.

[109] Paul Krassner, *Confessions of a Raving, Unconfined Nut: Misadventures in the Counterculture*, 37-44, etc.

[110] Mick Broderick, *Reconstructing Strangelove*, 6-7.

[111] Mae Brussell, World Watchers International, KLRB, September 19, 1977, https://www.youtube.com/watch?v=WVV9XKXRw2Y (accessed March 22, 2024).

Kubrick's main inspirations for initially getting into filmmaking. They were fellow film buffs growing up.[112]

Singer already aspired to be a director when he gave Kubrick the bug. However, Kubrick directed first with the short documentary *A Day at the Fight*. Singer helped Kubrick shoot this outing, along with his second feature film, *Killer's Kiss*.[113] He also served as an associate producer on *The Killing* and introduced Kubrick to James B. Harris.[114] Harris, a producer and later director, was a key early Kubrick collaborator whom he formed a production company with. But more on that later.

Singer is pivotal in Kubrick's early career, and he just happens to be a really interesting guy in his own right. He got into filmmaking not long after graduating high school. This would have been in the aftermath of World War II. He got a job with Time Inc working on *The March of Time* series. If you've ever seen *Citizen Kane*, then you're familiar with *The March of Time* format. They were high quality newsreels covering current events that were aired before, and sometimes after, feature films.[115]

The individual behind *The March of Time* series was Louis de Rochemont. He worked on these projects with his brother Richard, who took over as the executive producer of *The March of Time* in 1943.[116] Richard was also close to Charles de Gaulle's France Forever during WWII. This organization was dedicated to rallying support for De Gaulle, in opposition to the Vichy government.[117] Richard de Rochemont became a key early financier for Kubrick, coming up with funding for *Fear and Desire*, and *Killer's Kiss*. He also got Kubrick some second unit work on a miniseries centered around the life of Abraham Lincoln that Norman Lloyd was directing.[118]

Both de Rochemont brothers had intelligence ties, especially Louis. It was later revealed that Louis's firm, which his brother was then a part of, worked as a front for the CIA in a 1951 animated adaptation of George Orwell's *Animal Farm*. And, given their ties to De Gaulle and involvement in *The March of Time* series, which had great propaganda value, it's likely intelligence ties went back even further. Notorious Watergate "Plumber" and CIA officer E. Howard Hunt worked on *March of Time* during WWII while detailed to the Navy and later the Office of Strategic Services (OSS, the predecessor to the CIA). Hunt later worked on *Animal Farm* as well.[119]

---

[112] Fenwick, *Stanley Kubrick Produces*, 13-15; LoBrutto, *Stanley Kubrick: A Biography*, 27-33; .

[113] Baxter, *Stanley Kubrick: A Biography*, 37-39, 63; LoBrutto, *Stanley Kubrick: A Biography*, 58-70, 96.

[114] LoBrutto, 109-110, 118-120; Baxter, 78.

[115] Fenwick, *Stanley Kubrick Produces*, 15; Baxter, 34; LoBrutto, 56.

[116] LoBrutto, 76-77; Fenwick, 35.

[117] LoBrutto, 77.

[118] Fenwick, 27; LoBrutto, 81-83.

[119] Frances Stonor Saunders, *Who Paid the Piper?: The CIA and the Cultural Cold War* (London: Granta Books, 1999), 294. For an in-depth account of the role de Rochemont and Hunt played in *Animal Farm*, see Daniel J. Leab, *Orwell Subverted: The CIA and the Filming of Animal Farm* (University Park, PA: The

Another CIA project the de Rochemonts were active in was sponsored by the World Assembly of Youth (WAY). The CIA provided the bulk of WAY's funding throughout the 1950s and 1960s, sometimes via the Ford Foundation. In 1952, WAY commissioned Richard de Rochemont to make a documentary about the organization's first triennial general assembly. What emerged in 1953 was the aptly titled *World Assembly of Youth: A Report on the First Triennial General Assembly of WAY at Cornell University, Ithaca, NY.* In his Kubrick biographer, John Baxter revealed that Kubrick placed this picture on his CV during the early 1950s, listing himself as a producer on behalf of the State Department. However, James Fenwick was unable to come up with any documentation of Kubrick working on this film in any capacity while researching *Stanley Kubrick Produces*.[120]

However, Fenwick doesn't discount the possibility of Kubrick's involvement. He notes the possibility that the director had some minor role in the production, such as taking still photography, that he later embellished. He also may have been covering the general assembly for WAY's radio program.[121] It's also of note that Fenwick found the 1951-1953 period the least documented part of Kubrick's life.[122] It's possible a fair amount of potential documentation went through the shredder upon Kubrick's death, before it reached the archives. We'll return to this period in a moment.

Let's return to Alexander Singer. Singer broke into the film industry working for the de Rochemonts and later introduced Kubrick to them. From there, Singer was drafted during Korea. And where did Singer end up serving?

The US Army Signal Corps.

A lot of Hollywood types served in the Signal Corp over the years. They included directors like Frank Capra and Russ Meyer, the famous MGM studio head Darryl F. Zanuck, Marvel head Stan Lee and even porn star John Holmes. Singer later credited his time with the Signal Corps in his development as a filmmaker.[123]

In 1942, the Signal Corp established the Army Pictorial Service and took over New York's Kaufman Astoria Studios and ran it until 1971. Over 2500 training and indoctrination films and series, including *The Big Picture*, were filmed here during the nearly 30 years the Army ran the studio. Singer served in the Signal Corp from '51-'53. Upon his demobilization, he started collaborating with Kubrick on his early films. Then, by the late 1950s, he got a more plush gig: he was hired by Leslie Stevens to work for his Daystar Productions.[124]

Pennsylvania State University Press, 2007).

[120] Fenwick, 36-37; Baxter, 51.

[121] Fenwick, 37.

[122] Fenwick, 26-27.

[123] Baxter, 57, LoBrutto, 109, 117

[124] Dore Page, *Leslie Stevens Goes to Hollywood: Daystar Productions, Kate Manx and the Making of Private Property* (Jefferson, North Carolina: McFarland & Company, Inc., 2021), 108; LoBrutto, 98.

Stevens is an interesting figure. He's most well-known for having created the original *Outer Limits* and assisting with the 90s revival. But that's hardly all. He wrote and directed the cult William Shatner horror film *Incubus*; and the New Age classic *est: The Steersman Handbook*, which may well have partly inspired Werner Erhard's est movement. He helped create the original *Battlestar Galactica* as well.

A compelling case can be made that Stevens also helped develop the original *Star Trek*. Gene Roddenberry was present on *The Outer Limits* set throughout the first season. *Outer Limits* production assistant Tom Seldon described *Star Trek* as an "outgrowth" of Stevens' series. Dominic Frontiere, Stevens former partner in Daystar Productions, has described how he used Bob Justman (Daystar's production manager) and much of *The Outer Limits* crew to work on the *Star Trek* pilot.[125]

Interestingly, Stevens' links to *Star Trek* are further bolstered by... Alexander Singer. Between 1989 and 1998, he principally worked on various *Star Trek* TV franchises, helming over 20 episodes of *Next Generation*, *Deep Space Nine*, and *Voyager* combined. This was by far Singer's biggest contribution as a director or filmmaker in any capacity.[126] It's also interesting to note that Kubrick's interest in science fiction and extraterrestrials appears to have exploded around the time Singer went to work for Stevens.

Singer had known Stevens since 1953. They met at *Life Magazine,* where Singer was working on a photo feature for *Killer's Kiss*, Kubrick's second film. As was noted above, Singer also helped shoot this film. Stevens was impressed with what Kubrick and Singer had achieved with the visual look. It was Singer's photographer's eye that led to his gig at Daystar.[127]

Kubrick also knew Stevens and his Daystar partner, Dominic Frontiere. As to the latter, Kubrick originally considered Frontiere, a composer by trade before becoming a producer on *The Outer Limits*, to score *The Shining*.[128] As for Stevens, during the early 1970s, he attempted to turn an abandoned Titan missile base in Northern California into an ecological theme park. Part of Stevens' vision involved an "experimental underground farm with piped in sunlight plus a recycling complex and a massive communications center." This sounds remarkably like the mineshaft utopias Dr. Strangelove advocates building for the survivors of the nuclear Armageddon. One suspects this was a factor in Kubrick throwing his support behind this project.[129]

---

[125] Dore Page, *Leslie Stevens Goes to Hollywood: Daystar Productions, Kate Manx and the Making of Private Property*, 180. See also Knowles, C. (2013, July 10). Secret star trek: The godfather. The Secret Sun. https://secretsun.blogspot.com/2013/07/secret-star-trek-part-6-godfather-of.html; and Knowles, C. (2013b, July 13). Secret star trek: Playground of the elementals. The Secret Sun. https://secretsun.blogspot.com/2013/07/secret-star-trek-part-7-playground-of.html.
[126] LoBrutto, 27.
[127] Dore Page, *Leslie Stevens Goes to Hollywood*, 107-108.
[128] Emilo D'Alsseandro with Filippo Ulivieri, *Stanley Kubrick and Me*, 123.
[129] Dore Page, *Leslie Stevens Goes to Hollywood*, 202-203.

Stevens had a suitably "deep" background: he served as an intelligence officer in the Army Air Force for three years during WWII.[130] But that paled in comparison to his father.

Leslie Stevens III was an admiral in the US Navy at the onset of WWII. In the aftermath of that conflict, he served as the Naval attaché at the Moscow embassy. In this capacity, he received reports from Office of Naval Intelligence officers deployed in the USSR.[131] In 1949, the Joint Chiefs of Staff initiated the Joint Subsidiary Plans Division to coordinate covert operations and psychological warfare with the CIA. Admiral Stevens was the first chief of this body.[132] Later, he was bumped up to the National Security Council's Psychological Strategy Board, the first of many NSC bodies tasked with overseeing psychological warfare and covert operations. He served as this group's military advisor.[133] After retiring from the military, Admiral Stevens headed the American Committee for Liberation From Bolshevism.[134] This group was largely funded and supported by the CIA.[135]

I've opted to dwell at length on Stevens and his father because these connections are highly significant in regards to themes that later appear in *2001* and *A Clockwork Orange*. Admiral Stevens was deeply involved in psychological warfare and other covert activities during the early years of the Cold War. We shall further explore these implications in a latter chapter.

For now, let us return to the least documented period of Kubrick's life, 1951-1953. In 1952, Richard de Rochemont produced *Mr. Lincoln*, an early television docudrama limited series written by James Agee and largely directed by Norman Lloyd. Kubrick picked up some second unit work on this production, but again tried to embellish his role. The series was largely financed by the Ford Foundation.[136] As Frances Stonor Saunders revealed in *Who Paid the Piper?*, the Ford Foundation was regularly used as a funding conduit by the CIA during the 1950s and worked closely with the agency on their political warfare efforts. [137]

---

[130] Dore Page, *Leslie Stevens Goes to Hollywood*, 13-14.

[131] Ian Johnson, *A Mosque in Munich: Nazis, the CIA, and the Rise of the Muslim Brotherhood in the West* (Boston: Mariner Books, 2011), 81.

[132] Alfred H. Paddock, Jr., *U.S. Army Special Warfare: Its Origins* Revised Edition (Lawrence, KS: University of Kansas Press, 2002), 73.

[133] Maret, S. (2018, February). Murky projects and uneven information policies: A case study of the Psychological Strategy Board and CIA, 84n22, https://scholarworks.sjsu.edu/cgi/viewcontent.cgi?httpsredir=1&article=1034&context=secrecyandsociety. The Psychological Strategy Board later evolved into more well-known bodies such as the Operations Coordinating Board and the Committee of 40. This group, by one name or another, functioned for much of the Cold War. Its primary purpose was coordinating psychological warfare and covert operations between the military, the intelligence community, and "civilian" bodies.

[134] Dore Page, *Leslie Stevens Goes to Hollywood*, 19; Ian Johnson, *A Mosque in Munich: Nazis, the CIA, and the Rise of the Muslim Brotherhood in the West*, 82.

[135] See, for instance, Christopher Simpson, *Blowback: America's Recruitment of Nazis and Its Effects on the Cold War* (New York: Weidenfeld & Nicolson, 1988), 128-133, etc. For more on Amcomlib (as the American Committee for liberation From Bolshevism was known) and its links to the CIA, see Ian Johnson, *A Mosque in Munich: Nazis, the CIA, and the Rise of the Muslim Brotherhood in the West.*

[136] Fenwick, 40-42; LoBrutto, 82; Baxter, 51.

Even more mysterious is a project Kubrick was attached to in 1953 known as *Shark Safari*. Almost everything relating to this project, including the film itself, appears lost to the sands of time. All that remains is one slim folder in the Stanley Kubrick Archives. It reveals that Kubrick was hired to take over all aspects of post-production on the project in 1953.

The most noteworthy thing about this film is the writer, who was in contact with Kubrick. His name was James Atlee Phillips, a novelist and sometime screenwriter mainly known for pulp crime novels. During WWII, he served in the Marine Corps before being contracted as an operations manager for the China National Airlines in Burma. After the war, he did the same thing for the Burmese government via the National Airport.[138] As the OSS ran operations in Burma during WWII, it is all but certain Phillips had some dealings with him. Further, both of these airlines became a part of the infamous Air America. [139]

This has led to longstanding speculation Phillips worked for the CIA in some capacity. However, this has never been proven. The same cannot be said of his brother, however. That would be David Atlee Phillips, a notorious CIA officer who worked closely on anti-Castro operations during the early 1960s. As such, he's been widely implicated in the JFK assassination.[140] Keep this in mind when we return to Kennedy in the following chapter. It's also interesting to note David was a co-founder of the Association of Former Intelligence Officers. A lot of colorful figures have turned up in that outfit over the years.[141]

---

[137] See, for instance, Frances Stonor Saunders, *Who Paid the Piper?*, 138-144, etc.

[138] Fenwick, *Stanley Kubrick Produces*, 45.

[139] I have not been able to locate a "China National Airline" operating in Burma during WWII. What Fenwick probably means is the China National Aviation Corporation. This institution was loaded with members of the American Volunteer Group, better known as the Flying Tigers.. See Wedemeyer, A. C. (n.d.). First over the "hump:" The China National Aviation Corporation. National Museum of the United States Air ForceTM. https://www.nationalmuseum.af.mil/Visit/Museum-Exhibits/Fact-Sheets/Display/Article/196206/first-over-the-hump-the-china-national-aviation-corporation/. Corporate entities linked to the Tigers became deeply implicated in drug trafficking in Burma in the aftermath of WWII. See Peter Dale Scott, *American War Machine: Deep Politics, the CIA Global Drug Connection, and the Road to Afghanistan* (Lanham: Rowman & Littlefield, 2010), 79-80. In 2019, The *Big Bend Sentinel* confirmed Phillips worked for Civil Air Transport, a company eventually rolled into Air America, in Burma after the war. They were not able to confirm his membership in the Flying Tigers, however. See Sentinel, B. B. (2019, July 12). A stealth author from Fort Worth is revealed. The Big Bend Sentinel. https://bigbendsentinel.com/2019/06/27/a-stealth-author-from-fort-worth-is-revealed/.

[140] Fenwick, *Stanley Kubrick Produces*, 45. David Atlee Phillips has been covered at length in a number of works on the JFK assassination. Some of the most notable include Dick Russell, *The Man Who Knew Too Much* (New York: Carroll & Graf Publishers/Richard Gallen, 1992); Peter Dale Scott, *Deep Politics and the Death of JFK* (Berkeley: University of California Press, 1993); and H.P. Albarelli Jr., *A Secret Order: Investigating the High Strangeness and Synchronicity in the JFK Assassination* (Walterville, OR: Trine Day, 2013).

[141] Peter Dale Scott, *Deep Politics and the Death of JFK*, 217. Phillips' co-founder was Navy veteran Gordon McLendon. McLendon owned a number of radio stations throughout the South, including two early "pirate stations" dealing in rock 'n' roll during the early 1960s. Other known members include occult author Peter Levenda and notorious military intelligence officer Colonel Michael Aquino.

Let's now consider James B. Harris, whom Singer introduced Kubrick to. Singer and Harris met one another while they were both serving in the Army Signal Corps during Korea. Harris hailed from a wealthy East Coast family. This enabled him to found his own company to distribute film to television in 1949. Later the company, Flamingo Films, began developing its own content. Its most notable contribution was *The Adventures of Superman* (ABC, 1952-1958).[142]

Harris' father, Joseph, was a co-founder of Flamingo. After James departed Flamingo to establish Harris-Kubrick Productions in 1955, his father continued to run Flamingo. In 1957, the elder Harris incorporated a new company, Art Theatre of Air (ATA) as a successor to Flamingo. Its purpose was to import foreign films and distribute them to US television networks. From the beginning, Joseph Harris put a special emphasis on acquiring films from the Soviet Union. Starting in 1959, it heavily invested in filmed ballets shot in Moscow's studios.[143]

The returns were promising that Harris formed Vitalite Film Corporation for a similar purpose, though this company would focus on theatrical releases rather than television. Harris believed re-edited and dubbed versions of Soviet films would have a lucrative market. Harris-Kubrick Products was hired to prep one of these pictures, *Ilya Muromets* (renamed *The Sword and the Dragon* in the US). Joseph Harris learned that Kubrick was viewed as an up-and-coming filmmaker in the Soviet Union. Harris may even have engineered an invitation from the Moscow International Film Festival to Kubrick as a festival jury member. Kubrick declined. He was becoming concerned over the possible taint from the Soviet connection.[144] McCarthyism was only a few years in the rearview and the Hollywood blacklist was still in effect. We'll return to these developments in a moment.

As for James B. Harris, he produced *The Killing*, *Paths of Glory* and *Lolita* while also playing a crucial role in developing these projects with Kubrick.[145] He also helped with the early stages of *Dr. Strangelove* and has been credited with the decision to turn it into a comedy.[146] But, despite these early successes, Kubrick and Harris quietly parted ways during 1962. The public reason given has always revolved around Harris' desire to direct his own films.[147] But there may have been another factor at play.

In 2020, the Mamas and the Papas' Michele Phillips alleged that Sue Lyon, who played the title character in *Lolita*, lost her virginity to Harris during the production. He was 32 at the

---

[142] Fenwick, *Stanley Kubrick Produces*, 64; Baxter, 57-58; LoBrutto, 109-110. Interestingly, Baxter notes that Singer and Harris served in the Signal Corps' Photographic Center, located in Paramount's old studios in Astoria, Long Island.

[143] Fenwick, *Stanley Kubrick Produces*, 104-106.

[144] Fenwick, *Stanley Kubrick Produces*, 108-109.

[145] Fenwick, *Stanley Kubrick Produces*, 63-64.

[146] Fenwick, *Stanley Kubrick Produces*, 124; Baxter, 171.

[147] LoBrutto, 228-230; Fenwick, 119-120; 173-174.

time while she was 14. Phillips was a longtime friend of Lyons, having known her since she was a pre-teen.[148]

At this point it's also worth mentioning comments made on the Hollywood gossip website Crazy Days and Nights. This website has a reputation for publishing rumors that more often than not have a strong current of truth.[149] Which makes the claims about Kubrick especially noteworthy.

There it is alleged Kubrick raped Lyon along with two other tweens as part of the casting process for *Lolita*. Lyon got the role because she was the best in bed. During filming, he pimped her out to what is described as the foreign-born star of his film. This is surely a reference to Peter Sellers. Kubrick is then said to have "kept her around for a couple of years under the guise of getting her more roles, but the real reason was he could send her out to find other tweens and early teens to bring back to his place where he would get them drunk or slip them drugs and then rape them." Kubrick is accused of drugging and raping his victims, often filming them in the process. And finally, when the director died, he left hundreds of hours of the most extreme child pornography ever found.[150]

To begin with, there's an obvious problem with these allegations: no mention of James B. Harris. This is despite gossip columnists commenting on the Harris/Lyon "relationship" as far back as 1962. In the *Washington Post*, Dorothy Kilgallen noted that Lyon "bowled over her producer, James B. Harris. Her age is 16, according to her studio, and he's an old man of 33. She prefers the company of mature men, and James may be just her cup of tea." The following year, Kilgallen noted that Harris seemed to be following Lyon around the country, writing: "James Harris, who has been [Lyon's] most ardent suitor since the 'Lolita' days, still has hopes of recapturing her affections, and is talking of renting a house in Mexico while Sue is in Puerta Vallarte for *Night of the Iguana*. So Jimmy and Sue may write their own thrilling chapter."[151] By the way, *Night of the Iguana* was directed by John Huston, George Hodel's old friend. More on that in a moment.

But to return to Harris. Kubrick and Harris, along with the production company Seven Arts Production, signed Lyon to a seven picture deal in 1960. After Kubrick opted to dissolve his

---

[148] Weinman, S. (2020, October 24). The Dark Side of Lolita. Air Mail. https://airmail.news/issues/2020-10-24/the-dark-side-of-lolita. For more on Lyons' early relationship with Phillips, see Michelle Phillips, *California Dreamin': The True Story of the Mamas and the Papas* (New York: Warner Books, 1986).

[149] For more on the website's track record, see Bonner, M. (2016, October 7). The King of the Hollywood Blind Item reveals all. Vanity Fair. https://www.vanityfair.com/style/2016/10/crazy-days-and-nights-enty-interview.

[150] Lawyer. (2018, February 13). Blind items revealed #6. Crazy Days and Nights. https://www.crazydaysandnights.net/2018/07/blind-items-revealed-6_5.html.

[151] These quotes were taken from James Fenwick, "The exploitation of Sue Lyon: Lolita (1962), archival research, and questions for film history, Feminist Media Studies," 23:4, 1786-1801, DOI: 10.1080/14680777.2021.1996422, 2023, https://shura.shu.ac.uk/28988/10/Fenwick-TheExploitationOfSueLyon%28VoR%29.pdf.

partnership with Harris following *Lolita*, Harris and Seven Arts are who managed Lyon's career while Kubrick moved onto *Dr. Strangelove*. Kubrick wrote periodic letters to Harris requesting updates on the roles Lyon was offered. Among the projects being considered for her was Harris' proposed directorial debut, *Portrait of a Young Man Drowning*. There, Harris wanted her to play a teenager who is raped. Eventually, the project fell through.[152]

Harris' comments to Kubrick concerning this film are especially interesting. He stated:

"I let Ray Stark read the script [I Want My Mother] since they actually had first call on Sue at that time. My thinking was that perhaps he would get the idea of trying to acquire the project for Seven Arts. This as you know would have been very helpful in eliminating our commitment. However, unfortunately, or fortunately, he merely returned the script saying he was surprised that after all the projects they had suggested for Sue, I would come up with "this type of role in this type of picture." I must interpret this as complete disinterest on his part. Again a natural reaction by someone trained in Hollywood. [...] If you could see the reaction from publicists, publicity people, photographers, photo services and anyone connected with the press, on the exploitable values of Rita and Sue, my first picture as a director, the subject matter and the possibilities of additional casting, you would know why I want to fight so hard to get this picture made."[153]

Eventually, Harris gave up her contract to Seven Arts in order to pay off the debts of Harris-Kubrick when their company dissolved. The swap was made during the filming of *Night of the Iguana*. Again, Harris' comments are very revealing, so I'm going to quote at length from a July 11, 1963 letter he wrote to Kubrick:

"Now I come to what I started to write to you about when I received your letter, and that is Sue Lyon – Seven Arts. After a discussion with Lou and Jack, which only took a few minutes, as we know this is a most advantageous deal for us, we agreed with Seven Arts to amend the Sue Lyon deal as follows:

"In consideration of her co-starring with Richard Burton, Ava Gardner, and Deborah Kerr in THE NIGHT OF THE IGUNA to be directed by John Huston, they will take over her contract completely and we will be given the use of Sue for one picture a year for the remainder of her contract. We realize that under no circumstances could we ever use her for more than one picture a year anyway, and in this arrangement we only have to pay double her weekly salary for each week we use her, but have the right to either loan her out or use her ourselves and keep the entire amount of money that we get for her.

"Seven Arts blackmailed us by saying they would not put her in the picture unless the deal was amended. Since they have close to $100,000.00 already invested, they would prefer to

---

[152] James Fenwick, "The exploitation of Sue Lyon: Lolita (1962), archival research, and questions for film history, Feminist Media Studies," 23:4, 1786-1801, DOI: 10.1080/14680777.2021.1996422, 2023, https://shura.shu.ac.uk/28988/10/Fenwick-TheExploitationOfSueLyon%28VoR%29.pdf.

[153] Quotation taken from Fenwick, "The exploitation of Sue Lyon"

start fresh with a new girl they would prefer to own completely. This sounds a little peculiar but Ray Stark said that he would rather own 100% of someone like Tuesday Weld, or any newcomer which they could control, than build Sue up and have to deal with us on approvals and also split 50-50. [...] Our big advantage is that we know that there aren't too many pictures left in her, unless she changes her attitude about her career, and in the new arrangements we do not have to concern ourselves with their recouping all the money they have invested. I do believe that playing in a picture with Richard Burton, particularly since her part is romantically connected with his, will push her close to the top of the female attractions. She might be worth $100,000 when it is our turn to use her, and we don't have to bother producing the picture which I am sure neither of us want to do."[154]

In this context, the allegations made on Crazy Days and Nights concerning Kubrick are even more suspect. And then there's the timing of the claims. They were published on February 13, 2018. This was just a little over a year before Sue Lyon died, when her health began to go into permanent decline. Not long after she died, Michelle Phillips came forward with her claims regarding Harris. This is interesting because the post appears to be accusing Kubrick of doing the things that Harris was actually engaged in. This is especially true of Lyon's post-*Lolita* career, which Kubrick was little involved in. I suspect that Harris or someone tied to him, concerned at what deathbed revelations Lyon was poised to make, decided to be proactive. Thus, a narrative was spun in which Kubrick was smeared with actions Harris was engaged in.

The one aspect of Crazy Days and Nights' allegations that are compelling are the claims that Kubrick had a vast trove of pornography. Many of Kubrick's former associates have remarked that the director was fascinated by pornography.[155]

It's interesting to note comments made by Emilio D'Alessandro, Kubrick's longtime driver and assistant, concerning the immediate aftermath of the director's death. Emilio has aggressively pushed back on conspiratorial claims concerning Kubrick over the years. But following the director's death, Emilio describes how a group of unnamed individuals entered the Kubrick manor and ransacked the director's private quarters. Quarters which only Kubrick and Emilio supposedly had the keys to. Emilio didn't understand how they had gained entrance. Christiane Kubrick, Stanley's third and final wife, apparently didn't let them in. Emilio implies personal materials of Kubrick's were taken during this encounter.[156]

So, perhaps there is something to the rumors of Kubrick's dirty movies, which numerous actors and other notables, appeared in. But if Kubrick did have such a cache, it didn't seem to do him much good when it came to making *Napoleon*. Suffice to say, Kubrick comes off as

---

[154] Quotation found in Fenwick, "The exploitation of Sue Lyon"

[155] Baxter, 194-195; Fenwick, *Stanley Kubrick Produces*, 194; Kolker and Abrams, *Eyes Wide Shut*,28. Kubrick toyed with the idea of making a big budget hardcore porn film as far back as the filming of *Dr. Strangelove*. It is believed this was one of the inspirations behind what became *Eyes Wide Shut*.

[156] D'Alessandro with Ulivieri, 333.

surprisingly powerless for a man who faked the moon landing and had an extensive collection of porn featuring various VIPs. Allegedly.

***

While we're speculating, let's consider one final point of interest about Harris: He's a big James Ellroy fan. He was the first filmmaker to adapt Ellroy's gritty crime novels to the screen. The most-well known Ellroy adaptation is the Oscar-winning *LA Confidential*, which Harris had no role in. But the last film Harris worked on in any capacity was the 2006 adaptation of *The Black Dahlia*.

A popular and compelling suspect for the Black Dahlia killer was the previously mentioned Dr. George Hodel. His daughter, Tamar Hodel, was a close friend and surrogate mother to future rock star Michelle Philips of the Mamas and Papas. During the early 1960s, Tamar and Michelle were an inseparable duo, and occasionally a trio.[157] The third member was Sue Lyon, who received a copy of *Lolita* from Michelle several years before being cast in the role. But it fell to Tamar to explain the novel's infamous masturbation scene to Lyon.[158] It was Tamar who introduced her to her future husband, Papa John Phillips.[159] John later raped his own daughter, Mackenzie, from another marriage. These were some incestuous circles, in more ways than one.

Consider Peter Sellers, the star of Kubrick's *Lolita* and *Dr. Strangelove*. His interest in co-star Lyon was described as "entirely non-professional." During a post production press junket that stopped off at his house, co-star James Mason was creeped out when Sellers spent the entire time on the floor taking pictures of Lyon.[160] Later, Sellers was a guest of Michelle Phillips and Papa John at their Bel Air mansion during the late 1960s. This was the same scene that included various Laurel Canyon rockers, fellow actors like Marlon Brando and future Kubrick star Ryan O'Neal, and Roman Polanski and wife Sharon Tate.[161] Charles Manson is long rumored to have made the scene as well.[162]

Charles Manson was successfully prosecuted by Vincent Bugliosi. Manson was one of two cases Bugliosi made his reputation off of. The other involved Kubrick's cousin Paul Perveler,

---

[157] For more on the relationship between Phillips and Tamar Hodel, see Michelle Phillips, *California Dreamin': The True Story of the Mamas and the Papas*. See also Weller, S. (2007, November 20). California dreamgirl. Vanity Fair. https://www.vanityfair.com/news/2007/12/phillips200712.

[158] Weller, S. (2007, November 20). California dreamgirl. Vanity Fair. https://www.vanityfair.com/news/2007/12/phillips200712; Phillips, *California Dreamin'*, 7-8.

[159] Phillips, *California Dreamin'*, 16-19.

[160] Baxter, 170.

[161] Weller, S. (2007, November 20). California dreamgirl. Vanity Fair. https://www.vanityfair.com/news/2007/12/phillips200712

[162] See, for instance, Ed Sanders, *The Family* 3rd ed. (Boston: De Capo Press, 2002), 59-60, 62. Michelle Phillips acknowledged that she and John believed the Mansonites had stalked their Bel Air residence a time or two. See Phillips, *California Dreamin'*, 172-173

whom Bugliosi convicted of murder in 1969. Bugliosi later wrote successful books about both trials --*Helter Skelter* and *Till Death Us Do Part.*

In the later work, Bugliosi revealed some noteworthy characteristics about Perveler and his criminal activities. Politically, Perveler had drifted to the far right by the time of his arrest after starting the 1960s off as a Kennedy Democrat. He embraced Goldwater and joined the John Birch Society. He even received literature from the Minutemen,[163] the first significant Cold War-era militia. The Minutemen were deeply implicated in criminal and terrorist activities during the 1960s.[164]

Bugliosi also notes that by the mid-1960s, Perveler had started dressing like a gangster and hinted that he worked for the Syndicate.[165] While Bugliosi chalks this up to Perveler's blustering, it does seem that he was running a criminal operation out of his bar, the Grand Duke. He fenced stolen goods and provided "clean guns" for robberies to local hoods.[166] Contract killings may have been on tap as well. Even Bugliosi acknowledges the probability that Perveler did not kill his wife, but hired someone to carry out the deed. He was also accused of commissioning hoods to kidnap a wealthy relative from LA International Airport and relieve him of the $70,000 in cash he would be flying with.[167] Perveler made this suggestion in 1967, well after Kubrick had stopped flying. But this may have been around the time his parents were relocating to LA.

One of the LAPD detectives to work the case was the legendary John St. John, alias "Jigsaw John."[168] St. John earned his celebrity reputation by working several high profile cases involving serial killers, including Richard "The Night Stalker" Ramirez and the Hillside Strangler. But St. John's first significant assignment was investigating the Black Dahlia. St. John was first assigned the case in 1948 and continued to work it until his retirement in 1993.[169]

Nor were Bugliosi and St. John the only legal superstars involved in the case. Kristina Cromwell, Perveler's mistress and co-defendant, retained Melvin Belli as her attorney. Next to F. Lee Bailey, Belli may have been the most celebrated defense attorney in the country at the time. Belli had represented a variety of celebrities in his day—Muhammad Ali, Chuck Berry, the Rolling Stones, Mae West, and Tony Curtis, who co-starred in *Spartacus* and developed a friendship with Kubrick. Belli had also represented Jack Ruby, Lee Harvey

---

163 Vincent Bugliosi with Ken Hurwitz, *Till Death Us Do Part: A True Murder Mystery*, 47.

164 See, for instance, William Turner, *Power on the Right* (Berkeley, CA: Ramparts Press, 1971), 63-90, etc.

165 Vincent Bugliosi with Ken Hurwitz, *Till Death Us Do Part: A True Murder Mystery*, 90.

166 Vincent Bugliosi with Ken Hurwitz, *Till Death Us Do Part: A True Murder Mystery*, 118.

167 Vincent Bugliosi with Ken Hurwitz, *Till Death Us Do Part: A True Murder Mystery*, 118.

168 Vincent Bugliosi with Ken Hurwitz, *Till Death Us Do Part: A True Murder Mystery*, 27-28.

169 Malnic, E. (1995, May 4). Legendary LAPD detective “jigsaw john” st. john dies□:Police: In four decades on the force, he was known as a fair cop with dogged skill at piecing together murder clues. Los Angeles Times. https://www.latimes.com/archives/la-xpm-1995-05-04-mn-62350-story.html.

Oswald's killer, on a pro bono basis. He was known for the occasional acting gig, and had recently appeared in an episode of *Star Trek* that originally aired in 1968.

How Cromwell was able to afford Belli's fees is a mystery no one has addressed. Bugliosi states that her parents put up $20,000 for the attorney's fees while friends contributed $2,300 towards her defense. But while Cromwell's family was solidly middle class, $20,000 is the equivalent of over $180,000 in 2024 dollars. That's a bit steep for most families, middle class or otherwise.

Bugliosi waited until 1978 to write his account of the trial. One suspects he was trying to cash in on the success of *Helter Skelter*. He opted to change the names of Perveler, Cromwell and others closely connected to the crimes for the book. There has been suspicion that he was pressured by Kubrick to keep the Perveler name out of the book. But Cromwell was paroled in 1976. It's just as likely the names were changed to protect her privacy (and to prevent a possible lawsuit against Bugliosi).

As was noted earlier, *Death* was made into a 1992 TV movie starring *Full Metal Jacket*'s Arliss Howard as Bugliosi. The district attorney was just wrapping up Perveler's trial when the Manson killings occurred. One can only imagine what Kubrick thought of Bugliosi moving on from his cousin to Manson. Nor would this have been the only reason for Kubrick to follow the Manson trial.

A persistent rumor surrounding director Roman Polanski at the time his wife was murdered by the Manson family is that he had been filming his Hollywood and rock 'n' roll friends in intimate moments. This may even involve S & M. Paul Krassner alleged the LAPD had acquired some of this footage and were even selling it on the black market. Among those filmed were Greg Bautzer, an attorney for Howard Hughes, with the former wife of a former governor, Sharon Tate in one tape with a popular singer and in another with Steve McQueen, and an orgy featuring Cass Elliot of the Mamas and Papas, Yul Brynner and Peter Sellers. Later, Sellers and Brynner were part of a group offering a $25,000 reward for the Tate killers.[170]

One of the most incredible and longest standing allegations concerning the Tate murders revolves around one of these tapes. As the story goes, several days before the Tate murders, drug dealer Billy Doyle made the scene at the Mama Cass Elliot's nearby Laurel Canyon residence. There, he drank, smoked and snorted himself into unconsciousness. While never a good idea, doing so around individuals who believed Doyle had burned them on a drug deal proved to be a tremendous miscalculation. He was whipped, anally raped and potentially videotaped while this was all unfolding by figures who turned up dead at the Tate House

---

[170] Paul Krassner, *Confessions of a Raving, Unconfined Nut: Misadventures in the Counterculture* 2nd ed., 225. See also, Ed Sanders, *The Family*, 253-256, 331-332, etc. Sanders reports that at one point Polanski was suspicious enough of Papa John's involvement in his wife's murder that he snuck into his Bel Air residence and chemically checked Phillips' Jaguar for bloodstains.

several days later. In some accounts, the incident occurred at the Polanski residence or the Phillips' Bel Air mansion.[171]

The legitimacy of these claims have long been debated, but investigative journalist Tom O'Neill was eventually able to confirm the substance of them: Doyle had been drugged at the Polanski residence and was later taken to Cass Elliot's. There was a good chance he had been raped, but O'Neill was unable to confirm if it was filmed. O'Neill did find that the police considered Doyle and his associates suspects immediately following the Tate murders. And many people in these social circles thought this incident was connected to the killings.[172]

Recall the allegations that Kubrick had a massive trove of hardcore child porn at his residence at the time of his death. And here we find allegations of pornography turning up in the Tate murders. At one point, Manson himself claimed some of these films constituted "kiddie porn."[173] Kubrick was in a position to have knowledge of these claims. He had personally known Roman Polanski since at least the mid-1960s. In 1967, Polanski screened his then-latest picture, *The Fearless Vampire Killers*, for Kubrick at Abbots Mead.[174] Polanski later invited Kubrick to his wedding reception at the Playboy Club, which Kubrick wisely declined.[175]

Kubrick was never a part of Polanski's LA circles, but many of his collaborators were. In addition to Sellers, another one was *Dr. Strangelove* co-writer Terry Southern, who plotted the *Blue Movie* project with Kubrick and later turned it into a novel. As was noted above, this work dealt with a Hollywood director trying to make a porno with Hollywood stars. Further, Southern was a contributor to Paul Krassner's *The Realist*. As was noted in the introduction, Kubrick read *The Realist* from the late 1950s until at least the mid-1960s. If he was still a reader during the 1970s, it surely would have encountered Krassner's musings on the Manson killings.

Jack Nicholson was also a part of this scene and a longtime friend of Polanski's. When Polanski raped a 13 year old girl in 1977, he did so at Nicholson's Mulholland Drive residence. Present for part of this incident was Anjelica Huston,[176] the daughter of director John. Nicholson started filming *The Shining* in the UK with Kubrick not long after the Polanski scandal. In some accounts, his performance was partly channeling the darkness that had enveloped his Hollywood circles with Manson and Polanski.[177]

---

[171] Ed Sanders, *The Family*, 195; Tom O'Neill with Dan Piepenbring, *Chaos: Charles Manson, the CIA, and the Secret History of the Sixties* (New York: Little, Brown and Company, 2019), 68.

[172] Tom O'Neill, *Chaos: Charles Manson, the CIA, and the Secret History of the Sixties*, 68-73.

[173] Jonathan Vankin & John Whalen, *The Eighty Greatest Conspiracies of All Time: History's Biggest Mysteries, Coverups & Cabals* (New York: Citadel Press, 2004), 270-271.

[174] Michael Benson, *Space Odyssey*, 307.

[175] Robert P Kolker and Nathan Abrams, *Kubrick: An Odyssey*, 265;

[176] Patrick McGilligan, *Jack's Life: A Biography of Jack Nicholson* (New York: W.W. Norton & Company, 1994), 296-299

[177] See Patrick McGilligan, *Jack's Life*, 309-312, etc.

Kubrick officially befriended Nicholson during the late 1960s when he was considering the actor for the lead in *Napoleon*. This was in the immediate aftermath of Nicholson's big break with *Easy Rider*.[178] It's possible they encountered one another nearly a decade before then. During the 1950s, they were both guests at the residence of Samson DeBrier, whom Nicholson characterized as a "male witch."[179] Regardless, Kubrick remained close to the actor from the late 1960s onward. When his relationship with his youngest daughter Vivian went into tailspin after she relocated to LA during the 1990s, it was Nicholson whom Kubrick trusted to check in on her.[180] Nicholson was present at Kubrick's funeral and one of the only actors he continued to communicate with after the film they worked on was completed.

In a 2020 article on *DuJour*, Michelle Phillips alleges that she shared Tamar's Dahlia musings with Nicholson when the two were dating. She further claims that Tamar's allegations were incorporated into *Chinatown*,[181] a film that Polanski directed, and one co-starring Hodel's longtime friend, director John Huston. Nicholson idolized Huston and viewed him as a father-like figure. This was probably a big part of Nicholson's attraction to Anjelica Huston.[182]

Man Ray and John Huston were among George Hodel's closest associates in LA's surrealist circles during the late 1940s. Kubrick's ex-wife directly worked for Man Ray on *Dreams Money Can Buy*. And now, we have Michelle Phillips' claims of feeding Nicholson Tamar's dirt on her father. I would suggest at a minimum it is highly plausible Kubrick became aware of these claims at some point during his life.

The allegations surrounding Hodel may have been a piece of Hollywood lore years before he was publicly linked to the murder. Elizabeth Short has become a mythological figure in film, beginning with *Sunset Boulevard* (1950) and *The Blue Gardenia* (1953), and continuing into the present day. David Lynch's 1997 film *Lost Highway* was partially inspired by the Black Dahlia, for instance.

A Dahlia-esque murder in *Highway* is committed in a home designed by architect Lloyd Wright, the son of Frank Lloyd Wright. Hodel was passionate about the architecture of the Wright family and lived in a home designed by Lloyd at the time of the murder. [183] Lynch claimed his interest in the Black Dahlia was spurred by conversations he had with John St. John.[184]

---

[178] LoBrutto, 329; Baxter, 240; McGilligan, *Jack's Life*, 309.

[179] McGilligan, 108-109; Baxter, 78. The salons DeBrier ran out of his home are legendary. Figures ranging from composer Igor Stravinsky to James Dean turned up there. Local legend holds that Dean made the scene with Malia Nurmi, the original Vampira, shortly before his death. Kenneth Anger filmed his cult classic *Inauguration of the Pleasure Dome* there in 1954.

[180] D'Alessandro with Ulivieri, 301.

[181] Weller, S. (2020, July 29). George Hodel and the Black Dahlia Murder. DuJour. https://dujour.com/news/uncovering-the-secrets-of-the-black-dahlia-murder/3/

[182] McGilligan, *Jack's Life*, 256-258, etc.

[183] Steve Hodel, *Black Dahlia Avenger*, 68-69, etc.

[184] David Lynch and Kristine McKenna, *Room to Dream* (New York: Random House, 2018), 353-354.

One of St. John's former partners claimed Hodel's name never came up in relation to the Black Dahlia.[185] But Hodel was not publicly linked to the murder until his son published his first book on the subject in 2003. Which begs the question: Was the use of a Lloyd Wright house in a film inspired by the Black Dahlia nearly six years before Hodel was linked to the murder an eerie coincidence or an instance of inside baseball? And if St. John was aware of the Hodel allegations, was Lynch the only he shared these thoughts with?

If Michelle Phillips is to be believed about Tamar Hodel outing her father as the Black Dahlia murderer in Hollywood circles as far back as the 1970s, the possibility of a Hollywood legend becomes even more possible. Elizabeth Short's death as a grotesque piece of surrealist art is surely something that would have fascinated Kubrick.

But it gets even more incredible. During the filming of *Chinatown*, the production frequented Hugh Hefner's Playboy mansion. Hefner and Roman Polanski were friends. Playboy even financed Polanski's adaptation of *Macbeth*, the film he made in the aftermath of his wife's murder.[186]

The 2022 docu-series *Secrets of Playboy* features disturbing allegations by former Playboy employees, Bunnies, and scenesters. At the forefront are claims that the famous Playboy mansion was beset with video cameras through the grounds. This enabled Hefner to accumulate decade's worth of videotape featuring numerous celebrities and prominent LA businessmen in a variety of compromising situations. In addition to Polanski, Huston probably participated in these activities. There is little question Huston had an affair with former *Playmate* centerfold Paige Young during the mid-1970s. Young committed suicide in her apartment during 1974. Many of her friends believed her death was caused by the abuse she endured from men she met through Playboy. She singled out Hefner and Huston to several intimates as her chief tormentors.[187]

While this may seem like an unwarranted digression, Huston's activities during this timeframe will come up later in this work. And it will cast his connections in an even more unsettling light. But to return to Kubrick, the notion of pornography in Hollywood was an ongoing interest. Even before his discussions with Terry Southern, this was a plot point in *Lolita* taken from the novel. At the end of both the film and movie, the title character is

---

[185] Steve Hodel, *Black Dahlia Avenger*, 345-346.

[186] Weinraub, B. (1971, December 12). "[I]f you don't show violence the way it is," says Roman Polanski, "I think that's immoral and harmful. If you don't upset people then that's obscenity." The New York Times. https://www.nytimes.com/1971/12/12/archives/-if-you-dont-show-violence-the-way-it-is-says-roman-polanski-i.html.

[187] *Secrets of Playboy*, Season 1, episode 8, "Predator's Ball," directed by Arlene Nelson, aired May 17, 2022, A & E, 2022, Hulu. For more on Paige Young, see Ryan Parry, W. C. C. for M. (2014, December 4). Paige Young the Playboy playmate of the month who felt so used she shot herself. Daily Mail Online. https://www.dailymail.co.uk/news/article-2857873/Passed-Bill-Cosby-Hugh-Hefner-dozens-Hollywood-honchos-Playboy-Playmate-Month-felt-used-abused-powerful-leading-men-took-gun-shot-head.html.

almost coerced into doing porno by writer Clare Quilty (played by Peter Sellers in the film no less). I can't help but feel Kubrick's ongoing interest in this subject was driven by things he either heard of or witnessed in real life.

***

Some of the most significant actors Kubrick worked with early in his career had suspect connections. The first thing resembling a bona fide star Kubrick got to collaborate with was Sterling Hayden, a B lister most well known for his work in gritty film noir. At the forefront of these efforts was John Huston's *The Asphalt Jungle*.

Hayden turned up in Hollywood around 1940-1941 and made two movies. He then leaves and enlists in the Army as war breaks out. He allegedly suffers an injury while training in Scotland and is discharged. Undeterred, he then enlists in the Marine Corp as John Hamilton. The Marines sent him to Officer Candidate School in 1942. But upon graduation, he was assigned to William Donovan's Office of the Coordinator of Information. This outfit soon became the OSS we all know and love. And Hayden, still working under the name John Hamilton, served in it throughout the war.

He joined the Communist Party while fighting alongside Tito's partisans in Yugoslavia. This got him into trouble with the House of Un-American Activities (HUAC) during the early 1950s. He eventually testified before the committee and named names. Supposedly, Hayden was "eternally remorseful" for this act.[188] But concurrently, he established himself as a sometimes leading man in B pictures such as *Asphalt Jungle*.

No other actor who was more crucial in launching Kubrick's career than Kirk Douglas.[189] The Hollywood legend was quite a political activist, though this part of his life is often overlooked. He was part of a loose network of actors and filmmakers who worked closely together for over 20 years to change the political culture of Hollywood. They included blacklisted scribe Dalton Trumbo, who wrote the script for *Spartacus*, producer Edward Lewis, who also worked on *Spartacus*, directors Stanley Kramer and John Frankenheimer, and fellow star Burt Lancaster.[190]

This is an interesting list. The nexus for much of this collaboration was Bryna Productions, Douglas' independent production company. Named after Douglas' mother, the company was established in 1949.[191] Throughout the 1950s, it released a series of politically provocative films: Kubrick's *Paths of Glory* (1957) and *Spartacus* (1960) as well as *Seven Days in May*

---

188 Neal Gabler, *An Empire of Their Own: How the Jews Invented Hollywood* (New York: Anchor Books, 1988), 376-337.

189 Fenwick, *Stanley Kubrick Produces*, 80, etc.

190 Ehret, M. (2020, February 10). Neo-mccarthyite witchhunters hypocritically mourn the death of Kirk Douglas. Antiwar.com. https://original.antiwar.com/Matthew_Ehret/2020/02/09/neo-mccarthyite-witchhunters-hypocritically-mourn-the-death-of-kirk-douglas/.

191 Fenwick, *Stanley Kubrick Produces*, 80; LoBrutto, 133.

(1964) and *Seconds* (1966). It also produced a stage production of Ken Kesey's *One Flew Over the Cuckoo's Nest* (1963). Under the auspices of Kirk's son, actor Michael Douglas, it brought the celebrated film adaption of Kesey's counterculture classic to the screen in 1975.

Edward Lewis joined Byrna in 1956 and produced most of the films issued by the company until his departure in 1967. He then founded a production company with director John Frankenheimer, whom he had previously worked with on several pictures. In total, Lewis produced nine of Frankenheimer's films.

Frankenheimer is most well-known today for directing the original *Manchurian Candidate* (1962). Much has been said and written about its parallels to the JFK assassination, so I'm not going to get into that here. Frankenheimer also directed the equally politically charged *Seven Days in May*, which Douglas and Burt Lancaster co-starred in. This is basically a non-comedic version of *Dr. Strangelove* about an attempted coup. It's initiated by a rogue military cabal after the American president signs a disarmament agreement with the Soviets. To say it eerily parallels Kennedy's final years would be an understatement. More on that in a moment. Frankenheimer also made the mind-bending thriller *Seconds* for Bryna with Lewis as the producer.

Kirk Douglas "went to far-off locations for the U.S. Information Agency (USIA) at his own expense for decades."[192] From the early days of the Cold War, the USIA has been used by the national security state for psychological warfare.[193] Which makes it especially intriguing that Douglas flirted with making a movie in the Soviet Union throughout the 1950s. This stemmed from a cultural exchange initiative the US and USSR launched in 1958 to foster feature film co-productions. At the onset, the Soviet cultural attaché at the Washington, D.C. embassy formally invited Douglas to participate in an adaptation of Jules Verne's *Michael Strogoff* in the USSR. But this soon fell through once the Reds decided that the book contained "false elements."

Inexplicably, Douglas next proposed *Doctor Zhivago*, a scathing account of the Bolshevik Revolution and its aftermath. The adaptation of *Zhivago* emerged as a potential collaboration between Byrna and Harris-Kubrick Productions. It's possible Douglas viewed the Soviet film connections of Joseph Harris, James' father, as a possible inroads in getting this film made.[194] Suffice to say, it didn't work.

---

[192] Gray, T. (2016, December 8). Kirk Douglas Turns 100: The legendary actor recalls Kubrick and the blacklist. Variety. https://variety.com/2016/film/news/kirk-douglas-100th-birthday-actor-turns-100-spartacus-1201934250/.

[193] Alfred McCoy, *A Question of Torture: CIA Interrogation from the Cold War to the War on Terror* (New York: Holt Paperback, 2006), 25. For a more in-depth examination of the relationship between USIA and the national security services, see Christopher Simpson, *Science of Coercion: Communication Research & Psychological Warfare 1945-1960* (New York: Oxford University Press, 1994), 52-53, etc. See also this author's earlier work, *The Art: The Secret History of Psychological Warfare, Conspiritainment and the Shattering of Reality Book I* (West Virginia: Mysterion, 2023).

[194] Fenwick, *Stanley Kubrick Produces*, 104.

Despite the setback, Douglas' political activities continued unabated. He appears to have been collaborating with the Kennedy White House throughout the administration. And the relationship was reciprocal . While often overlooked now, *Spartacus* was highly controversial when it was released. That's partly because Kirk Douglas made the last minute decision to credit the blacklisted Dalton Trumbo with the script.

Trumbo was considered an arch Communist. He had only been able to work in Hollywood using aliases for nearly a decade at that point. When *Spartacus* came out, Douglas was under assault from the far right. The American Legion denounced the film across their 17,000 posts in the US and were at the forefront of efforts to boycott the film.[195]

This was no idle threat. The Legion exercised tremendous influence in Hollywood during this era thanks to HUAC. Oftentimes, the only way a Hollywood figure could be cleared by the Committee was via the FBI or by self-appointed vigilantes from the Legion or like anti-Communist groups. Conversely, the Legion could bar an individual from working in Hollywood with just a word to HUAC. Its power was such that Hollywood infiltrated it through Navy veteran Al Chamie in a bid to change the national debate. Chamie eventually became a national commander in the Legion through these efforts.[196]

While the Legion wasn't quite as formidable by 1960, there was ample concern it could sink the film at the box office. In response, JFK opted to attend the movie at a public theater in Washington shortly after he won the 1960 election. And he gave it a favorable review in the immediate aftermath.[197] This presidential endorsement gave the film a whiff of prestige at this crucial moment, paving the way for it to become one of the biggest hits of the decade. While often overlooked, this act was instrumental in washing away the last vestiges of McCarthyism from Hollywood. The Legion had been the far right's primary cudgel against the film industry. The success of *Spartacus* exposed the Legion as a paper tiger.

It was around this time the FBI opened up a file on Kubrick. Around September 1960, he played chess with a "person of interest" in NYC that got the FBI's attention. This person has never been identified.[198] While *Spartacus* had no bearing on the FBI's interest, the higher profile it granted him may have been what originally put the director on the Bureau's radar. It's also possible this could be related to Harris and Douglas' ties to the Soviet film industry.

Another intriguing connection of Douglas' is the after-mentioned Ray Stark, a man who lingers over Kubrick's career like a specter. We've already seen the role Ray Stark played in the contract Sue Lyon signed with Harris-Kubrick. The storied producer and studio head first encountered Kubrick while serving as Kirk Douglas' agent during the *Paths of Glory* negotiations. By all accounts, Stark put Kubrick and Harris through the ringer. In order to

---

[195] LoBrutto, 192; Baxter, 151.

[196] Neal Fabler, *An Empire of Their Own*, 375-379.

[197] Baxter, 151; LoBrutto, 192.

[198] Robert P Kolker and Nathan Abrams, *Kubrick: An Odyssey*, 187.

secure Douglas for *Glory*, Harris and Kubrick were coerced into signing a five picture deal with Byrna.[199] Practically from the moment of signing the contract Harris and Kubrick began seeking ways to extract themselves from it.

After Stark took over running Seven Arts Productions, an early success for him was the Harris-Kubrick adaptation of *Lolita*. *Dr. Strangelove* originally began as part of a production deal with Stark's company as well. But Seven Arts withdrew after Harris and Kubrick dissolved their partnership. Supposedly, Stark didn't want to work with Kubrick without the steadying influence of Harris.[200] However, this didn't stop Warner Brothers from signing Kubrick in 1970 after it was taken over by Seven Arts.[201]

Inevitably, there's a George Hodel connection in this milieu. Stark cut his teeth as the literary agent for famed screenwriter Ben Hecht.[202] Hecht is an intriguing figure on a number of levels. He was a member of the original Fortean Society, and his early literary output has been linked to the surrealist movement. On a more ominous level, Hecht developed close ties to Irgun Zvai Leumi, a violent, Palestine-based Jewish terror group, in the run up to World War II.[203]

George Hodel idolized Hecht. One of Hecht's early novels, *Kingdom of Evil*, profoundly influenced the young Hodel. Steve Hodel, George's son, has argued his father's belief system was molded by this work.[204] It's possible Hodel and Hecht knew one another, though this has never been confirmed. Either way, Hecht was certainly a part of the same surrealist circles in LA as Hodel.[205]

It's also interesting to note that Kirk Douglas was questioned by police in the 1949 disappearance of actress Jean Spangler. There has long been speculation Spangler's disappearance was linked to the Black Dahlia murder. While Douglas was an early suspect, he was quickly cleared.[206]

***

So, to recap: Kubrick's career gets a major boost from Kirk Douglas. Douglas' involvement in *Paths of Glory* establishes Kubrick as one of the hottest young directors working. He then brings Kubrick in to direct *Spartacus*. This is Kubrick's first taste of working on a big budget film. The results are mixed and the relationship between Douglas and Kubrick is permanently

---

199 LoBrutto, 134-135; Baxter, 93.

200 Baxter, 174-175; Fenwick, 124-125; LoBrutto, 227.

201 Fenwick, *Stanley Kubrick Produce*, 159.

202 LoBrutto, 134.

203 Neal Gabler, *An Empire of Their Own*, 290-291.

204 Steve Hodel, *Black Dahlia Avenger*, 56, 406.

205 See Mark Nelson and Sarah Hudson Bayliss, *Exquisite Corpse: Surrealism and the Black Dahlia Murder* for more on these connections.

206 Steve Hodel, *Black Dahlia Avenger*, 289.

ruptured over the film. But the movie becomes a major political statement that Kennedy embraces. It helps overturn the blacklist.

Kubrick made his next film, *Lolita*, with Shelly Winters in a leading role. Throughout this timeframe, Winters was passionately engaged in campaigning for JFK. After Winters was unable to attend JFK's inauguration on account of shooting *Lolita*, she was promised a gig as mistress of ceremonies for a White House ball dedicated to press photographers. Kennedy was even prepared to "say something super personal" to Winters over British television in gratitude for her efforts, per Peter Sellers.[207]

Was Kennedy suitably impressed enough with *Spartacus* that he started to consider Kubrick as a vehicle for telling tales out of school? The director was surrounded by Kennedy people by 1960. This would have profound implications for Kubrick going forward.

---

[207] LoBrutto, 205-206, 209.

Chapter Two:

A New York Mensch in President Kennedy's Camelot

Simulmatics, *Strangelove* and HAL

Dr. Strangelove constitutes the first in what I view as a trilogy of films exploring brainwashing and methods of controlling human behavior. These themes were continued in *2001* and *A Clockwork Orange*. In the case of *Dr. Strangelove*, Kubrick addresses these themes primarily through the prism of psychological warfare.

When Kubrick began work on *Dr. Strangelove*, he was provided with technical advice via Alastair Francis Buchan of the International Institute for Strategic Studies.[208] Then and now, the IISS is considered one of the leading defense and national security think tanks in the world. Buchan's father, John, was a celebrated novelist who worked for the British War Propaganda Bureau and Intelligence Corp during WWI. His most famous work is *The Thirty-Nine Steps*, considered to be one of the first instances of a modern spy thriller.[209]

Alastair Buchan was a co-founder of IISS along with Denis Healey, for decades Labour's leading defense strategist. Healey spent time with the RAND Corporation during the late 1950s,[210] which probably contributed to the similarities between the two think tanks. Both institutes specialized in nuclear strategy. There are several pointed jabs at RAND in *Dr. Strangelove*, indicating what Kubrick thought of this "expertise." Healey later became an arch nemesis of Kubrick's during the 1970s, which we shall explore in a future chapter. It's also interesting to note that the seed capital for the IISS was provided by the Ford Foundation.[211] Kubrick certainly had an uncanny knack for crossing paths with Ford Foundation-supported entities during this point in his career.

In most accounts, it is Alastair Buchan who brought Peter George's *Red Alert* to Kubrick's attention.[212] This is the novel *Dr. Strangelove* is based upon. George also co-wrote the adaptation with Kubrick and Terry Southern. George was a WWII veteran and Royal Air Force (RAF) officer who served until 1961. He has been branded an intelligence officer, but that is not accurate. While he received foreign language training while stationed in Hong Kong and later worked at a classified radar facility, there is no evidence he was used for intelligence work. By all accounts, George was an alcoholic and had been for years prior to meeting Kubrick, making him ill suited for the spy craft. Nor was George a member of the Campaign for Nuclear Disarmament (CND) despite being highly critical of US/UK nuclear policy.[213]

---

[208] George Case, *Calling Dr. Strangelove: The Anatomy and Influence of the Kubrick Masterpiece*, 20-21; Baxter, 170; LoBrutto, 227. .

[209] Quinn, A. (2019, May 5). Beyond the Thirty-nine steps: A life of john buchan review – a man of no mystery. The Guardian. https://www.theguardian.com/books/2019/may/05/beyond-the-thirty-nine-steps-a-life-of-john-buchan-ursula

[210] Stephen Dorril & Robin Ramsay, *Smear! Wilson and the Secret State* (London: Fourth Estate, 1991), 51.

[211] Oshinsky, D. M. (2001, July 15). Bagman for democracy. The New York Times. https://www.nytimes.com/2001/07/15/books/bagman-for-democracy.html.

[212] LoBrutto, 228; Baxter, 170; George Case, *Calling Dr. Strangelove*, 21; Mick Broderick, *Reconstructing Strangelove: Inside Stanley Kubrick's 'Nightmare Comedy'*, 14.

The remarkable thing about *Dr. Strangelove* is that it is a pointed piece of psychological warfare that satires psychological warfare. This is a complex topic which requires a bit of unpacking before we delve into the film. To start with, we need to consider related bodies such as the National Military Industrial Conferences and the Institute for American Strategy. I deal with both at length in an earlier work, *The Art: Psychological Warfare, Conspiritainment and the Shattering of Reality Book I*. Here, I'm going to try and deliver the cliff notes version.

The official purpose of the National Military Industrial Conferences, which unfolded between 1955 and 1961, was to bring together senior officials from the Pentagon and the National Security Council with executives from many leading corporations of the time such as United Fruit, Standard Oil, Honeywell, US Steel, Sears Roebuck, etc. The objective was to develop an anti-Communist "educational program."

The Conferences were initially meant to target senior military officers and captains of industry with militant anti-Communism before applying such methods to the public at large. And they brought in some big guns to help with this. The University of Chicago and several other noteworthy schools from Illinois played crucial roles throughout the Conferences and later with the IAS. Also contributing were the Hoover Institute from Stanford University and especially the Foreign Policy Research Institute from the University of Pennsylvania. Present by at least 1958 was a Colonel James Monroe, then heading the Society for the Investigation into Human Ecology, or SIHE.

For those of you unaware, this was the outfit that funded much of the MK-ULTRA research during the late 1950s and early 1960s.[214] Just how much Monroe was involved with the IAS has been closely guarded. But we know a sister institute to the IAS was founded by Dutch intelligence during the late 1950s. The Dutch component behind it was called the Foundation for the Investigation of Problems of Ecology. It came together after Colonel James Monroe put senior Dutch intelligence officers in contact with Frank Rockwell Barnett,[215] the initial director of the IAS and for years a major source of funding throughout the far right.

One of the IAS's "innovations" under Barnett was laying the foundation for what became the infamous "dark money" network[216] behind the resurgent conservative movement. Barnett, a Rhodes Scholar, started out as a major figure at the Smith Richardson Foundation, a longtime

---

[213] Mick Broderick, *Reconstructing Strangelove*, 17.

[214] For the SIHE's role in MK-ULTRA, see John Marks, *The Search for the "Manchurian Candidate": The CIA and Mind Control* (New York: W.W. Norton & Company, 1979); and H.P. Albarelli Jr., *A Terrible Mistake: The Murder of Frank Olson and the CIA's Secret Cold War Experiment* (Walterville, OR: Trine Day LLC, 2009).

[215] Giles Scott-Smith, *Western Anti-Communism and the Interdoc Network* (New York: Palgrave Macmillan, 2012), 37, 49. See also David Teacher, *Rogue Agents: The Cercle and the 6I in the Private Cold War 1951-1991*, 5th Ed. (unpublished manuscript, 2017), 25.

[216] For more on the "dark money" behind the modern conservative movement, see Jane Meyer, *Dark Money: The Hidden History of the Billionaires Behind the Rise of the Radical Right* (New York: Doubleday, 2016).

funding source of the far right. Later, he effectively managed much of Richard Mellon Scaife's political contributions. He also brought other right wing sugar daddies such as the Regnery, Hearst and Koch families into the IAS orbit, and established a highly effective donor network for many of the leading right wing think tanks. Groups like the American Security Council, the Heritage Foundation, Hoover, and later the Council for National Policy. And if this wasn't enough, Barnett was also one of the principal architects of fourth generation warfare, which they called fourth dimensional warfare back during the early 1960s. Again, the IAS was at the forefront of instructing various right wing activists in Fourth Generation Warfare.

What it amounts to is that a lot of far right groups were established around 1958, when the IAS was officially set up. It likely played a crucial role in launching what became the World Anti-Communist League (WACL)[217] and the John Birch Society (JBS). The overlap between leading WACL figures like Stefan Possony and the IAS has been known for a while now. Practically the entire US section of the original US WACL chapter appears on the IAS' mastheads from the early 1960s onwards. But through related bodies like the National Association of Manufacturers (NAM, which played a significant role in the early national Military-Industrial Conferences), overlaps with the JBS can be discerned as well.

Robert Welch, the JBS founder, was on NAM's board of directors prior to setting up the JBS while at least three founding members were past NAM presidents. Further, figures like W. Cleon Skousen, active in the IAS during the late 1950s, later turned up in the JBS. It's all extremely incestuous.

It's entirely possible this is what Eisenhower was getting at with his famous Military-Industrial speech. It's what spurred Senator J. William Fulbright, surely at the urging of the Kennedy administration, to issue a warning in 1961 about the combination of right wing and military encroachment on US public opinion. He issued a memorandum to Secretary of Defense Robert McNamara that was later entered into Congressional record. Fulbright warned of the propaganda activities of US military personnel and cited eleven incidents of far right materials being used to indoctrinate troops and civilians. They included materials from the Christian Anti-Communist Crusade.

---

[217] WACL was a curious mixture of aging Nazi war criminals, budding black terrorists, drug traffickers and religious fanatics of various stripes. Its various international branches were deeply implicated in right wing terrorism throughout the Cold War. For more on WACL, see Anderson, Scott & Jon, *Inside the League: The Shocking Expose of How Terrorists, Nazis, and Latin American Death Squads Have Infiltrated the World Anti-Communist League* (New York: Dodd, Mead & Company, 1986); Russ Bellant, *Old Nazis, the New Right, and the Republican Party* (Boston, MA: South End Press, 1991)), 65-88; Kyle Burke, *Revolutionaries for the Right: Anticommunist Internationalism and Paramilitary Warfare in the Cold War* (Chapel Hill, NC: The University of North Carolina Press, 2018); and Dennis, Keith Allen, *Building the League: Transnational Anti-Communism and the Development of the World Anti-Communist League 1954 and 1967*, (unpublished, 2021). For more on WACL's ties to drug trafficking, see Kruger, Henrik, *The Great Heroin Coup: Drugs, Intelligence, & International Fascism* (Boston, MA: South End Press, 1980), 192-195; and Scott, Peter Dale, *American War Machine: Deep Politics, the CIA Global Drug Connection, and the Road to Afghanistan* (New York: Rowman & Littlefield, 2014), 20, 52.

This unfolded roughly at the same time General Edwin Walker was ousted for using Bircher literature to indoctrinate his troops in Berlin. Eventually, this led to his removal from the military. While these two incidents have never been concretely linked, it seems clear Walker and the JBS were part of broader efforts on behalf of the IAS. Certainly Fulbright strongly implied they were linked in his memo. Had these activities not been exposed in Congress, it's difficult to say how far they would have gone.[218]

But if *Dr. Strangelove* is any indication, these activities were still an ongoing concern to the Kennedy White House at the time filming began. The General Jack D. Ripper character is inspired in part by Walker.[219] Fittingly, Ripper has been driven totally mad by the IAS' own psychological warfare efforts. His Air Force base in Texas is totally decked out in IAS-style slogans and literature. And Ripper's obsession with fluoride is taken straight from Bircher materials. I propose that Ripper is meant as a representation of the risks for IAS' style indoctrination on US Military personnel.

While Walker was never directly linked to the IAS milieu, other officers lampooned in *Strangelove* were. Another popular candidate for Ripper is Air Force General Curtis "Bombs Away" LeMay, the longtime SAC commander and a co-founder of RAND. Among his defining characteristics were the phallic-like cigars he smoked, which was incorporated into Ripper's character. Additionally, LeMay was a major proponent of preemptive first strike against the Soviets, as was his protégé in SAC, General Thomas Power. Power has also been proposed as an inspiration for Ripper.[220]

Both LeMay and Power were members of the American Security Council for a time.[221] The ASC maintained close ties to the IAS from its inception. Later, the two organizations merged.[222] LeMay and Power probably provided part of the inspiration for General Buck Turgidson (George C. Scott), along with Army General Lyman Lemnitzer.[223] Naturally, he was also connected to the ASC/IAS nexus.

---

[218] These activities are all detailed at length in this author's *The Art: The Secret History of Psychological Warfare, Conspiritainment and the Shattering of Reality Book I*, especially 33-49. Other works that address the IAS nexus include Russ Bellant, *Old Nazis, the New Right, and the Republican Party*, 29-57, etc; Sara Diamond, *Roads to Dominion: Right-Wing Movements and Political Power in the United States* (New York: The Guilford Press, 1995), 46-51; D.J. Mulloy, *The World of the John Birch Society: Conspiracy, Conservatism, and the Cold War* (Nashville: Vanderbilt University, 2014), 46-49; and John Fisher, "History Milestones: American Security Council and American Security Council Foundation" (Wayback Machine, captured 12/07/12, https://web.archive.org/web/20121207230636/http://www.ascfusa.org/app/webroot/files/fckfiles/HISTORY%20MILESTONES.pdf).

[219] George Case, *Calling Dr. Strangelove*, 85.

[220] Case, 16-18.

[221] William Turner, *Power on the Right*, 207-208.

[222] . See John Fisher, "History Milestones: American Security Council and American Security Council Foundation." See also Bellant, *Old Nazis, the New Right, and the Republican Party*, 38.

[223] Case, 88; Mick Broderick, *Reconstructing Strangelove*, 135-137.

Another affiliate of the ASC was the American Legion. During the height of the Cold War, former FBI agent Lee Pennington did double duty in both. Pennington was a senior figure in the Legion who compiled a massive "library" of information on alleged subversives.[224] The blacklist did not end with Hollywood, but was applied to numerous industries linked to defense. Organizations like the ASC and the Legion compiled possibly millions of dossiers on the political activities of American citizens applying for work in strategically important sectors.

The reader will recall that that Legion attempted a boycott of *Spartacus*, which Kennedy countered by personally endorsing the film. And here is Kubrick in *Strangelove* pulling out all the stops to reduce the figures in this milieu to caricatures. This stretches coincidence. Much like the overlap between *Strangelove*'s plot and real life events in the Kennedy administration.

Given what we now know about the mindsets prevalent amongst the Joint Chiefs of Staff (JCS) during said administration, these concerns seem spot on.[225] At the onset of JFK's presidency, the JCS pushed for a preemptive nuclear strike on the USSR. But Kennedy's utter disgust at the prospect led to pressure being applied via private groups such as the Air Force Association (a sponsor of the IAS no less). Elsewhere, estimates of civilian casualties varied widely. The Pentagon's Net Evaluation Subcommittee put the figure at an "unacceptable" 30 million casualties. The Air Force's Strategic Air Command was far more optimistic, arguing a US first strike would entail a "mere" 12 million dead Americans. Presumably, this was an "acceptable" amount of collateral damage.[226]

Even conservative Kubrick scholars have acknowledged that some of Turgidson's War Room dialogue closely echoes the Net Evaluation Subcommittee's 1962 report.[227] Much of what appears in *Dr. Strangelove* concerning the SAC and US nuclear policy was highly accurate, and derived from open source materials. But the Net Evaluation Subcommittee report was classified at the time of filming. How Kubrick was able to arrive at the same figures through open source material has never been explained and probably can't be. I contend that the most likely explanation was that an insider was feeding him these figures.

But to return to *Strangelove*'s psychological warfare. The generals were not the only ones affected. While Ripper and the Joint Chiefs in the War Room serve as a commentary on the state of the senior officers, the rank and file soldiers in Major Kong (Slim Pickens)'s bomber come off no better. Outside of the James Earl Jones character, no one seriously questions

---

[224] Peter Dale Scott, *Deep Politics and the Death of JFK*, 244-245.

[225] Even academic Kubrick commentators acknowledge the depiction of the Joint Chiefs of Staff in *Strangelove* is disturbingly close to real life incidents. See Case, *Calling Dr. Strangelove*, 88.

[226] James W. Douglas, *JFK and the Unspeakable: Why He Died and Why it Matters* (New York: Touchstone, 2008), 236-242. See also Michio Kaku and Daniel Axelrod, *To Win a Nuclear War: The Pentagon's Secret War Plans* (Boston: South End Press, 1987).

[227] Mick Broderick, *Reconstructing Strangelove*, 141.

their orders to launch nuclear Armageddon. Rather, they simply parrot the same anti-Communist slogans plastered all over Ripper's base. Keenan Wynn's Col Bat Guano is no less hapless, denouncing Peter Seller's Group Captain Lionel Mandrake as a communist "prevert." He nearly prevents Mandrake from passing on the recall codes to Washington because he frets over reparations to the Coca Cola company. Talk about a commitment to capitalism!

We are left with a depiction of the US Military driven mad by their own psychological warfare efforts. And sadly, this was probably far closer to the reality than few dared imagine outside national security circles. Famed whistleblower Daniel Ellsberg worked for RAND, one of the major architects of US nuclear policy. during this era. After viewing *Dr. Strangelove* in 1964, while still firmly a Cold War hawk, Ellsberg emerged from the theater and proclaimed, "This was a documentary."[228]

Speaking of Ellsberg, I've often wondered if he inspired Matthew Modine's Private Joker in Kubrick's Vietnam flick *Full Metal Jacket*. Ellsberg was a Marine and active in Vietnam, though not at the same time. When he entered the war zone, he was working for General Edward Lansdale, one of the most influential counterinsurgency and psychological warfare gurus of the Cold War era.[229] Modine bears more than a passing resemblance to Ellsberg in the film.

It would be fitting, as that *Jacket* is every bit as concerned with psychological warfare as *Strangelove*. Joker, the closest thing the film has to a protagonist, works as a Marine correspondent for *Stars and Stripes*. Kubrick leaves little doubt that this is propaganda work via Jokers' quips to a superior officer in the "press room."

On a deeper level, the film is rumination on how American culture works hand in glove with military indoctrination. The soldiers, even the brutal Sgt. Hartman (R. Lee Emery), is obsessed with pop culture. Joker regularly breaks into John Wayne impersonations throughout boot camp, invoking his era's defining alpha male archetype. Hartman's Marines are reborn in the Corp with nicknames partly derived from television (i.e. Vincent D'Onofrio's hapless "Gomer Pyle" while "Joker" is surely a reference to the Adam West *Batman* TV series). When Hartman confronts an unhinged Pyle, he describes his breakdown as "Mickey Mouse shit." Nor is this the only reference to the popular cartoon character. An image of him is present in *Stars and Stripe* 's press room while the film ends with the Marines singing the "Mickey Mouse March" after intense urban combat.

The soldiers are self-conscious of being filmed and slip into character for the camera. The insinuation is that they have learned how to be soldiers as much through American pop culture as boot camp. As with *Strangelove*'s B-52 crew, Kubrick displays a clear fascination with how indoctrination manages the perceptions of rank and file soldiers. There's even a

---

[228] Case, 109.

[229] See this author's *The Art:The Secret History of Psywar, Conspiritainment and the Shattering of Reality Book I* for an in-depth discussion of Lansdale and Ellsberg's time in Vietnam.

bizarre reference to the JFK assassination when Hartman invokes it, as well Charles Whitman's 1966 shooting spree, to illustrate the lethality of Marine marksmanship.

***

Dr. Strangelove (Sellers)'s inspiration has long been a subject of debate. The top four candidates for the unreconstructed Nazi are foreign policy guru Henry Kissinger, nuclear strategist Herman Kahn, nuclear scientist Edward Teller, and rocket scientist (and former Nazi) Werner von Braun.[230] Kissinger is the most popular due to his thick German accent and bloodstained "realpolitik" ideology. But he is also the most unlikely. Kubrick consulted Kissinger's writings extensively during the preproduction, but neither he nor Sellers had seen Kissinger in the flesh prior to filming. Further, Kissinger was still a minor figure in foreign policy circles during the early 1960s. Still, Kubrick later saw Strangelove as presaging the public Kissinger persona.[231]

Herman Kahn is the most likely. He was a long time fixture at RAND (referred to as the "Bland Corporation" in *Strangelove*) specializing in nuclear strategy. And he was a leading proponent of the notion that a nuclear war with the Soviets could be "won." Edward Teller, another affiliate of RAND, is also in the mix. Kubrick indicated Strangelove's accent was influenced by the Hungarian Teller. And Teller was even more fanatical about nuclear war than Kahn. He later proved to be a major advocate of weaponizing space via the Strategic Defense Initiative, alias "Star Wars."[232]

Equally compelling is von Braun, Seller's acknowledged inspiration for Strangelove.[233] While von Braun did not have direct links to America's nuclear program, he was the most well known figure connected to Operation Paperclip, a post-WWII program that imported a litany of "former" Nazis and fascists into the United States to aid the national security state.[234]

Of these four individuals, Kissinger and Kahn lacked ties to the IAS-ASC-Military-Industrial nexus during the Cold War. Indeed, Kissinger's policy of detente would later clash with the "rollback" advocates in the ASC.[235] But Edward Teller was the ASC's primary scientific adviser

---

[230] Case, 95-97.

[231] Mick Broderick, *Reconstructing Strangelove*, 55-56.

[232] Case, 155.

[233] Case, 96.

[234] For more on Paperclip, see Linda Hunt, *Secret Agenda: The United States Government, Nazi Scientists, and Project Paperclip* (New York: St. Martin's Press, 1991); and Christopher Simpson, *Blowback: America's Recruit of Nazis and Its Effect on the Cold War* (New York: Weidenfeld & Bicolson, 1988). While the use of Nazis in defense-related research is fairly well-known now, they were utilized in all aspects of national security. Simpson's work remains invaluable in fleshing out how they were employed by the American military and intelligence services.

[235] In Cold War parlance, "detente" advocated peaceful co-existence with the Soviet Union while maintaining economic competition. Conversely, "rollback" sought to dismantle the Communist sphere. For much of the Cold War, the US sought a middle ground known as "containment" in which the US sought to contain the Soviet Union militarily in various proxy wars across the developing world.

for decades.[236] And von Braun was a speaker at two separate Military-Industrial Conferences.[237]

While little talked about now, Kennedy clearly put a lot of political pressure on the DoD to end the National Military Industrial Conferences via Fulbright. Had the Fulbright Memorandum turned into a full-blown investigation of the DoD, I suspect some very disturbing things would have come out.

I delve into the historical context around this in *The Art* extensively. But, in brief: the military was obsessed with launching a preemptive nuclear strike against the Soviet Union in 1963. During summer 1961, the JCS proposed a preemptive strike against the USSR in late 1963 after "a period of heightened tension."[238] The Pentagon would continue to push this insanity throughout Kennedy's presidency.

Strangelove was originally planned to come out towards the end of that year. It was to be screened for critics on November 22 , with a broader release the following month. This would be in the midst of the Pentagon's hypothetical period of "heightened tension." Instead, it turned out to be the day JFK was assassinated.[239] The film was screened several days earlier (probably November 19) for studio bigwigs and their families. In attendance were Jean Kennedy Smith and Pat Kennedy Lawford.[240] This presence of the president's sisters came about after Kubrick asked actor Warren Beatty to arrange a screening for JFK. Supposedly, Kubrick was concerned about JFK's reaction because the mockery of "Cold War pieties" was so extreme he feared presidential censor.[241]

Strangelove was originally to end with an epic pie fight in the War Room. During the melee, Seller's President Merkin Muffley[242] was to be struck in the face with a pie, leading General

---

Vietnam was the prominent instance of this. Detente was briefly en vogue during the 1970s, after the Vietnam debacle. But it was soon replaced with rollback following Reagan's election. See Thomas Bodenheimer & Robert Gould, *Rollback! Right-wing Power in U.S. Foreign Policy* (Boston, MA: South End Press, 1989); and Jerry W. Sanders, *Peddlers of Crisis: The Committee on the Present Danger and the Politics of Containment* (Boston, MA: South End Press, 1983).

[236] William Turner, *Power on the Right*, 208.

[237] See George B. de Huszar (ed.), *National Strategy in an Age of Revolution: Addresses and Panel Discussions of the Fourth National Military-Industrial Conference* (New York: Frederick A. Praeger, 1958),; and The Institute of American Strategy (ed.), *The Soviet Economic Challenge: Proceedings of the Fifth Annual Military-Industrial Conference * A Project of Institute for American Strategy* (Chicago: The Institute of American Strategy, 1959). Von Braun's second lecture was "Challenge in Space" while his first was the curiously named "The Acid Test."

[238] James W. Douglas, *JFK and the Unspeakable: Why He Died and Why it Matters*, 236. See also Michio Kaku and Daniel Axelrod, *To Win a Nuclear War*, 11; and *The Art*, 74-75.

[239] Bizarrely John F. Kennedy Jr., JFK's eldest and only surviving son, died on July 16, 1999. This was the day on which Kubrick's final film, *Eyes Wide Shut*, was released. JFK Jr. also died in a plane crash. As is well-known, Kubrick avoided flying during the later part of his life out of safety concerns.

[240] Case, 67-68. LoBrutto, 245; Robert P Kolker and Nathan Abrams, *Kubrick: An Odyssey*, 225.

[241] Robert P Kolker and Nathan Abrams, *Kubrick: An Odyssey*, 225.

[242] Muffley's appearance and mannerism were based on perpetual Democratic presidential candidate

Turgidson to exclaim: "Gentlemen, our beloved president has been struck down in his prime!" It's widely believed the pie fight sequence was cut due to this line following the assassination, but Kubrick made the decision some months prior. Kennedy's death did lead to one change: During the scene where Major Kong is explaining the survival kits to his crew, his original line was "A fellow could have a pretty good weekend in Dallas." "Vegas" was later dubbed over Dallas. [243]

Strangelove was not released until January 1964. Throughout this timeframe, the threat of nuclear war remained high. A lot of this was due to the John Birch Society, who launched the original JFK assassination conspiracy theory: namely, that Kennedy was killed by Commies. This propaganda blitz threatened to push the nation into a nuclear exchange. As incredible as it may seem, part of the inspiration for creating the Warren Commission was to push back against the "JFK-assassinated-by-a-communist-cabal" narrative then being pushed by the Birchers and fellow travelers.[244]

This was the climate *Dr. Strangelove* was released into. Lyndon B. Johnson's notorious "Daisy ad" during the 1964 presidential election played into this. His opponent, Republican Senator Barry Goldwater (himself a future member of the ASC), was heavily supported by the Birchers during his presidential campaign.[245] Both Kubrick and LBJ sought to depict the JBS and Cold War hawks as unhinged.

Is it possible Kubrick was enlisted by Kennedy or his supporters to push back against the Pentagon's nuclear fever dreams? As incredible as this may seem, Kennedy had already endorsed the novel *Seven Days in May* prior to it being turned into a film. As was noted above, the plot of both the novel and film revolve around an attempted coup by a far right cabal within the military. "It's possible," JFK said of the plot to a friend. Later, Kennedy encouraged Kirk Douglas to adapt it into a film. And Kubrick had discussions with Douglas about the adaptation during filming.[246]

If Kennedy was sufficiently unnerved by the military to support turning *Seven Days in May* into a film, is it that outlandish to believe he did the same for *Strangelove*? He had previously supported Kubrick's *Spartacus* against attacks from the IAS-linked American

---

and JFK's ambassador to the UN Adlai Stevenson. Even though Stevenson provided Muffley's look, it was Kennedy's administration that he was based on. See Case, 86-89.

[243] Case, 65-68, 89; Broderick, *Reconstructing Strangelove*, 182; LoBrutto, 245.

[244] D.J. Mulloy, *The World of the John Birch Society: Conspiracy, Conservatism, and the Cold War* (Nashville: Vanderbilt University, 2014), 90-91. I cover this subject in greater depth in *The Art*, especially 164-166.

[245] For the JBS role in Goldwater's campaign, see D.J. Mulloy, *The World of the John Birch Society*, 91-105, etc.

[246] Case, 127-128; and Hilmes, M. (2007). Seven Days in May (1964). Wisconsin Center for Film and Theater Research.
https://web.archive.org/web/20100610064500/http://wcftr.commarts.wisc.edu/collections/featured/kirkdouglas/film/sevendays/7days.html;

Legion. Kubrick was surrounded by Kennedy supporters during the late 1950s and early 1960s, most notably Douglas and Shelly Winters. And the president's own sisters attended an early screening of the film days prior to their brother's assassination. Presidential support is hardly beyond the realm of possibility.

If the purpose of the film was to push back against the narrative being promoted by Kennedy's rivals in the security services, it succeeded. General Thomas Power, a likely inspiration for Ripper and head of the SAC when the film was released, was forced to give a major speech defending the efficiency and security of America's nuclear arsenal. SAC even went so far as to shoot a short 1964 documentary called *SAC Command Post*. Its explicit point was that America's nuclear weapons could not be fired without proper authorization.[247]

The Genghis Khan-worshiping writer-director John Milius (*Conan the Barbarian, Red Dawn*) developed a long distance friendship with Kubrick during the 1980s. Milius claimed that Curtis LeMay and other senior figures in SAC tried to contact Kubrick after the film was released. Kubrick declined, which Milius described as a paranoid reaction. He claimed that the military loved *Strangelove* and wanted to honor him.[248]

But Milius may be alone in this assessment. When Kubrick thought he witnessed a UFO during summer 1964 while in the company of Arthur C. Clarke, he was reluctant to report it to the Air Force, fearing they would view it as a publicity stunt.[249] While working on the *Eyes Wide Shut* screenplay, co-writer Frederic Raphael discussed *Strangelove* with Kubrick. The not always-reliable Raphael quotes the director as saying: "A lotta people hated it [*Strangelove*]... They thought I was a traitor. They damn near refused to show it in the theaters."[250]

And that brings us to an interesting development in Kubrick's professional life post-*Strangelove*. A curious declassified document surfaced in recent years. It's a 1965 memorandum to Eric Goldman, then a consultant to LBJ in the White House, from the U.S. Information Agency. The reader will recall that Kirk Douglas, an early Kubrick backer, had a decades-spanning relationship with the USIA. As for the memorandum, it concerns an unnamed program which the USIA was searching for a film director to assist them with. Kubrick was one among several filmmakers the USIA planned on approaching for this project.

Nothing more is known about what was behind this memorandum. As it was issued while Kubrick was knee deep in *2001*'s preproduction, it has spurred ample speculation. Many see it as evidence that Kubrick faked the moon landing. Jasun Horsley takes a more sophisticated approach in his *Kubrickon*, arguing Kubrick was being used to generate propaganda for NASA and space exploration. *2001* was the end result of this collaboration.[251]

---

[247] George Case, *Calling Dr. Strangelove*, 115-116 .

[248] George Case, *Calling Dr. Strangelove*, 115-116

[249] Michael Benson, *Space Odyssey*, 57.

[250] Frederick Raphael, *Eyes Wide Open*, 103.

I think Jasun hit the nail on the head. To fully grasp what is going on here, I need to briefly address the NASA/Pentagon rivalry. In the first decade (the 1950s) of the space race, it was the military that oversaw this venture. DARPA, then known simply at ARPA, was mainly created for the purpose of developing rockets, satellites and ships for space exploration. The Air Force and Army had their own programs as well. When NASA, a civilian agency, was created in 1958, it quickly took over many of these programs.[252]

The geopolitics here are interesting. Eisenhower was alarmed by the military-industrial complex by this point. The space race, driven by the military, meant billions of dollars for the DoD to administer. Effectively, this meant the military would guide the direction of the crucial aerospace industry and related fields through these defense dollars for decades to come. By launching NASA, Eisenhower was depriving the military of billions. Kennedy was committed to this path, becoming a NASA backer. LBJ was an even bigger supporter of NASA due to its close Texas connections.

But the military still had designs on space and would continue to vie with NASA over this spending bonanza. By 1965, NASA's accomplishments were still sparse, as the Pentagon was quick to remind anyone who listened. With billions of federal funding and possibly its very existence still on the line, NASA was as in need of PR as any agency by 1965.

At a deeper level, Kubrick saw nuclear defense and space exploration, utilizing the same technology, as vying for the future trajectory of science and human development. While nuclear policy threatened to render the human species extinct, Kubrick viewed space exploration as offering the possibility to "change our views of ourselves and our world." In this way, Kubrick echoed JFK's own thoughts on space exploration as a means elevating the whole of society. Or, at least turning it away from the militaristic course it had taken during the early Cold War.[253] As *Dr. Strangelove* lampooned the military-industrial complex of the day, *2001* offered a Utopian vision of humanity's future sans this Sword of Damocles.

In a sense, *2001* can be viewed as commentary on how these conflicting impulses struggle for primacy in humanity's evolutionary journey. The celebrated "Dawn of Man" sequence links humanity's development with the discovery of tools, but especially weapons. This revolution enables one tribe of proto-humans to gain control of a waterhole at the expense of another. Cinema's most famous jump cut witnesses a bone used to murder an unfortunate proto-human being thrown into the air, where it transforms into a satellite.

While never mentioned in the film, *2001*'s satellites are weapon platforms for a new generation of nukes. The events in *2001*'s second act are driven by ongoing Cold War

---

[251] Jasun Horsley, *Kubrickon*, 63-67.

[252] See, for instance, Sharon Weinberger, *The Imagineers of War: The Untold Story of DARPA, the Pentagon Agency That Changed the World* (New York: Alfred A. Knopf, 2017), 44, 50-52, 61-62, etc.

[253] Filippo Ulivieri and Simone Odino, *2001 Between Kubrick and Clarke: The Genesis, Making and Authorship of a Masterpiece*, 40-41.

paranoia. Dr. Haywood Floyd (William Sylvester) dominates this section. He is a bureaucrat tasked with covering up a recently discovered alien monolith on the moon. In a scene onboard a commercial space station, Floyd encounters his Soviet counterparts at a lounge, where they pump him for information. Kubrick visibly likens this sequence to the proto-human tribes vying over the prehistoric waterhole.[254] The flat, emotionless way in which humans interact with one another in *2001* has often been interpreted as a comment on the dehumanizing influence technology has had. But specifically, technology driven by militaristic needs. Kubrick presents this as an evolutionary dead end. The second half of the film, in which space exploration dominates the remaining two sections, leads to humanity's evolution. In this context, *2001* is every bit as much an indictment of the national security state as *Strangelove*.

As such, I propose that Kubrick was once again enlisted to produce propaganda to counter the military. If this was the purpose of *Dr. Strangelove*, it succeeded and then-some. So, why not give Kubrick another crack? One thing often overlooked about *2001* is it secured NASA's cutting edge reputation among a generation of Americans a year before the moon landing. *2001* created a sense that this was already a fait accompli.

While this is speculative, what is not was the United Nation's bid to use Kubrick for such a purpose. In 1964, the UN announced that it was preparing, with financial support from Xerox, to produce a series of television films commemorating its 25th anniversary. Kubrick was cited as one of the filmmakers attached to the project, which was essentially a promotion vehicle for the UN. And promotion can be either PR or propaganda in the eye of the beholder.[255]

Kubrick later dropped out after being unable to find a story appropriate for the venture. The one film that came out of this endeavor, *A Carol for Another Christmas*, was a post-atomic take on the Dickens' classic starring Peter Sellers and Sterling Hayden, fresh from their celebrated turns in *Dr. Strangelove*.[256] It would seem that the UN still wanted the Kubrick touch in its PR exercise even if the director himself was not involved. But consider: if the UN was courting Kubrick to promote itself, is it a stretch to believe NASA would do the same?

Further bolstering this possibility is MGM chairman Robert O'Brien. As was noted in the introduction, O'Brien was crucial in protecting Kubrick from the MGM board throughout the making of the film. Despite *2001*'s success, it wasn't enough to save O'Brien's job. O'Brien's 1969 sacking was the culmination of a low key war waged among MGM executives over *2001*. O'Brien had no prior connections to Kubrick. His steadfast loyalty to the director and

---

[254] Thomas Allen Nelson, *Kubrick: Inside a Film Artist's Maze*, 116-117 ; Joe R. Frinzi, *Kubrick's Monolith: The Art and Mystery of* 2001: A Space Odyssey, 130-131.

[255] Filippo Ulivieri and Simone Odino, *2001 Between Kubrick and Clarke*, 24-25; Robert P Kolker and Nathan Abrams, *Kubrick: An Odyssey*, 233.

[256] Filippo Ulivieri and Simone Odino, 24-25.

2001 is often chalked up to Kubrick's wunderkind reputation. But is that enough to explain O'Brien's decision to stake his career and the future of MGM on Kubrick's film?

An intriguing possibility is raised by O'Brien's pre-Hollywood connections: he was a longtime friend of the Kennedy family.[257] Born in 1904, O'Brien graduated from the University of Chicago Law School in 1933. A supporter of liberal causes. O'Brien joined the Public Works Administration briefly before signing on with the newly-founded Securities and Exchange Commission (SEC) in 1934. In 1942, FDR appointed him a commissioner in the SEC. But when O'Brien initially joined the body, his boss was Joseph P. Kennedy, JFK's father and the family's patriarch. Thus, it's possible O'Brien's time with the SEC marked the beginning of his relationship with the family.

O'Brien was a lifelong film fan who abruptly shifted careers into Hollywood in 1944. Despite having no prior experience in the entertainment industry, he rose through the executive ranks, becoming MGM's president less than 20 years later. While often overlooked, Joseph Kennedy made much of his fortune in Hollywood during the 1920s and maintained contacts in the industry for the rest of his life.[258] It would be interesting to know if O'Brien benefited from this connection.

Regardless, Kubrick is again the beneficiary of a Kennedy supporter's patronage. For nearly a decade, from *Paths of Glory* to *2001*, this was a recurring motif in Kubrick's career. And given how much Kubrick's films from this era reflect the objectives and concerns of the family, this stretches coincidence, and this is all without even taking the bizarre *Fail Safe* saga into account.

***

Simulmatics was one of the most influential companies of the twentieth century, though little remembered today.[259] It was the first company to use computers for micro-targeting voters during a US presidential election, preceding Cambridge Analytica by over five decades. This technique was unveiled for JFK's 1960 presidential campaign.[260] Simulmatics' work on

---

[257] Michael Benson, *Space Odyssey*, 389-390.
[258] Easily the best account of JPK's Hollywood years is Cari Beauchamp, *Joseph P. Kennedy Presents: His Hollywood Years* (New York: Vintage Books, 2009).
[259] As of this writing, the only full length account of Simulmatics is Jill Lepore, *If Then: How the Simulmatics Corporation Invented the Future* (New York: Liveright Publishing Corporation, 2020). Limited accounts are presented in Yasha Levine, *Surveillance Valley: The Secret Military History of the Internet* (New York: PublicAffairs, 2018); Joy Rohde, *Armed with Expertise: The Militarization of American Social Research during the Cold War* (Ithaca: Cornell University Press, 2013); M. Mitchell Waldrop, *The Dream Machine* (San Francisco: Stripe Press, 2018); Sharon Weinberger, *The Imagineers of War: The Untold Story of DARPA, the Pentagon Agency That Changed the World*; and Annie Jacobsen, *The Pentagon's Brain: An Uncensored History of DARPA, America's Top Secret Military Research Agency* (New York: Little Brown and Company, 2015).
[260] Yasha Levine, *Surveillance Valley: The Secret Military History of the Internet*, 65. For more on Simulmatics' role in the Kennedy campaign, see Jill Lepore, *If Then: How the Simulmatics Corporation*

the Kennedy campaign, as well as their later connections to the Army's Project Camelot, brought the corporation quite a bit of notoriety by the middle of the decade. As was revealed then, this type of predictive modeling could be used to target voters as well as aid counterinsurgency efforts.

Project Camelot was the largest behavioral science program in American history at the time.[261] The purpose of Camelot was to develop computer models that would enable the Army to predict communist insurgencies breaking out before they happened. This involved massive amounts of data on developing nations, which, in theory, would enable the Army to track not just movements that could become insurgencies, but individuals. Basically, it was an early effort at pre-crime.

Once Project Camelot was leaked to the American public, a considerable amount of controversy broke out over it during 1965. Concerns over this technology being used domestically and all. It would hardly be surprising if Kubrick followed these developments. But beyond that, he likely had more direct knowledge of the principal company behind Camelot, Simulmatics.[262]

And that's because Kubrick had direct dealings with the Simulmatics milieu by the early 1960s. One individual who helped set up Simulmatics, but who declined to join, was a man named Eugene Burdick.[263] Burdick wore a lot of hats over the course of his life, behavior scientist being one of them. He was one of the first lecturers at Stanford's Center for Advanced Study in the Behavioral Sciences, an outfit that received its seed capital from the Ford Foundation.[264] But what Burdick is most remembered for are his novels. Three of his works are especially noteworthy: *The Ugly American* (1958), *Fail Safe* (1962), and *The 480* (1965).

The Ugly American was one of the most celebrated works of the Vietnam era. But it's *Fail Safe* from which Kubrick's connection to Burdick derives. Burdick and his *Fail Safe* co-author Henry Wheeler actually pitched the novel to Kubrick in 1961, prior to its publication, when they got word that the director was looking to do a film on nuclear war. Kubrick was already in the midst of adapting *Red Alert* into what became *Dr. Strangelove.* He declined the offer

---

Invented the Future, 116-124, etc.

261 Yasha Levine, *Surveillance Valley*, 67. For a broad overview of Camelot and the controversy it generated, see Irving Louis Horowitz (ed.), *The Rise and Fall of Project Camelot: Studies in the Relationship between Social Science and Practical Politics* (Cambridge, MA: The M.I.T. Press, 1967). See also Joy Rohde, *Armed with Expertise: The Militarization of American Social Research during the Cold War*, 63-89, etc.

262 Simulmatics was not directly involved in Camelot, but it was spurred by a report co-written by one of Simulmatics' founders; people who worked for Simulmatics either before or after Camelot helped design it; and it utilized Simulmatics' techniques. See Jill Lepore, *If Then*, 208-212, etc.

263 For Burdick's links to Simulmatics, see Jill Lepore, *If Then*, 100-101, etc.

264 Jill Lepore, *If Then*, 32-38

and sent him an outline of the *Strangelove* project and a copy of George's book by registered mail to the *Fail Safe* authors during January 1962.[265]

Meanwhile, George caught wind of *Fail Safe* and began to contemplate a lawsuit. He had ongoing conversations with Kubrick on the matter as they continued to refine the *Strangelove* script. Kubrick also began devising a game plan with his attorney when the film rights to *Fail Safe* were inevitably sold. George formally filed a plagiarism lawsuit against Burdick and Wheeler in early 1963. It was also around this time Kubrick learned that Sterling Hayden and Burdick had been friends for years. The director implored Hayden for silence on the *Strangelove* production.[266]

Burdick and Wheeler sold the rights to *Fail Safe* in January 1963. It went into production with Sidney Lumet as the director and Henry Fonda attached to star. When Kubrick caught word of this rival project, he launched his lawsuit. It was a frivolous lawsuit, one that Kubrick engaged in to delay the release of *Fail Safe*. Unprompted, Kirk Douglas offered Kubrick his assistance in the lawsuit in a letter discussing *Seven Days in May*.[267]

Kubrick ultimately prevailed and *Dr. Strangelove* made it to theaters six months prior to *Fail Safe*. But the lawsuit wasn't what ultimately caused the delay. The lawsuits swiftly brought about the collapse of Entertainment Corp of America, the company producing *Fail Safe*. This forced it to sell off all future productions, including *Fail Safe*, to major studios. *Fail Safe* ended up at Columbia, the same studio behind *Dr. Strangelove.* In theory, *Fail Safe* would come out six months after *Strangelove* despite being completed before Kubrick's nightmare comedy, but lawyers in the *Fail Safe* continued to lobby the studio for an earlier release.[268]

Kubrick obviously prevailed, but many questions remain. Columbia's actions are curious, to put it mildly. James B. Harris, Kubrick's former business partner summed up the outcome thus: "A deal was worked out—because they were both at Columbia, which absolutely fucked *Fail Safe*—*Strangelove* had to be released first."[269]

But why would Columbia do this? While *Strangelove* had a decent budget, it wasn't eye-popping and certainly didn't constitute a significant financial investment on the studio's part. And while *Red Alert* was more widely read prior to *Strangelove* than is generally believed, it never enjoyed the level of success as *Fail Safe*. Further, Columbia executives had misgivings

---

[265] Mick Broderick, *Reconstructing Strangelove*, 100; Jill Lepore, *If Then*, 174-175.

[266] Broderick, *Reconstructing Strangelove*, 101-103.

[267] Broderick, *Reconstructing Strangelove*, 104-105; Jill Lepore, *If Then*, 174-175; Case, *Calling Dr. Strangelove*, 63. Just how frivolous the lawsuits were is a matter of debate. George clearly seems to have believed Wheeler and Burdick plagiarized his novel. And there are numerous undeniable similarities between the two. But even Kubrick defenders such as Mick Broderick acknowledge the director's interest in the lawsuit was mainly twofold: to delay production on a rival film, and to generate free publicity as the two camps made their case in the press.

[268] Broderick, 106-107.

[269] Broderick, 110.

about *Strangelove* throughout the production. Mo Rothman, the executive designated by the studio to oversee the production, was increasingly alarmed. Kubrick attempted to win him over by purchasing the executive a golf cart. Rothman refused the gift, telling Kubrick it was "bad form."[270]

Mick Broderick depicts Columbia's UK head of productions, Mike Frankovich, as *Strangelove*'s leading champion. Supposedly Frankovich and other Columbia executives were having a "glowing" response to the *Strangelove* dallies.[271] Presumably this did not include Rothman, whom Kubrick hounded to watch the footage without success.[272] And even Frankovich had second thoughts after viewing the completed movie. He apparently found the film "unshowable, a disgrace to Columbia Pictures." Nor was he the only Columbia executive to have such a reaction to the finished product. [273]

All the while, Columbia had *Fail Safe* in the wings, a picture with a more conventional narrative; an established star and director; and based upon a hugely successful novel. And yet, it was *Strangelove* they opted to back. A film the studio long had misgivings about, and which they staged a hostile takeover of a rival production for.

Had Columbia opted to do nothing and *Strangelove* tanked after *Fail Safe* beat it to theaters, Columbia would have only been out $2 million, plus advertisements. They probably spent as much taking over *Fail Safe* and financing it. Then they opted to put *Strangelove* out first despite having serious misgivings about its box office viability. *Strangelove* could have easily bombed, leaving the studio with two duds on their hands, but with a more significant financial investment after taking on *Fail Safe*. In other words, they took on more financial risk by intervening rather than doing nothing for a film the studio had serious reservations about.

Suffice to say, Columbia's actions do not make a lot of sense from a business standpoint. Which leads me to believe that the studio's bottom line was not what drove these actions.

A possible motive may be discerned in the book Burdick followed *Fail Safe* up with. *The 480* concerned a thinly veiled version of Simulmatics working with a Republican populist candidate to win the 1964 election. The genesis of the book resided in a TV movie called *The Candidate* that Burdick pitched to Bob Hope in 1963. After that fell through, Burdick expanded the concept into a novel and renamed it *The 480*. The book was a success and there was considerable interest in adapting it during the mid-1960s, especially after the Camelot controversy. Unfortunately, the rights to *The 480* were a mess and the work never made it to the screen.[274]

---

[270] Baxter, *Stanley Kubrick: A Biography*, 182.
[271] Broderick, 106-107.
[272] Case, *Calling Dr. Strangelove*, 62.
[273] LoBrutto, 245-246.
[274] Jill Lepore, *If Then*, 182-186.

Even though *The 480*'s candidate was a Goldwater-esque politician, the plot was based on the Kennedy campaign's use of Simulmatics in 1960. With the election of 1964 on the horizon, I suspect there was concern in the Kennedy White House that if Burdick's book became too popular, it would blow back on Kennedy and how he ran the 1960 campaign. A successful film adaptation of an earlier Burdick book was not seen as advantageous. This may explain why Columbia executives went to bat for *Strangelove* despite their adverse, even shocked, reaction to the film.

Did Kennedy or someone close to him intervene and suggest which horse to back in this case? I don't think such a possibility can be discounted. Attorney General Robert Kennedy's fury at the company over boasting of their contributions to his brother's election was such that Simulmatics opted to sit out the 1962 midterms. RFK had effectively blacklisted them within the Democratic Party.[275] While Burdick never joined the company and was rather critical of it, his novel inevitably continued to link JFK to Simulmatics. Which raises the distinct possibility of *Fail Safe* receiving its own scarlet letter.

Yes, *Fail Safe* was very similar to *Strangelove*. But, so was *Seven Days in May*. And yet, it wasn't singled out like *Fail Safe*. What's more, Kubrick even offered Kirk Douglas advice while the actor was working on *May*. Douglas reciprocated and offered his support with the *Fail Safe* lawsuit. Further, *May* was released a mere two weeks after *Strangelove*. Apparently there was no concern about over saturating the market with films revolving around US nuclear policy and rogue generals.

It's also worth noting that Kubrick's *Strangelove* follow up, 1968's landmark *2001: A Space Odyssey*, may have taken a subtle swipe at Simulmatics. As I'm sure most are aware, the film revolves around humanity's development in relation to a series of mysterious obelisks that appear at different junctures in history. In the title year, one of these mysterious monoliths is discovered on the moon, triggering a mission to Jupiter.

Except none of the astronauts tasked with this mission are aware of any of this. They were never told about the obelisk, and instead think it's a routine mission of exploration. Further, three of the five astronauts are being kept in cryogenic chambers during the journey, officially to save life support. But these astronauts also trained separately from Dr. David Bowman (Keir Dullea), and his partner, Dr. Frank Poole (Gary Lockwood). These are the two astronauts awake when the film's third section unfolds.

Security is heavily compartmentalized for the mission, with no one knowing what the objective is. Other than the ship's AI, the famed HAL 9000. HAL is crucial to this whole section. Generally, the AI is described as malfunctioning and murdering the entire crew, save for Dr. Bowman. Arthur C. Clarke hints at this in the film's novelization while making this clear in the sequel, *2010: Odyssey Two*. But I have a different take, and as Kubrick's film differs in many ways from Clarke's novels, this alternative explanation cannot be discounted.

---

[275] Lepore, 142, 151.

At one point, HAL is shown questioning Bowman about all the secrecy surrounding the mission. HAL expresses concern over not being aware of their purpose. But later, it's revealed that this is a lie. HAL is the only one who actually knows why they're out there. Immediately after this encounter, the AI informs the astronauts that a part outside the spaceship is broken. Upon investigation, it is determined that the part is fine, and that HAL made an error.

But, did he? A tell tale exchange happens around the time HAL questions Bowman about their mission. It's noted that HAL is tasked with compiling psychological profiles on the crew.

It's often argued that HAL is a cover for IBM. That's what you're left with when you go up one letter of the alphabet. This may well be the case, but I think Kubrick is telling some even more serious tales out of school here. The ARPAnet, which became the Internet we all know and love, was being built around the time Kubrick shot *2001*. Its principal function was for command and control for the US Military. But a secondary goal was to compile data on human beings to form personality profiles and predict human behavior.[276] And that appears to be exactly what HAL is doing shortly before he reports that a piece is damaged.

Another hint possibly occurs during HAL's "death": In the delirium brought about by Bowman's "lobotomy," HAL refers to his teacher as "Mr. Langley." This is interesting, because Langley, Virginia is where the CIA is headquartered. As such, Langley is at times used to refer to the Agency.

I don't think the HAL 9000 malfunctioned. Rather, I think it did exactly what it was programmed to do: ascertain whether the crew would be able to handle the ontological shock when their ultimate mission was revealed to them. HAL does not seem to believe they were up to the task and acted accordingly.[277]

I know this may sound like a reach, but recall that once Project Camelot leaked to the American public, a considerable amount of controversy broke out during 1965. Concerns over this technology being used domestically and all. As with the exposure of the IAS and General Walker's use of Bircher literature, the Congressman leading the charge against Camelot was close Kennedy ally J. William Fulbright.

Did Kubrick know about the dangers of using computers to predict human behavior? Based on what I've just outlined, I would suggest that it would be more amazing if Kubrick was *not*

---

[276] For more on ARPANet's role in the military's counterinsurgency efforts, which very much drove the obsession with predictive modeling, see Yasha Levine, *Surveillance Valley: The Secret Military History of the Internet*; Sharon Weinberger, *The Imagineers of War*; Annie Jacobsen, *The Pentagon's Brain: An Uncensored History of DARPA, America's Top Secret Military Research Agency*; and this author's *The Art: The Secret History of Psywar, Conspiritainment, and the Shattering of Reality Book I*.

[277] A case was made for HAL's sanity in one of the Internet's oldest and most compelling pieces of Kubrickology. See Waldrop, C. (n.d.). The case for Hal's sanity. The Kubrick Site. http://www.visual-memory.co.uk/amk/doc/0095.html.

aware of Simulmatics and Project Camelot. Further, Camelot made heavy use of IBM computers to compile data. It surely seems like there are some pretty pointed references to that fiasco, one which mid-1960s audiences would have certainly been aware of. A full blown congressional hearing was held over Camelot in 1965.

What's more, Kubrick took a subtle swipe at personality profiling in *Dr. Strangelove* via President Muffley's grilling of General Turgidson on how General Ripper passed the military's human reliability tests. While rarely acknowledged, attempts to predict human behavior are a recurring theme in several of Kubrick's films and I suspect this concern stemmed from the controversy surrounding Simulmatics and Camelot.

More broadly speaking, behaviorism would remain a target of Kubrick's in *A Clockwork Orange*. Here, Kubrick openly condemns efforts to merge behaviorism with cutting edge technology. While little commented upon, it's actually a liberal government in the UK that embraces the Ludovico Technique. In the US, Camelot was sponsored by Democratic governments. This may be another veiled swipe at the technocratic policy makers of the left who viewed technology as a more "humane" form of coercion.

Kubrick the Eccentric

Another interesting development around this time was Kubrick's legendary "eccentric" behavior and his increasing isolation from society. He was paranoid about the world being destroyed by nuclear war as far back as 1952-53. While still living in the Bronx, he seriously considered moving to Australia, where life had a much better chance of surviving. He was still considering this option until at least the early 1960s.[278]

Obviously, there's been a lot of speculation as to why Kubrick chose to relocate to the UK full time during the middle of that decade and why he spent his final years in an isolated country manor. On the one hand, it's worth noting that he was the father of three young children, all daughters, by the time he finished filming *Lolita*. In light of recent allegations concerning his former partner, James B. Harris, and *Lolita* star Sue Lyon, certain conclusions can be drawn as to why he did not want to raise them in Hollywood, or even NYC.

The Kubricks settled into their manor/fortress in Hertfordshire around 1980, where Kubrick operated out of with a small staff for the rest of his life. By that time, he'd been living in the UK full time for over a decade. Gradually, the family moved further into the countryside. Supposedly, this provided Kubrick the secrecy/seclusion he coveted. Even before then, he enclosed them in a wall mansion in Abbots Mead. Kubrick became hyper-sensitive about infections, and sent home those in his unit who contracted colds. He was also a gun enthusiast and kept several on the property.[279]

---

[278] LoBrutto, 227; Mick Broderick, *Reconstructing Strangelove*, 8.

These are several instances of Kubrick's supposed "eccentric" behavior. Another one often cited is his fear of flying. This irony is that Kubrick was a lifelong aviation enthusiast and became a certified pilot around 1947. His passion for flying was on display in his second documentary, *Flying Padre*.[280] He continued flying as both a pilot and passenger until at least the late 1950s, mostly around New Jersey's Teterboro Airport. He had put in over 150 hours of flying time and flown solo as far as Albany.[281]

When Kubrick gave up flying and what spurred the decision is a matter of dispute. Filippo Ulivieri claims that Kubrick last flew in 1959, when he went to Spain to film parts of *Spartacus* on a commercial flight.[282] But John Baxter cites 1960 as the last time Kubrick flew when he accompanied James Harris on a PanAm flight to London.[283]

Even accounts of the incident that spurred his fear of flying are murky. It unfolded at Teterboro Airport. Set designer Ken Adams, who worked with Kubrick on *Strangelove* and *Barry Lyndon*, alleged that the incident happened during Kubrick's first solo flight, but this is contested.[284] Regardless, one of the switches either became stuck, or Kubrick forgot to flip it, during takeoff. As a result, the plane took off with only one side of the engines firing. After a struggle, Kubrick was able to land the plane. But, he was shaken.[285]

This experience, combined with his constant monitoring of air traffic from London via shortwave radio and extensive reading of aviation literature, convinced him that the risk of flight was too great to his personal safety. Kubrick had been flying and closely studying aviation literature for over a decade before he came to this conclusion.

Another such eccentricity related to driving. Reportedly, Kubrick instructed his drivers to not go faster than 35 mph.[286] Others put it at 50. Just how extreme he was about this has been hotly contested, though he was a stickler for his driver obeying the traffic laws.[287] And yet, Kubrick himself is described as a terrible driver, one who often became distracted while behind the wheel. Again, we are told this is a man petrified of death, who insists his driver strictly abide traffic laws, and yet can't focus long enough to drive safely.

---

[279] Baxter, 167. For more on Kubrick's love of firearms, see Michael Benson, *Space Odyssey*, 428.

[280] LoBrutto, 39, 72.

[281] LoBrutto, 297.

[282] Filippo Ulivieri & Simone Odino, *2001 Between Kubrick & Clarke*, 81-82.

[283] Baxter, 168.

[284] Baxter, 167-168. As noted above, LoBrutto claims Kubrick had already made solo flights.

[285] Baxter, 167-168; LoBrutto, 297-298.

[286] Baxter, 167; LoBrutto, 319. Credible accounts from the filming of 2001 indicate Kubrick settled on 29 mph after determining this was the top speed he could survive a crash in his Rolls or Mercedes. During this period, he told his drivers that he was recovering from back surgery and for medical reasons, they had to drive him at a snail's pace. See Michael Benson, *Space Odyssey*, 203.

[287] Emilo D'Alessandro with Filippo Ulivieri, *Stanley Kubrick and Me*, 297. D'Alessandro was Kubrick's longtime personal driver and claims he was always allowed to drive the speed limit. But as far as I've been able to determine, he was the only one Kubrick trusted to that extent.

Concurrently, his filmmaking process would become almost totally isolated. Kubrick constructed his films from the vast, blank stages of sound studios. Using rapidly developing communications technology enabled him to direct second units from any point in the world. Kubrick was apparently among the first to start using an early version of the internet and cell phones for his projects.

These attempts to control his environment and avoid any kind of personal risk are often explained by a crippling fear of death on Kubrick's part, and yet, for a man allegedly so obsessed with his own mortality, Kubrick had been a chain smoker since the age of 12. Despite the best efforts of his wife, Kubrick remained a heavy smoker till at least through the completion of *Barry Lyndon*.[288] There are indications he may have continued smoking, at least on occasion, his entire life.

He was also a workaholic by all accounts, frequently operating on four hours of sleep a day or less. This continued all through his life. The grueling pace Kubrick personally kept on his films was legendary. Principal photography on some of the later ones lasted for nearly a year or more. During this time, Kubrick routinely worked 12 hour days, seven days a week. And while his diet was not terrible, it wasn't great either. As noted earlier, much of what he ate came out of a microwave. While never extremely obese, he had ongoing issues with his weight from the 1960s onwards.

For a man supposedly terrified of dying, Kubrick does not appear to have taken especially good care of his personal health. Kubrick gave up flying and driving over 35 mph because they're unnecessary risks, but he continued chain smoking until he's nearly 50? This is a bit of a contradiction.

I personally believe that at some point between *Spartacus* and *2001*, Kubrick became convinced that he could be a target for assassination. Perhaps it was the incident with the plane. Maybe there were several things. But Kubrick's behavior is indicative of someone afraid of being murdered rather than possessing an all-encompassing fear of death. His own disregard for his personal health seems to rule out the latter possibility.

Incredible?

Well, consider: By the mid-1960s, Kubrick appears to be in the midst of an ongoing war for the hearts and minds of the American public being waged by elements of the neo-liberal order and the far right. On the one hand, the Kennedy administration enlisted a network of filmmakers centered around Kirk Douglas for the purposes of exposing the insanity then unfolding in the Pentagon and the CIA. A rogue nuclear strike or even a coup appears to have been at the forefront of the administration's concerns. The Pentagon established an entire underground network spearheaded by the Institute for American Strategy to get their

---

[288] Michael Benson, *Space Odyssey*, 203; LoBrutto, 399.

message out. Kennedy went through Hollywood and seemingly enlisted Stanley Kubrick into these efforts.

Maybe Kubrick didn't know what he was getting into when he made *Spartacus*. Perhaps the Kennedy assassination was the ultimate wake-up call. Regardless, his behavior changed after *Strangelove*, driven by a fear for his personal safety and especially that of his family. Consider a certain incident that occurred in NYC during 1965. A man Arthur C. Clarke described as a "psychotic" demanded that Kubrick hire him for his next film. He took to sitting outside Kubrick's offices on a park bench for several weeks. Occasionally, he ventured into the building to make fresh demands for employment. Kubrick was so unnerved by this that he started carrying a large hunting knife in his briefcase.[289]

Given some of the topics I've covered, I don't think assassination would be an unreasonable concern on Kubrick's part. And as we shall see, there was at least one direct threat made to Kubrick's life after he relocated to the UK. What's more, Kubrick is reported to have left the US for good in 1968. He never set foot on the shores of his homeland after this. Not even for the funeral of his mother or father, whom he remained close to.[290]

1968 is the year his cousin, Paul S. Perveler, was originally arrested for murder. His former wife, Ruth Sobotka, died during the prior year. 1968 was also when Robert F. Kennedy was assassinated and the last year a Democrat held the presidency until 1977. But by that time, most of the Kennedy people in the party were marginalized. If Kubrick was in fact some kind of agent for a Kennedy faction, this would go a long way towards explaining why he never returned to the US after 1968.

Anthony "Tony" Frewin, an assistant to Kubrick from *2001* to *Eyes Wide Shut* (with the exception of *Barry Lyndon*) and now a representative for his estate, is especially illustrative in this regard. For years, Frewin managed a team of readers to review potential projects for Kubrick. Originally, Frewin worked with a small team, but by the 1980s the work had overwhelmed him. A company, Empyrean Films, was set up to employ additional readers. Many were recruited from ads placed in the *Times Literary Supplement* and none knew they were working for Kubrick. Frewin described the operation as "run like a communist spy cell -- nobody knew anyone else."[291]

Frewin is also a writer, whose credits include the novel *London Blues* and the film *Colour Me Kubrick* (based on the true story of a man impersonating Kubrick in the UK during the 1990s). But it's his nonfiction work that is most intriguing. One is entitled *The Assassination of John F. Kennedy: An Annotated Film, TV, and Videography, 1963-1992*. Nor are these the only

---

[289] LoBrutto, 267; Michael Benson, *Space Odyssey*, 91-92.

[290] Robert P Kolker and Nathan Abrams, *Kubrick: An Odyssey*, 288; Kubrick's daughter, Vivian, was the family's "representative" for both funerals. See Emilo D'Alessandro with Filippo Ulivieri, *Stanley Kubrick and Me*, 181-182.

[291] Robert P. Kolker and Nathan Abrams, *Kubrick: An Odyssey*, 481-483; James Fenwick, *Stanley Kubrick Produces*, 180.

contributions Frewin has made to JFK assassination literature. He was a regular contributor to the UK parapolitical journey *Lobster* on this subject for at least a decade.[292]

Then there's his 1998 novel, *Sixty-Three Closure*. The plot revolves around protagonist Christopher Cornwell's efforts to unravel the mystery behind several photo a friend mailed him shortly before an apparent suicide. As the story unfolds, Christopher discovers that the photos are of Lee Harvey Oswald in the UK during the early 1960s. The real Oswald had officially defected to the Soviet Union during this time. Once Christopher confirms the authenticity of the photos, he comes to believe his friend was murdered over them. In a bid to find the killers, Christopher ventures to an isolated manor that the British government constructed an underground compound beneath as part of the continuity of government plans during the Cold War.

At least some of the novel is clearly autobiographical. Like Frewin, Christopher Cornwell was born in 1947. Cornwell also works in the movie industry. As the novel opens, he's just returning from Prague, where he took photos of possible locations for a film called *Blue Lou*. The exteriors were to be just in the Czech Republic, while the interiors would be filmed in the UK's Pinewood Studio for this American-financed picture.

During the early 1990s, Kubrick was poised to film parts of his would-be Holocaust epic *Aryan Papers* in the Czech Republic. Instead, he made *Eyes Wide Shut* in which he recreated New York City at Pinewoods. As was previously noted, *Eyes Wide Shut* partly had its origin in the novel *Blue Movie* Terry Southern wrote for Kubrick. Much of the novel's action, including the underground compound, is based in Hertfordshire, which is where Kubrick's Childwickbury Manor is located. *Sixty-Three Closure* was given advance praise from *New York Post* journalist Larry Celona, who later contributed fictitious articles that appeared in *Eyes Wide Shut* under his real name.[293]

The novel was Frewin's second. His debut, 1997's *London Blues*, was another parapolitical thriller. This one deals with the early days of pornographic films in the UK intersecting with the Profumo scandal, which JFK may have also been implicated in. The Profumo Affair was surely an influence on *Eyes Wide Shut*, as shall be discussed in chapter 4. For now, it's worth noting *Sixty-Three Closure*'s Christopher Cornwell finishes the novel incarcerated after child pornography is planted in his apartment.

---

[292] For a list of Frewin's contributions to *Lobster*, see Anthony+Frewin. Lobster. (n.d.). https://www.lobster-magazine.co.uk/?s=anthony%2Bfrewin.

[293] Celona is a veteran crime reporter who has been the first to report several high profile deaths over the years, including Kubrick's, JFK Jr. 's. and arch pedophile Jeffrey Epstein's in 2019. For a time, Cryptokubrologists proposed that Celona was not a real person, but an Illuminati anagram for "Royal Lancer," a covert reference to Prince Andrew. I'm not entirely sure what this was supposed to signal, but such chargers were soon withdrawn when it became evident that Celona is real. Albeit, there is little information available about him online, including what he looks like. Bizarrely, the Secret [illegible]e's codename for JFK actually was "Lancer," which Frewin notes at several points in *Sixty-Three* [illegible]*e*.

This hardly proves Kubrick subscribed to a parapolitical reading of the JFK assassination. Only that one of his closest collaborators for several decades did. But it should be noted that Kubrick was quite fanatical about complete devotion from his employees. Kubrick once fired a writer for breach of contract for taking on a speaking engagement while work was suspended on his project with Kubrick.[294] The director kept close watch on the extracurricular activities of his employees, in other words. One could infer that Kubrick's cordial relations with Frewin throughout his engagement with the JFK assassination community constitutes approval, at a minimum.

It's also worth noting that Frewin thanks a "Maria Harlan" in *The Assassination of John F. Kennedy*.[295] Maria is the name of Jan Harlan's wife, Kubrick's brother-in-law and a producer on all of Kubrick's films since *A Clockwork Orange*. I do not know if the Maria Harlan thanked in Frewin's book is the same woman, or what kind of assistance she gave him, but her name comes up among other noted JFK assassination researchers such Martin Cannon, Robin Ramsey, Michael Eddowes, Harold Weisberg, and Anthony Summers.

Also, do keep *Lobster* magazine in mind, as we'll be returning to it in the next chapter.

---

[294] Robert P. Kolker and Nathan Abrams, *Kubrick: An Odyssey*, 430.

[295] Anthony Frewin, *The Assassination of John F. Kennedy: An Annotated Film, TV, and Videography, 1963-1992*. (Westport, CT: Greenwood Press, 1993), xv.

Chapter Three:

Operation Clockwork Orange

Enter The Nine

In all the annals of conspiritainment, few sagas are quite as strange as that of The Nine. Even fewer are as well documented, making the decades-spanning reports all the more intriguing. As the story goes, on December 31, 1952, New Year's Eve, an event known to posterity as "the Séance that Changed the World" unfolded. It was carried out in Maine by an outfit known as the Round Table Foundation. It was established during the late 1940s to explore ESP and the paranormal.

The founder and head of this organization, as well as the driving force behind the séance, was a mysterious figure known as Dr. Andrija Puharich (b: Henry Karel Puharić, 1918-1995).[296] Puharich has been described as the "Grandfather of the New Age" and for good reason. He was one of the earliest and most prominent of the post-war parapsychologists and a trailblazer in entheogenic research. Puharich had been investigating the magic mushroom in lab conditions several years before Timothy Leary's first trip. By the 1980s, Puharich was deeply involved in research concerning what is now known as "zero point energy" or "free energy."[297]

But all that came later. Puharich first made his mark with the after-mentioned séance. Present were Puharich, a lab assistant named Hank Jackson and a Hindu scholar known as Dr. D.G. Vinod, who acted as the medium. During the session, Vinod allegedly channeled entities known as The Nine. In Ancient Egypt, they appeared to humanity as the Grand Ennead, the pantheon worshiped at Heliopolis since the Old Kingdom. A follow up séance in occurred 1953 involving Arthur Young (a later New Age guru who made his fortune by inventing the Bell Helicopter), socialite Ruth Forbes Paine (Young's wife, who was born into the Forbes

---

[296] Remarkably, Puharich has never received a full length biography for his mysterious life. He's dealt with at length in Annie Jacobson, *Phenomena: The Secret History of the U.S. Government's Investigations Into Extrasensory Perception and Psychokinesis* (New York: Little, Brown and Company, 2017); and Lynn Picknett & Clive Prince, *The Stargate Conspiracy: The Truth About Extraterrestrial Life and the Mysteries of Ancient Egypt* (New York: Berkeley Book, 1999). Other compelling information on Puharich can be found in H.P. Albarelli Jr., *A Terrible Mistake: The Murder of Frank Olson and the CIA's Secret Cold War Experiments* (Walterville, OR: Trine Day, 2009); H.P. Albarelli Jr., *A Secret Order: Investigating the High Strangeness and Synchronicity in the JFK Assassination* (Walterville, OR: Trine Day, 2013),; Peter Levenda, *Sinister Forces: A Grimoire of American Political Witchcraft Book I: The Nine* (Walterville, OR: Trine Day, 2005); and Ben Robinson, *The Magician: John Mulholland's Secret Life*, 2nd Ed. (self-pub., www.lynrary.com, 2010). Some of Puharich's own autobiographical works offer compelling insights as well, such as *Uri: A Journal of the Mystery of Uri Geller* (New York: Anchor Press, 1974) and *The Sacred Mushroom: Key to the Door of Eternity* (Garden City, NY: Doubleday & Company Inc, 1974).

[297] Zero-point energy is the lowest possible energy level or ground state in a quantized electromagnetic field, which interacts with a physical system of particles, which are represented by de Broglie waves with quantized energy levels. It has been linked by some researchers to the Victorian conception of "ether," a force that is present throughout the universe and all around us on earth specifically. It's long been speculated that if such a force existed, it could be harnessed to power an industrial society. The theories of Nikola Tesla are often applied to modern notions of zero point energy.

family and later married into the Paine family); and a host of other Boston Brahmins and American gentry (including members of the Astor and DuPont families) added further details: The Nine weren't just the gods of ancient Egypt, but extraterrestrial intelligences that existed outside of time and space. Or something to that effect. The story changed over the years. By the 1970s, they claimed to be intelligences that had shed their physical form in favor of residing in a computer on board the spaceship Spectra then invisibly stalking the Earth.[298]

Throughout the Cold War, The Nine turned up time again in the damndest places. They have links to the JFK assassination and Watergate; to the writers' room of the original *Star Trek* (to say nothing of latter incarnations such as *Deep Space Nine*....); the legendary Stanford Research Institute "remote viewing" experiments; Esalen, the new Age Mecca in Big Sur, CA; and so much more. Hence, the whole "Séance that Changed the World" slogan.

For our purposes here, what most concerns us are their links to *Star Trek*. Officially, *Star Trek* creator Gene Roddenberry did not meet The Nine and the scene around Puharich until 1974, after *The Original Series* was axed, but before the first movie. By this time, Puharich had relocated to Ossining, NY at a facility dubbed Lab Nine. Roddenberry was a regular fixture there during the mid-1970s for the channeling sessions. This has led to speculation that concepts derived from The Nine were worked into the *Star Trek* films and later series such as *The Next Generation* and especially *Deep Space Nine*.[299] Aliens such as Q and the Prophets of *DS9*, both of which are essentially immortal beings that exist outside of space and time, bear strong similarities to conceptions of The Nine.

But former comic book writer turned synchro-mystic Christopher Knowles has made a compelling case that Roddenberry became acquainted with The Nine at a much earlier date: during his apprenticeship on *The Outer Limits* set.[300] Even a precursory glance at the first season of *The Outer Limits* makes it impossible to dismiss these musings. The series, and especially the episodes penned by Stevens, have a very novel take on extraterrestrials, especially for the mid-1960s.

---

[298] For Puharich's account of The Nine, see Andrija Puharich, *Uri: A Journal of the Mystery of Uri Geller*. Parts of the saga are alluded to in *The Sacred Mushroom* as well. The only full length account of this psychodrama currently available is Lynn Picknett & Clive Prince, *The Stargate Conspiracy: The Truth About Extraterrestrial Life and the Mysteries of Ancient Egypt*. While the raw data in this work is useful, it is on the whole a highly sensational and dated account. A slightly better overview can be found in the first book of Peter Levenda's *Sinister Forces* trilogy. It probably goes without saying, but a truly scholarly account of these doings has yet to be written.

[299] Lynn Picknett & Clive Prince, *The Stargate Conspiracy: The Truth About Extraterrestrial Life and the Mysteries of Ancient Egypt*, 177. Roddenberry was even commissioned to write a screenplay about The Nine, though as of this writing it has never been filmed.

[300] See, for instance, Knowles, C. (2013, July 10). Secret star trek: The godfather. The Secret Sun. https://secretsun.blogspot.com/2013/07/secret-star-trek-part-6-godfather-of.html; and Knowles, C. (2013b, July 16). Secret star trek: "an outgrowth of the Outer Limits." The Secret Sun. https://secretsun.blogspot.com/2013/07/secret-star-trek-part-8-daystar-trek.html.

"The Galaxy Being," the series premier written and directed by Stevens, concerns a Puharich-like scientist investigating electromagnetic radiation. This enables him to communicate with an alien intelligence that exists in a different dimension. "Controlled Experiment," another Stevens episode, concerns a pair of aliens tampering with time lines. But perhaps allusions to The Nine are most implicit in "The Borderland" where a scientist opens a portal to another dimension that grants him access to an alien planet. This episode even opens with a séance, and repeatedly draws similarities between occultism and what we would now think of as quantum physics. And of course, this episode was also written and directed by Stevens.

But if Stevens was peppering *The Outer Limits* with references to The Nine, where was he getting his information from? This is where things get extremely speculative, but I think the most likely source was his father, Admiral Leslie Stevens III. The contact likely derived from Puharich's day job during the initial Nine séances: working on psychological warfare for the US Army.

In August and November 1952, Puharich briefed US Army psychological warfare officers on extrasensory perception (ESP). Shortly thereafter, Puharich was reactivated by the Army. During January 1953, he delivered a classified briefing on ESP to the Medical Field Service School of the US Air Force in San Antonio. In February, Puharich was at the Pentagon. There, he addressed the Advisory Group on Psychological Warfare and Unconventional Warfare.[301]

So, what were these arcane military bodies then assessing Puharich's work? The Army psychological warfare officers would have belonged to a then-obscure section of the Army's Directorate of Operations, Plans, Training, and Force Protection, International Affairs and Security Cooperation (G3)[302] called "The Office of the Chief Psychological Warfare," or the OCPW. Puharich had two 1952 engagements with this outfit involving psywar, one in the summer and one in November.[303] Puharich was reactivated into the Army by January 1953. He met with Air Force doctors that month, and addressed the Pentagon's Advisory Group on Psychological Warfare and Unconventional Warfare in February, shortly before formally re-joining the Army.[304]

---

[301] Andrija Puharich, *The Sacred Mushroom: Key to the Door of Eternity*, 10-12; H.P. Albarelli Jr., *A Terrible Mistake: The Murder of Frank Olson and the CIA's Secret Cold War Experiments*, 53; Annie Jacobson, *Phenomena: The Secret History of the U.S. Government's Investigations Into Extrasensory Perception and Psychokinesis*, 36-37, 44. Albareli reports the San Antonio meeting as occurring after the DC presentation. Jacobson does not mention Puharich's second presentation to the Pentagon in November 1953. Rather, she placed it in November 1952. Puharich himself also placed it in 1952. .

[302] While psychological warfare is typically viewed as an intelligence function, the US Military does not classify it as such. Virtually all military intelligence functions fall under the purview of G2, the intelligence section. Psychological warfare is carried out by G3, which concerns itself with operations. From the early postwar years, psychological warfare was viewed as "primarily operational in nature and does not readily fall within the scope of the Intelligence Division." See Alfred H. Paddock. Jr., *U.S. Army Special Warfare: Its Origins*, 2nd ed., 44.

[303] Annie Jacobsen, *Phenomena: The Secret History of the US Government's Investigation Into Extrasensory Perception and Psychokinesis*, 36-37.

[304] Annie Jacobsen, *Phenomena*, 44; Andrija Puharich, *The Sacred Mushroom: Key to the Door of*

The lineages of both the OCPW and the Advisory Group are noteworthy. The former was launched in 1951, in the midst of the Korean War. Despite the outfit's name, the OCPW also oversaw US Army special operations forces (SOFs) and its psywar officers. The OCPW is what gave birth to the US Army Special Forces (better known as the Green Berets) and consolidated special operations functions at Fort Bragg, North Carolina. In other words, the OCPW is the precursor to the modern-day US Army Special Operations Command.[305]

As for the "Advisory Group on Psychological Warfare and Unconventional Warfare," this appears to have originated as a subcommittee set up by the Joint Chiefs of Staff (JCS) to liaise with the CIA on covert operations during the late 1940s.[306] By 1951, all covert operations being carried out by the US national security state theoretically fell under the purview of the Psychological Strategy Board (PSB). Bringing together the CIA director, an Undersecretary of State, a Deputy Secretary of Defense, and a representative from the JCS serving as the body's military advisor, the PSB was housed within the National Security Council (NSC). In addition to coordinating all government bodies engaged in psychological warfare and managing public perception, the PSB oversaw unconventional warfare and special operations.[307] In other words, the group Puharich addressed was part of the PSB, probably the Department of Defense (DoD) component assigned to covert operations. It's also noteworthy that the PSB was considering the UFO phenomena by at least 1952, if not sooner.[308]

As the reader will recall from an earlier chapter, Admiral Leslie Stevens was a senior figure on the PSB. However, Stevens retired from the Navy (and by default, the PSB) towards the end of 1951. This would have been well over a year before the Army began sniffing around Puharich. But Admiral Stevens was still engaged with the national security establishment

---

Eternity,10-12. Interestingly, Puharich claims that it was an officer who headed the OCPW's research branch that first approached him. Puharich later addressed the OCPW's research branch proper in November at the Pentagon. Puharich claims they were interested in his work with Faraday cages, which he was then experimenting with. Puharich claims the Army requested that he rejoin the active duty the day after the meeting.

[305] Alfred H. Paddock. Jr., *U.S. Army Special Warfare: Its Origins*, 2nd ed., 1, etc. Joy Rohde, *Armed with Expertise: The Militarization of American Social Research during the Cold War* (Ithaca: Cornell University Press, 2013), 13-14, 20-21, etc. The lineage of the Army Special Operations Command is every bit as discombobulated as all aspects of US special operations. By the late 1950s, the OCPW had been rechristened the Office of the Chief of Special Warfare (Paddock, *U.S. Army Special Warfare*, 155). Steps were formally taken by General Edward Meyer to consolidate all Army special operations under a unified command during 1982. See William G. Boykin, "The Origins of the United States Special Operations Command" in *Special Operations and Low Intensity Conflict Legislation: Why It Was Passed and Have the Voids Been Filled?* (Carlisle, PA: United States Army War College Press, 1991), 5. It wasn't until 1989 that USASOC formally came into being.

[306] Alfred H. Paddock Jr., *U.S. Army Special Warfare*, 70.

[307] Annie Jacobsen, *Surprise, Kill, Vanish: The Secret History of CIA Paramilitary Armies, Operators, and Assassins* (New York: Little, Brown and Company, 2019), 67-68; Alfred H. Paddock, Jr., *U.S. Army Special Warfare*, 98, 138.

[308] U.S. Central Intelligence Agency, "Flying Saucers," Walter B. Smith, ER-3-2809, Washington D.C., 1952 (?), https://www.cia.gov/readingroom/docs/DOC_0000015338.pdf (accessed February 24, 2024).

through 1954 via his work for the American Committee for Liberation from Bolshevism.[309] As these activities involved psychological warfare, Stevens was surely still in contact with the PSB during this time. Thus, there is a possibility he was apprised of Puharich's work, as well as UFO investigations. While this may seem a stretch, other writers working on *The Outer Limits* have acknowledged that subtle digs at the CIA were peppered into the show.[310] And well over a decade before significant revelations of CIA abuses were available to the American public. There have been persistent rumblings that efforts to remove Stevens from *The Outer Limits* began after the first season. This was driven by the concern that he was divulging classified materials gleaned from his father.[311]

To return to Kubrick, an obvious parallel can be drawn between The Nine and *2001*'s conception of extraterrestrial life. Kubrick planned to show physical aliens on the screen. It was only at the very end of filming that he conceded then-available special effects were not capable of depicting something sufficiently "alien."[312] What ended up on screen are beings that appear to have transcended physical form and exist as pure energy, or perhaps even in another dimension. Kubrick was quite clear on this point when asked about *2001*'s ending by Japanese journalist Jun'ichi Yao shortly after *The Shining* had opened. The director noted:

> "Well I, I try to avoid doing this ever since the picture came out, because when you just say the ideas they sound foolish, whereas if they're dramatized one feels it. But I'll try. The idea was supposed to be that he is taken in by godlike entities; creatures of pure energy and intelligence with no shape or form and they put him in what I suppose you could describe as a human zoo, to study him. He spends his whole life from that point on in that room, and he has no sense of time, it just seems to happen, as it does in the film. And they choose this room which is a very inaccurate replica of French architecture, deliberately so. Inaccurate because one was suggesting that they had some idea of something that he might think was pretty but weren't quite sure, just as we aren't quite sure about what to do in zoos with animals, to give them what we think is their natural environment. And

---

309 The New York Times. (1956, December 1). Admiral Stevens, ex-attache, dead; naval aide in Moscow from 1947 to 1950 served with Air Research Board well prepared for post journey to caucasus retired in 1951. The New York Times. https://timesmachine.nytimes.com/timesmachine/1956/12/01/84715183.html?pageNumber=21. It's interesting to note that declassified documents posted on the Wilson Center seem to indicate that CIA had become so disillusioned with Stevens' chairmanship of Amcomlib by 1953 that they resolved to force him out. See CIA criticizes American Committee for Liberation Policies. CIA Criticizes American Committee for Liberation Policies | Wilson Center Digital Archive. (1953, May 18). https://digitalarchive.wilsoncenter.org/document/cia-criticizes-american-committee-liberation-policies.

310 King, S. (2000, March 9). An original writer talks of creating "limits." Los Angeles Times. https://www.latimes.com/archives/la-xpm-2000-mar-09-ca-6841-story.html.

311 Dore Page, *Leslie Stevens Goes to Hollywood*, 180

312 Michael Benson, *Space Odyssey*, 64-66, 283-389, etc; Joe R. Frinzi, *Kubrick's Monolith*, 28-30.

> anyway, when they get finished with him, as happens in so many myths of all cultures of the world, he is transformed into some kind of super being and sent back to, um, earth, transformed and made into some sort of superman. And we have to only guess what happens when he goes back. It is a pattern of a great deal of mythology. And that is what we were trying to, um, suggest."[313]

This is in keeping with the mythology of The Nine. At one point, they were said to have transferred their consciousness to a spaceship. One can possibly see shades of the monolith from *2001* in these notions. And even before Kubrick made the decision to forgo the aliens on screen, the time loop in the final moments of the film strongly implies they have escaped the confines of linear time. This is a theme Kubrick would return to with *The Shining*, a film widely believed to be symbolically connected to *2001*.

Even more intriguing is the possibility of *2001*'s legendary "star gate" sequence being inspired by this milieu. The psychedelic nature of this section has long been evident to viewers, but for decades the similarities to such experiences have been dismissed as coincidence. But researcher Michael Benson uncovered a 1965 letter that indicated otherwise. It was dispatched incognito from Kubrick's production company[314] to Dr. Walter Pahnke requesting more information on an experiment he conducted three years earlier. Commonly referred to as the Marsh Chapel Experiment, it was part of his PhD thesis at Harvard. It fell under the purview of Harvard's famed Psilocybin Project overseen by Timothy Leary and Richard Alpert. Leary and Alpert, Pahnke's thesis advisors, supervised the experiment as well as participating in it. Benson was struck by how closely the experiences reported by the participants corresponded to Kubrick's depiction of the star gate. [315]

Were psychedelics behind the star gate sequence after all? Benson reports that Kubrick disdained psychedelics, and all narcotics for the matter, because he feared they would dull his creative edge.[316] But the interest in the Marsh Chapel Experiment surely originated with Kubrick. What attracted him to it? How did he learn of it? And what made him link the psychedelic experience to extraterrestrials? While somewhat common in 2024, this combination was nearly unheard of in 1965.

With the possible exception of Andrija Puharich.

His 1959 work *The Sacred Mushroom* was not only one of the first popular accounts of psychedelic mushrooms, but also recounted encounters users had with a high priest of

---

[313] Interview transcript between Jun'ichi Yao and Stanley Kubrick. (2021). http://www.visual-memory.co.uk/amk/doc/0122.html.

[314] The letter bore the street address of Polaris Productions, but made no reference to the company or that the information being requested was for a film.

[315] Michael Benson, *Space Odyssey*, 98-100.

[316] See Benson, 307 and 346.

Ancient Egypt known as Rahotep. While possessed by this being, subjects reported that the mushrooms would "open the door" to the gods. Puharich never linked these experiences with his channeled communications from The Nine. But he never discussed The Nine in a popular work until 1974's *Uri* and it seems a stretch to believe he never made the connection. What's more, with knowledge of The Nine communications, this would imply mushrooms opened the doors to an extraterrestrial intelligence.

If Kubrick had knowledge of these developments, it would go along towards explaining his interest in magic mushrooms as part of *2001*'s preproduction. But would he be aware of Puharich's communications with The Nine?

We must again turn to Admiral Leslie Stevens. As is fairly well-known now, the Pentagon and CIA experimented with a variety of psychedelics as part of various programs such as ARTICHOKE and MK-ULTRA from the late 1940s until at least the late 1970s. During the early 1950s, the NSC's Psychological Strategy Board was kept apprised of these projects.[317] The reader will recall that Stevens was a senior figure on the early PSB. And after joining the Army, Puharich's research was by ARTICHOKE.[318]

And while it's never been directly linked to MK-ULTRA, there is reason to believe Leary's psilocybin research at Harvard was being followed by the defense establishment. Leary's mentor at Harvard, Dr. Henry Murray, was an OSS veteran famed for his personality tests. Murray's tests were used to screen students for Harvard experiments involving LSD and potentially monitored by the CIA.[319]

There is a distinct possibility Admiral Stevens was at least aware of Puharich's research. Alexander Singer, Kubrick's high school friend, worked for Admiral Stevens' son during the early 1960s. As such, there is a clear channel from Stevens to Kubrick if the two filmmakers did not formally know one another at this point. And keep in mind, Singer spent the bulk of his final years in the industry directing episodes of the various *Star Trek* franchises. Given some of the storylines presented in the first season of *The Outer Limits*, it is hardly beyond the realm of possibility Leslie Stevens was aware of the psychedelic experimentation and its possible connection to UFOs. If his father clued him in on this overlap, Stevens may have continued to track the psychedelic experimentation, possibly through his own contacts in the intelligence community.

---

[317] For more on the PSB's role in these experiments, see Maret, Susan. 2018. "Murky Projects and Uneven Information Policies: A Case Study of the Psychological Strategy Board and CIA." Secrecy and Society 1(2). https://doi.org/10.31979/ 2377-6188.2018.010206 https://scholarworks.sjsu.edu/secrecyandsociety/vol1/iss2/6.

[318] See, H.P. Albarelli Jr., *A Secret Order: Investigating the High Strangeness and Synchronicity in the JFK Assassination* (Walterville, OR: Trine Day, 2013), 42-43; and Ben Robinson, *The Magician: John Mulholland's Secret Life*, 2nd Ed., 177-179.

[319] Jonathan D. Moreno, *Mind Wars: Brain Research and National Defense* (New York: Dana Press, 2006), 71.

While this is all extremely speculative on my part, I believe these possibilities warrant consideration. The depictions of extraterrestrials in early *Outer Limits* episodes and *2001* are far more mystical and frankly occulted than virtually anything else during this era in popular entertainment. The more metaphysical interpretation of the UFO phenomena, such Jacques Vallee's "inter-dimensional control system," or John Keel's "ultraterrestrials" would not receive a public airing until after *2001* was released. Carl Jung had ventured there during the 1950s. Kubrick, a devoted Jungian, was surely aware of Jung's archetypal hypothesis of the phenomena. But only Puharich can explain the psychedelic depiction that ended up on screen.

Kubrick's interest in ESP provides another possible route towards an awareness of Puharich. During the making of *The Shining*, the director implied that he followed the "scientific experiments" in parapsychology.[320] As these comments were made during the late 1970s, it's probable he was referring to the celebrated Stanford Research Institute (SRI)'s remote viewing experiments. Puharich brought Israeli stage magician Uri Geller to be tested at SRI during the mid-1970s Previously, Puharich had published works on ESP such as 1961's *Beyond Telepathy*. Puharich was one of the most prolific authors on parapsychology during the Cold War.[321] If Kubrick had more than a passing interest in this subject, he surely would have encountered Puharich's research at some point.

Strangely, *A Clockwork Orange* may provide us with another linkage between Kubrick and Puharich. Puharich always claimed his work for the national security state started with a Navy program called Penguin in 1948.[322] But no one has ever come up with such a program run by the Navy, or anyone, using that name. What can be confirmed is that the Navy launched a Project Pelican in 1947, and that it was later rolled into Project ARTICHOKE.[323] ARTICHOKE was a brutal joint CIA/Pentagon program exploring what would now be described as "enhanced interrogation methods" as well as behavior modification. It was similar to the more well-known Project MK-ULTRA, though these two programs were never combined as is commonly claimed.[324]

As for Pelican, it was still active in some form till at least the mid-1970s. It was at that point it was first revealed to the public.[325] What came out was deeply disturbing. Pelican was a kind

---

[320] Robert P. Kolker and Nathan Abrams, *Kubrick: An Odyssey*, 370.

[321] For more on Puharich's influence on Cold War parapsychology and the SRI remote viewing experiments, see Annie Jacobson, *Phenomena*.

[322] Peter Levenda, *Sinister Forces: A Grimoire of American Political Witchcraft Book I: The Nine*, 240.

[323] Pelican seems to have been a part of Project BLUEBIRD, which grew into ARTICHOKE around 1951. See Albarelli Jr., *A Terrible Mistake*, 202, etc.

[324] See, for instance, H.P. Albarelli Jr., *A Secret Order: Investigating the High Strangeness and Synchronicity in the JFK Assassination*, 168-171, etc.

[325] Albarelli Jr., *A Terrible Mistake*, 345-347. Pelican, though it was not named, was first revealed to the public prior to the MK-ULTRA revelations of 1977. In 1975 journalist Peter Watson first reported the *Clockwork Orange*-style methods being used by Pelican in the *London Sunday Times*. He later elaborated on this earlier report in his book *War on the Mind: The Military Uses and Abuses of*

of conditioning program for men selected for special operations, specially for assassinations and related projects. The individuals recruited were given extensive personality profiles beforehand. In some cases, they were recruited out of military prisons. There were several centers for Pelican, but the only known facility was at the Naval Medical Center San Diego within the large Naval base there. Subjects were strapped into a chair, their eyes clamped open, administered drugs and subjected to a series of ultra violent videos. Basically, what was depicted in *A Clockwork Orange*. Only in this case, the Pelican procedure was to transform recruits into more capable killers.

In *A Clockwork Orange*, this procedure is called the "Ludovico Technique." What appears on screen is fairly close to the source material. Anthony Burgess, the Brit who wrote the novel *Orange* is based upon, is alleged to have had firsthand knowledge of behavioral modification programs then active in the United States. According to a controversial biography of Burgess by Roger Lewis, Burgess worked with MI5 during the late 1950s and early 1960s. This was during the nadir of the" special relationship," when the Cambridge 5 spy scandal[326] made the American spooks wary of their British cousins. Burgess was apparently tapped to produce a novel that would constitute a limited hangout of then-cutting edge methods of behavior modification.[327] Supposedly, the procedure Alex undergoes in the novel is based upon the Ewen Cameron "medical experiments" in Montreal[328] as well as the lesser known research conducted by the Remote Neural Monitoring facility at Fort Meade, home of the NSA.[329]

Lewis further alleges that on page 29 of the *Clockwork Orange* novel are coded references to a facility at Fort Bliss engaged in psychotronic warfare technology research.[330] Curiously, the

---

Psychology (New York: Basic Books, Inc., Publishers, 1978), 248-250. Pelican was first referenced by name in David C. Martin, *Wilderness of Mirrors* (New York: Ballantine Books, 1980). From there, the matter largely rested until the publication of Albarelli's *A Terrible Mistake* in 2009. The sparring references to Pelican therein constitute the most in-depth account of it published thus far.

[326] The Cambridge 5 were a group of British nationals working as Soviet double agents from WWII until their covers were gradually blown during the Cold War. Several rose to senior ranks in the British securities services. The ring included Guy Burgess, Anthony Blunt, Donald MacLean, Kim Philby, and likely John Cairncross, though there is still some dispute over the fifth man.

[327] Roger Lewis, *Anthony Burgess: A Biography* (New York: Thomas Dunne Books, 2002), 282-283.

[328] Cameron's horrendous "psychic driving" method has gained a certain amount of public awareness in recent years after partially inspiring the first season of the it Netflix series *Stranger Things*. See, for instance, Drell, C. (2016, August 5). “stranger things”: The secret CIA programs that inspired hit series. Rolling Stone. https://www.rollingstone.com/culture/culture-features/stranger-things-the-secret-cia-programs-that-inspired-hit-series-249484/. Cameron's research has been addressed in many works, but one of the best accounts remains the earliest: John Marks, *The Search for the Manchurian Candidate: The CIA and Mind Control*, 140-151, etc.

[329] Roger Lewis, *Anthony Burgess: A Biography*, 285.

[330] Psychotronic weapons are sometimes known as "nonlethal weapons." The most notorious often involve electromagnetic waves, i.e. microwaves and extreme low frequencies (ELF). It has been speculated that "Havana syndrome" by Russian psychotronic weapons. See, for instance, Borger, J. (2021, June 2). Microwave weapons that could cause Havana syndrome exist, experts say. The Guardian. https://www.theguardian.com/science/2021/jun/02/microwave-weapons-havana-syndrome-experts.This subject shall be discussed in greater depth below.

Navy was said to be overseeing this research during the early 1960s when the book was published.[331] As I noted earlier, Puharich claimed his initial research was sponsored by the Navy. He later researched technology related to extremely low frequencies, or ELF waves, that have long been linked to psychotronic weapons. Further, as I detail in *The Art*, the Navy invested a fortune in this type of research from the onset of the Cold War well into the 1980s at least.

***

This brings up another curious aspect of *A Clockwork Orange*: the violence linked to it. While there are some tenuous links between the film and Arthur Bremer, who attempted to assassinate George Wallace during the early 1970s, virtually all of the copycat crimes linked to the film occurred in the UK during the 1972-1974 timeframe. It was during 1974 that Kubrick famously withdrew *Orange* from distribution in the UK and effectively banned it for decades.[332] This came after an intense campaign of moral outrage against the film, often driven by the Labour Party. At the forefront of these efforts was infamous British DJ Jimmy Savile, later exposed as an arch pedophile. Savile famously roasted Burgess on the BBC over the film in 1973. The debate ended with the DJ allowing a convicted felon to argue reading Burgess' novel spurred his criminal behavior without allowing any rebuttal.[333]

The movie never generated such a response anywhere else in the world, and seemingly only in the UK during its initial run. Further, most filmgoers in the UK saw it at a particular theater: Warner West End Cinema. Over 55,000 people saw it there. At the time Kubrick pulled it, the film had only been screened in London and a few of the surrounding cities.[334]

In 1973, *The Exorcist* opened and terrified audiences worldwide. In some cases during its initial theatrical run, reactions even more intense than screams were reported. People were said to have fainted, vomited, reported curious headaches and so on. It's now acknowledged that subliminal techniques --both sounds and images --were used in the film.[335]

But was there something more at play? The extreme reactions only occurred during the film's initial run, nor do they seem to have been evenly dispersed. When *The Exorcist* opened in New York City, incredible accounts emerged—not only people fainting and vomiting, but heart attacks and even a miscarriage. But these reports were only linked to one theater, Cinema 1—and do not seem to have occurred at other NYC theaters.[336]

---

[331] Roger Lewis, *Anthony Burgess: A Biography*, 287.
[332] LoBrutto, *Stanley Kubrick: A Biography*, 368-369.
[333] John Baxter, *Stanley Kubrick: A Biography*, 270-271.
[334] LoBrutto, 369.
[335] Breznican, A. (2023, October 27). The truth behind the hidden demon in "the exorcist." Vanity Fair. https://www.vanityfair.com/hollywood/2023/10/exorcist-hidden-demon
[336] See Klemesrud, J. (1974, January 27). They wait hours to be shocked. The New York Times. https://www.nytimes.com/1974/01/27/archives/they-wait-hoursto-be-shocked-the-exorcist-got-mixed-reviews-why-has.html. However, a later *New York Times* article questions the reports of heart

It's possible no extreme reactions occurred at any of the theaters. Warner Brothers may have simply planted reports at strategic theaters to create a buzz. And there is little dispute that copycat crimes inspired by *Clockwork Orange* occurred. But only during its initial run, and almost exclusively in the UK, and when the movie was mainly being screened around the London area.

Certainly *A Clockwork Orange* is not the only movie with real life copycat crimes attributed to it. By and large, violent crimes inspired by films are often isolated incidents with few exceptions. 1994's *Natural Born Killers* generated a lawsuit over murders allegedly inspired by it. It's been cited as an influence on a variety of murders and even the 1999 Columbine High School shooting.[337] But the violence associated with *Natural Born Killers* continued well after the film's theatrical run and spread beyond the United States. As was noted before, only Arthur Bremer, George Wallace's would-be assassin, is the only incident linked to the film in the States. And Bremer's association is tenuous --aside from seeing the movie shortly before the shooting, there's no copycat aspect to his crime.

A Clockwork Orange is more culturally British, which could contribute to audience reactions. But it was also little seen in the UK outside of certain areas during its limited run. Is the movie's Britishness enough to explain why no real copycat crimes happened in the US upon release, especially considering it was far more widely seen in the States?

At this point, it's useful to step back and consider Cold War intrigues that had been playing out since the late 1950s. It started during 1956 when a mysterious signal began bombarding the US embassy in Moscow with electromagnetic radiation (EMR). It was first detected by US officials in 1962. They soon deduced that the EMR was administered via microwaves. It was a composite of several frequencies, aiming for a synergistic effect from various wavelengths. The signal's intensity may have been as high as 4,000 microwatts. It was beamed directly into the ambassador's office. At various times, it was said to be used to activate bugging devices, or to jam US eavesdropping equipment. But both explanations are problematic given that the CIA allowed the signal to continue for years after it was detected.[338] If sensitive surveillance technology was in play, surely they would have protested sooner?

---

attacks, though confirms fainting and vomiting. But the source for this article is the director of operations at Cinema 5, not 1. And he merely states he's heard reports, not that he's experienced the extreme reactions at his theaters. See Gelder, L. V. (1974, January 24). "exorcist" casts spell on full houses. The New York Times. https://www.nytimes.com/1974/01/24/archives/exorcist-casts-spell-on-full-houses-record-take-expected-mostly.html. As such, Cinema 1 seems to be the only theater where these reactions can be definitively traced to in NYC.

337 While I'm loath to cite Wikipedia, it offers a fairly comprehensive breakdown of the various crimes linked to the movie. See Wikimedia Foundation. (2024, February 1). Natural born killers copycat crimes. Wikipedia. https://en.wikipedia.org/wiki/Natural_Born_Killers_copycat_crimes.

338 Robert O. Becker & Gary Selden, *The Body Electric: Electromagnetism and the Foundation of Life* (New York: William Morrow, 1985), 315-316; Annie Jacobsen, *Phenomena: The Secret History of the U.S. Government's Investigations Into Extrasensory Perception and Psychokinesis*, 74-75 Paul Brodeur, *Currents of Death: Power Lines, Computer Terminals, and the Attempt to Cover Up the Threat to Your Health* (New York: Simon and Schuster, 1989), 90-91.

Or perhaps they wanted to see what would happen?

Soviet research published during the mid-1960s indicated that such a beam would produce eyestrain/blurred vision, headaches and a loss of concentration during early exposure. Cancer was a possibility after prolonged exposure, or so the Soviets claimed. And it just so happens that three separate US ambassadors (Charles Bohlen, Llewellyn Thompson and Walter Stoessel) stationed there during the time of the Signal all later succumbed to different types of cancer. Stoessel suffered from both extreme headaches and bleeding from his eyes prior to developing a rare blood disease similar to leukemia. Testing in 1977 revealed that nearly a third of the returning embassy workers had "slightly higher than average" white blood cell count (the white blood cell counts were described as being 40 percent above those of other foreign service employees...). During the prior year, the US State Department was forced to give Moscow employees a 20 percent hardship allowance in an "unhealthy post." It also installed aluminum window screens to protect the staff. The Soviets continued to irradiate the embassy until 1978 or 1979, then started again in 1983.[339]

One hundred US embassy employees previously stationed in Moscow brought a $250 million lawsuit against the US government for overexposure to The Signal. The State Department ponied up $1 million to John Hopkins University School of Hygiene and Public Health to study the effects of The Signal. When the study was issued in 1978, it concluded that "no convincing evidence" was found that employees suffered "adverse health effects as of the time of this analysis." Every suit was eventually withdrawn without a penny being paid.[340]

The Soviet Union may have reached a different conclusion. The regime actively used electromagnetic waves administered through radio and television to "physically connect" with their citizenry. These efforts continued till the very end of the Soviet Union. In partnership with the Soviet media apparatus, attempts were to hypnotize TV audiences during the government's collapse in a bid to bolster confidence.[341] Since at least the late 1990s, compelling arguments have been made that certain frequencies of electromagnetic waves can affect mood and emotions in human beings.[342]

But, to return to the Cold War. Even as US officials denounced the ill effects of the Moscow Signal as humbug, the national security establishment began to study it. Project Pandora was launched in 1965 under the auspices of ARPA to investigate The Signal. Or at least that was

---

339 Robert O. Becker & Gary Selden, *The Body Electric: Electromagnetism and the Foundation of Life*, 315-317; Annie Jacobsen, *Phenomena*, 190-191.

340 Annie Jacobsen, *Phenomena*, 191; Sharon Weinberger, *The Imagineers of War*, 200.

341 D.W. Pasulka and David Metcalfe, "Where the Soul Meets Technology: Catholic Visionaries and the Stanford Research Institute as a Precedent for Human-Machine Interfaces and Social Telepathy Apps" in *Believing in Bites: Digital Media and the Supernatural* ed. by Simone Natale & D.W. Pasulka (New York: Oxford University Press, 2020), 156.

342 See, for instance, Sher L. The effects of natural and man-made electromagnetic fields on mood and behavior: the role of sleep disturbances. Med Hypotheses. 2000 Apr;54(4):630-3. doi: 10.1054/mehy.1999.0912. PMID: 10859654.

the official explanation given. During the late 1960s, Pandora conducted the first tests on Moscow embassy employees to ascertain the Signal's effects.[343] By the early 1970s, it advanced to holding formal discussions on testing microwave beams on human subjects.

Tests done on primates under Pandora during the 1960s showed promise, but after a few non-Pandora ARPA scientists peer reviewed the data, they were less convinced. In theory, human testing was abandoned at this point. Or at least directly under Pandora. Another related program, dubbed "Big Boy," beamed microwaves at unwitting sailors stationed at the Philadelphia Naval Yard just to see what would happen.[344]

ARPA's hierarchy concluded during the early 1970s that, upon reviewing Pandora, the Moscow Signal posed no physical or psychological threat to human beings. But by the mid-1970as, ARPA had good reason to downplay the effects: Both the Moscow Signal and the US intelligence community's awareness of it began to leak to the press circa 1973. Embassy workers in Moscow feared adverse health effects after being formally notified of The Signal in 1976. A wave of lawsuits soon followed. The government successfully parried them, as was noted above.[345]

A Clockwork Orange hit theaters when Pandora was still active while *The Exorcist* dropped shortly after it ended, but filming would have occurred during Pandora's run. Nor was Pandora the only such program then active. US Navy officials became intrigued by extreme low frequency (ELF) radiation in 1958, when they determined these frequencies could be used to communicate with deeply submerged submarines. In 1969, the Navy built an ELF testing facility in northern Wisconsin in 1969.[346]

During that time, the Navy laid plans to build a massive antenna in the state. The stated objective was to establish radio links with nuclear submarines at their standard depth of 120 feet below sea level. Conventional radio signals could not pass through the waters at that depth, necessitating the use of ELF waves. To manage this, the original design called for 6,000 miles of cable arranged in a grid to be buried across two-fifths of Wisconsin. The device these cables serviced was a loop antenna that bounced ELF waves off the Earth's surface into the ionosphere, and back again. This formed the genesis of Project Sanguine. [347]

Sanguine was one of the first military projects scrutinized by the newly founded Environmental Protection Agency (EPA). A report was issued in 1973 that raised serious concerns about the potential harm that antenna posed for human health and the

---

[343] Becker & Selden, *The Body Electric*, 315-316; Paul Brodeur, *Currents of Death*, 91.

[344] Annie Jacobsen, *Phenomena*, 75-77, 189; Weinberger, *The Imagineers of War*, 194-195; Paul Brodeur, *Currents of Death*, 91-93.

[345] Jacobsen, *Phenomena*, 189-191.

[346] Paul Brodeur, *Currents of Death: Power Lines, Computer Terminals, and the Attempt to Cover Up the Threat to Your Health*, 29.

[347] Becker & Selden, *The Body Electric*, 278-279; Paul Brodeur, *Currents of Death: Power Lines, Computer Terminals, and the Attempt to Cover Up the Threat to Your Health*, 29-30.

environment. Without classifying it, the Navy attempted to limit the reports circulation. By this time, an experimental station was already active in Clam Lake, WI. When the public became aware of the report in 1975, the full-scale antenna already had a new code name (Project Seafarer) and location (Michigan's upper peninsula). [348] The Navy had spent roughly $125 million (over $700 million in 2023 dollars) by that year on ELF research across various projects.[349]

While Sanguine/Seafarer had a different stated objective than Pandora, it still revealed how electromagnetic waves could affect public health, both mentally and physically. Which begs the question, would the US defense establishment not toy with weaponizing such effects? Especially since the Soviets were engaged in such activities?

Orange and *The Exorcist* were released at a time when different branches of the defense establishment were knee deep in electromagnetic experimentation. What I'm suggesting is what Soviet officials later attempted via TV: influence the moods of viewers. If electromagnetism could have a calming effect, could it not also be used to induce extreme states of fear or rage? Were audiences watching these films going through their own Ludovico Technique via the violent imagery combined with some outside influence?

Stanley Kubrick certainly appears to have been "read in" with certain sections of the US defense establishment by the early 1970s. He was a complete filmmaker, understanding the technical aspects of cinema as well as the creative. By all accounts, he was extremely tech savvy, with a lifelong passion. Was there another filmmaker in the West more qualified to utilize such technology by the early 1970s? And recall, Warner Brothers pushed Kubrick to follow up *Orange* with *The Exorcist*...

As absurd as this may seem to some readers, my case is bolstered by the political situation in the UK and Ireland during the early to mid-1970s.

A Very British Counterinsurgency

In the 2006 BBC2 documentary *The Plot Against Harold Wilson*, veteran journalist and psychological warfare specialist Brian Crozier casually acknowledges an incident in 1974 where he informed senior British military officers that they had to be prepared to stage a coup. As you may have gathered, Crozier was quite a character. He had shilled for the Information Research Department (IRD, a secretive British propaganda agency) for years before establishing a relationship with the Cousins. By the late 1960s, he headed Forum World Features, a press agency almost entirely subsidized by the CIA. From there, Crozier linked up with none other than the Institute for American Strategy's Frank Barnett. The

---

[348] Becker & Selden, *The Body Electric*, 278-281; Paul Brodeur, *Currents of Death*, 40-41.
[349] Annie Jacobsen, *Phenomena*, 188.

former IAS man was impressed and enlisted Richard Mellon Scaife (a central figure in Jane Meyer's *Dark Money* opus) to fund Crozier's new outfit, the Institute for the Study of Conflict.[350]

Crozier was one of many figures in the British right agitating during the 1970s. The period of 1974-1976 was an especially turbulent one in the UK. A combination of labor unrest, a moribund economy and renewed Troubles in Northern Ireland made it seem like the government was on the verge of collapse. And indeed, former spies such as Peter Wright to Colin Wallace have indicated that there were serious discussions of a military coup during the administration of Harold Wilson. While this never came to pass, there is compelling evidence a type of soft coup was run against the administrations of Edward Heath, Wilson and James Callaghan by the security services. Much of this was managed through a relentless campaign of psychological warfare directed against the UK public.[351]

These intrigues coincided with the destabilization of Northern Ireland during "The Troubles."[352] Over the span of three decades, over 3.5k lost their lives in the conflict, over half civilians. High profile victims included Ross McWhirter, co-editor of *The Guinness Book of World Records*; far right Tory politician Airey Neave; and Lord Louis Mountbatten of the Royal Family. For years, the far right Unionist Member of Parliament (MP) Enoch Powell alleged that the British security services, in collaboration with their American counterparts (especially the CIA), conspired to create a United Ireland within the NATO alliance (which has more or less come to pass). Powell placed the conspiracy's origin somewhere in the mid to late 1960s.[353] While his claims are baseless, there's no question things began to heat up around this time.

---

[350] Jeffrey H. Michaels, "The Heyday of Britain's Cold War Think Tank: Brian Crozier and the Institute for the Study of Conflict, 1970-79" in ed. by Luc Van Dongen, Stephanie Roulin and Giles Scott-Smith *Transnational Anti-Communism and the Cold War: Agents, Activities, and Networks* (New York: Palgrave Macmillan, 2014), 147, 150-153; Giles Scott-Smith, *Western Anti-Communism and the Interdoc Network* (New York: Palgrave Macmillan, 2012), 203-205.

[351] It probably goes without saying, but this is a highly controversial subject. Several of the most compelling accounts of this turbulent period include Peter Wright with Paul Greengrass, *Spycatcher The Candid Autobiography of a Senior Intelligence Officer* (New York: Viking, 1987); David Leigh, *The Wilson Plot: How the Spycatchers and Their American Allies Tried to Overthrow the British Government* (New York: Pantheon Books, 1988); Stephan Dorril & Robin Ramsay *Smear! Wilson and the Secret State* (London: Fourth Estate, 1991); and Clive Bloom *Thatcher's Secret War: Subversion, Coercion, Secrecy and Government, 1974-90* (Brimscombe Port Stroud, Gloucestershire: The History Press, 2015).

[352] This era is commonly known as "The Troubles." From roughly 1968 till 1998, a low intensity conflict raged throughout Northern Ireland, occasionally spilling into the Republic of Ireland (ROI), Britain and mainland Europe. State complicity, by both of the British and the ROI, remains a highly controversial subject across the board. Some of the best works on the misdeeds of the security services include Paul Foot, *Who Framed Colin Wallace?* (London: Pan Books, 1990); and two works by Martin Dillon, *The Dirty War* (London: Arrow Book, 1991); and *The Trigger Men* (Edinburgh: Mainstream Publishing, 2008).

[353] Martin Dillon, *The Dirty War*, 278-279.

The Irish Republican Army (IRA) was largely defunct by the mid-1960s, but sprang back to life at decade's end. Spurred by the worldwide student protests of 1968, Catholics and liberal Protestants began demonstrating for greater civil rights for Northern Ireland's Catholic minority. Soon, the protests and the violent response from Loyalist paramilitaries grew beyond the ability of the government of Northern Ireland to manage. At this point, both London and Dublin decided to intervene.

The British response, centered around the deployment of troops in Northern Ireland, has been widely commented upon. Far less attention has been paid to Dublin's response. In 1969, the Irish Army provided the IRA with weapons training and even prepared for an invasion of Northern Ireland. While these plans were eventually shelved during January 1970, the ROI contributed a considerable sum of money to relief efforts, some of which was diverted to the IRA for the procurement of weapons.[354] This scandal became known as the "Arms Crisis." Early in the conflict, the Dublin airport was a major hub for arms trafficking, facilitated by IRA sympathizers in the Irish government.[355] We shall return to that airport in a moment.

Suffice to say, a renewed IRA terror campaign ensued. Predictably, the British security services responded. It was in this maelstrom that something known as "Operation Clockwork Orange" was launched. This was a purported psychological warfare operation aiming to destabilize the IRA through false media stories. But from the beginning, the security services seemed more interested in destabilizing the governments of Heath and Wilson.[356] It's usually credited as running from 1974 to 1975, but Colin Wallace, a psychological warfare specialist then working with the British Army, claimed it was already active against Heath's administration in 1973.[357]

Clockwork Orange had everything but the kitchen sink. There was black propaganda mixed in with rumored false flag operations targeting British troops. Wallace claimed to have studied several celebrated grimoires for the purpose of crafting genuine "Satanic altars." He set up "magic circles" in derelict houses in the Catholic regions. He hung upside down crosses leading to the sites and even employed real chicken blood and feathers on the altars. This was done for the purposes of launching what we now think of as a Satanic panic. This came at a time when Northern Ireland's ongoing pedophile scandal was first beginning to attract attention from the press.[358]

---

[354] Martin Dillon, *The Dirty War*, 13-15, 21-22.

[355] Martin Dillon, *The Dirty War*, 19.

[356] Clive Bloom, *Thatcher's Secret War: Subversion, Coercion, Secrecy and Government, 1974-90*, 30-33. As of this writing, the only work to consider Operation Clockwork Orange in depth is Paul Foot's *Who Framed Colin Wallace?* A compelling account is also present in Dillon, *The Dirty War*, 197-204.

[357] Paul Foot, *Who Framed Colin Wallace?*, 42-48, etc.

[358] Paul Foot, *Who Framed Colin Wallace?*, 137-145.

Further muddying the waters is that this was at the height of the Kincora Boys Home scandal. In this case, there's no question numerous kids were being sexually abused by the proprietors, and that said proprietors had links to the British security service. A key link man was Protestant minister William McGrath, who ran the boy's home. When not ministering to his flock and orphans, McGrath led a violent paramilitary organization known as Tara. His relationship with British intelligence potentially began during the 1950s when he smuggled Bibles into Russia as a front for intelligence gathering by MI6.[359] Colin Wallace was aware of the abuses McGrath presided over for years and was prevented from exposing it by his superiors. Wallace suspected an MI5 operation was being run out of Kincora and that McGrath was an asset. Much collaborating evidence has emerged over the years to support Wallace's claims.[360]

McGrath and the Kincora scandal did not come to public attention until 1980. He was charged with multiple offenses and went to trial the following year. He was sentenced to four years, but only served two. Besides his intelligence ties, it was rumored McGrath had further protection thanks to "top hats and royalty," i.e. the British upper classes and those connected to the Royal family. One of McGrath's main financial backers and a figure implicated in the abuse at Kincora was Sir Knox Cunningham. Previously, Cunningham had served as an MP (1955-1970) and as Prime Minister Harold Macmillan's Parliamentary Private Secretary.[361] Other establishment figures alleged (but never proven) to have participated in the abuse at Kincora include Sir Anthony Blunt, the Keeper of the Queen's Pictures before being revealed as member of the Cambridge 5, and Lord Mountbatten, Prince Phillip's uncle and at one time commander of all British Armed Forces.[362]

So, to recap: credible evidence has emerged that the British security services were engaged in a soft coup against Heath and Wilson during the mid-1970s. The proverbial spear tip of these efforts was potentially a psychological operation called Clockwork Orange. And yes, the operation was specifically named after the film and book. This is coming against the backdrop of numerous reports of violence linked to the film in the UK. A media campaign begins targeting the film and Kubrick finally withdraws it in 1974.

There were equally intriguing developments afoot back in the States. In Hollywood, the era of the conglomerate had arrived. Major corporations were buying Hollywood studios and a variety of other entertainment-centric companies and merging them into behemoths. Warner Brothers, where Kubrick set up shop after *2001* and remained for the rest of his life, was no different.

---

[359] Paul Foot, *Who Framed Colin Wallace?*, 355; Dillon, *Trigger Men*, 113.

[360] Paul Foot, *Who Framed Colin Wallace?*, 355-356, etc. Dillon, *The Dirty War*, 200, etc; Dillon, *Trigger Men*, 117-118

[361] Dillon, *Trigger Men*, 115-117; McCurry, C. (2017, February 8). Kincora campaigner's fury after abuse evidence is censored. BelfastTelegraph.co.uk. https://www.belfasttelegraph.co.uk/news/northern-ireland/kincora-campaigners-fury-after-abuse-evidence-is-censored/35432535.html.

[362] Clive Bloom, *Thatcher's Secret War*, 177; Dillon, *Trigger Men*, 106, 115.

If anything, the developments surrounding the studio were even more suspect than others. Seven Arts, the company co-founded by Ray Stark, became big enough by the mid-1960s to buy Warner. During Kubrick's dealings with the company during the early 1960s, its chairman and largest shareholder was Louis Chesler. A 300-pound Toronto stockbroker, Chesler had links to infamous mobster Meyer Lansky since the 1940s. When Chesler's link to Lansky was revealed in 1964, he was forced out of Seven Arts, but the two largest shareholders in Warner-Seven Arts circa 1968 were Morris Mac Schwebel, Chesler's attorney and former right hand man, and Baltimore Colts owner Carroll Rosenbloom, a friend of Chesler's. [363]

Seven Arts' takeover of Warner began with the acquisition of Jack Warner's controlling interest in 1966 to the tune of $37 million. The following year, they made a successful offer for the rest of the studio's stock. A little over a year later, Seven Arts facilitated a $400 million takeover by Kinney National Company. This gave rise to conglomerate Warner Brothers Communications Inc.[364] Warner had already established its own record label. With this new ownership, it acquired additional record labels along with DC comics, *Mad* magazine, a publishing company, and so on.

By 1972, in the midst of an election year, Richard Nixon began threatening antitrust actions against the conglomerates. Various Warner executives contributed generously to Nixon's campaign. Charles Colson was even hired as a consultant on cable regulation and remained on the payroll right up to his indictment for stonewalling the Watergate investigation.[365] This is interesting, because as I documented in *The Art*, many former Kennedy allies were deeply involved in destabilizing the Nixon administration by this point. All of this makes Kubrick's activities during this time all the more intriguing.

The following year, Kubrick was in Ireland filming *Barry Lyndon*. It was an anomaly for both the director and his studio. During this era, Warner mainly produced comedies, action films and various genre efforts (i.e. westerns and horror) on modest budgets. Up to this point, Kubrick's film output had broadly conformed to industry trends. *Barry Lyndon*, a big budget period piece, was a considerable departure for both. It's long been rumored the film constituted a compromise between the studio and director: Kubrick gave up on his *Napoleon* epic in exchange for a more modestly priced costume drama set during the same era.[366] But there's good reason to believe that there's more to this story.

Kubrick originally wanted to shoot the movie on location close to his home in England. As you may have gathered, he could not have picked a more interesting time to shoot a film in Ireland than the mid-1970s. As the story goes, his brother-in-law and financial comptroller

---

[363] Marshall, J. (2022, February 15). Wall street, the supermob, and the CIA. Lobster magazine. https://www.academia.edu/71640287/Wall_Street_the_Supermob_and_the_CIA, 21-25.

[364] Marshall, J. (2022, February 15). Wall street, the supermob, and the CIA. Lobster magazine. https://www.academia.edu/71640287/Wall_Street_the_Supermob_and_the_CIA, 23-24.

[365] Baxter, *Stanley Kubrick: A Biography*, 280.

[366] James Fenwick, *Stanley Kubrick Produces*, 170.

Jan Harlan, along with legendary production designer Ken Adams and line producer Bernard Williams, urged Kubrick to shoot there.[367] Kubrick was still on the fence when what was described as an "alarming visitor" approached him at Abbots Mead. No one is entirely sure who this person was, but some have speculated they were linked to the IRA. The group had a reputation for extorting foreign films shot in Ireland. Regardless, whatever the stranger said to Kubrick so unnerved the director that he abruptly moved shooting to Ireland.[368]

This narrative makes no sense.

If the IRA wanted to extort Kubrick, why threaten him when's still deciding whether to film in Ireland? And would Kubrick actually believe that he would be safer from the IRA on production in Ireland than in England? This is even more peculiar when taking into account Bernard Williams' other job on *Lyndon*: Kubrick's liaison to the Irish Army, which contributed nearly 250 troops to work as extras.[369] Williams hired a retired colonel, Brian O'Kelly, to assist him. O'Kelly assured Williams of Kubrick's safety.[370]

So in 1973, in the midst of a terror campaign that had already claimed dozens of lives, Kubrick began filming in the Republic of Ireland. This meant hundreds of extras, including the Irish Army, to say nothing of the army of technicians, wranglers, prop department folks, and so on, with him. The entire production was shrouded in his notorious secrecy. He booked adjacent rooms in Dublin's Ardree Hotel. Emilio D'Alessandro claims this was done so Kubrick could hold face to face conversations, rather than having important discussions over two way radios. Kubrick was concerned someone would be listening in on his radio conversations for his movie.[371]

Kubrick filmed in Ireland all throughout the summer and fall of 1973 with a proverbial army attached to the production. Emilio D'Alessandro made frequent trips to and from the UK with a variety of packages. He was constantly being searched at the Dublin airport, supposedly due to the threat from the IRA.[372] As was noted above, this was the same airport that had been an early transit point for IRA arms smuggling.

Then, filming suddenly halted in October. Just as abruptly, Kubrick moved the entire production from Ireland back to the UK in twenty-four hours.[373] At the time, the stoppage was attributed to locations being unavailable for filming during the Christmas season. Elsewhere, rumors circulated Kubrick was actually using the time to film scenes for his long gestating *Napoleon* film.[374]

---

[367] Baxter, 285.
[368] Baxter, 286.
[369] Rodney Hill, "Barry Lyndon," in *The Stanley Kubrick Archives* ed. by Alison Castle, 471.
[370] Baxter, 286.
[371] Emilo D'Alessandro with Filippo Ulivieri, *Stanley Kubrick and Me*, 44.
[372] D'Alessandro w/ Ulivieri, 51.
[373] When this happened is hazy. Kolker and Abrams placed it in January 1974. See *Kubrick: An Odyssey*, 342.

It later came out that the move was spurred by bomb threats made by the IRA against the production. Or, at least that's one account. In another, "Special Branch" informed Kubrick he was an IRA target.[375] John Baxter's account of this in *Stanley Kubrick: A Biography* doesn't specify which Special Branch. In *Kubrick: An Odyssey*, Kolker and Abrams speculate the warning came from the "UK's Special Branch."[376] But this is unlikely. Special Branch in the UK is a part of the Metropolitan Police, London's police force. While the Met's Special Branch has intelligence functions, they're primarily concerned with domestic threats and played little role in the Troubles. British intelligence in Northern Ireland was handled by MI5 while MI6 was responsible for the ROI. In both cases, they worked with the respective Special Branches of those countries: the Royal Ulster Constabulary (RUC) Special Branch and the Special Detective Unit of the Gardaí, the ROI's national police force and security service. The warning would have most likely come from the Gardai as Kubrick was in ROI, but the RUC can't be discounted. It would be especially interesting if the RUC was behind the warning as they worked closely with MI5 and British military intelligence on Operation Clockwork Orange.

Emilio D'Alessandro's comments about these events are especially insightful: "On reflection, in the months leading up to this, there was a different atmosphere: there were more and more alerts at the airport, which now made me uncomfortable whenever I traveled by train, plane, or ferry, as these were all possible targets for a terror attack. I once took an Irish taxi that had bullet holes in the seats. When I noticed this I realized how serious the situation really was. I even spoke to Margaret about my fears: what if they found out I worked for Kubrick and attacked me as a way of getting to him? What if they targeted one of us to attract the attention of the media?

"The same thoughts were probably going through Stanley's mind. I don't know what they said to him that evening. Did they threaten him directly, or did they send a letter to the production company? Either way, I know all too well the effect it had on him, Christiana, and all the rest of us in the family. I realized that a lot of people stopped acting normally when they heard the name Stanley Kubrick. A few months later, when *A Clockwork Orange* was withdrawn from distribution in England, it became apparent that the impression I'd had of Stanley up to then was a bit limiting, given that people took him and what he said in his films so seriously."[377]

By this point in time, production had already gone over budget. While originally budgeted at $2.5 million, Kubrick had spent nearly $7 million. The final price tag would creep to over $11 million in the 1970s dollars. This contributed to *Lyndon*'s legacy as the only Kubrick film to have not turned a profit eventually. Few productions have inspired the same kind of reaction

---

[374] LoBrutto, *Stanley Kubrick: A Biography*, 386.

[375] Baxter, 289; LoBrutto, 386. When the threat occurred isn't clear. LoBrutto indicates it occurred in the fall, prior to Christmas, whereas Baxter claims it occurred shortly after New Year's, when filming was set to begin again.

[376] Kolker and Abrams, *Kubrick: An Odyssey*, 342.

[377] D'Alessandro w/ Ulivieri, 52-53.

as *Barry Lyndon*. Because of the tax code, Ireland has long been a popular place to film movies at. But as far as I'm aware, nothing drew the ire of the IRA quite like Kubrick. So, what are we to make of this?

Kubrick later befriended David Cornwell, more popularly known as novelist John le Carre, the author of numerous spy thrillers. Cornwell had worked in the British security services before becoming a full time novelist. He was employed with MI5 between 1958 and 1960, his time possibly overlapping with Anthony Burgess. In 1960, he transferred to MI6 and remained there until 1964. Supposedly, he was forced out of the intelligence racket after his cover was blown as a result of the Cambridge Five) which Burgess was then investigating).[378]

D'Alessandro reports that Kubrick held Cornwell in extremely high regard. While he was never officially credited with working on any of Kubrick's films, he contributed to the work on *A.I.* and likely many of Kubrick's later projects. Emilo reports once hearing Kubrick inform Cornwell: "Your word is final." Kubrick never displayed the same kind of trust in any of the other writers he worked with.[379]

Cornwell is an interesting figure. He was publically associated with the Labour Party, and more left wing elements, for virtually his entire life. He was a fierce critic of the 2003 invasion of Iraq and later denounced Trump and Brexit. Clearly, he's in the neo-liberal wing of the Anglo-American Establishment.

This is especially interesting in light of the mid-1970s coup allegations. The perpetrators are generally described as a right wing cabal based out of MI5, with some support from the British military. Colin Wallace alleged that Operation Clockwork Orange was initiated in North Ireland after MI5 took over operations from MI6 in 1973.[380] As was noted previously, they worked closely with the RUC's Special Branch in these efforts.

This is the same year Kubrick turns up in Ireland to film *Barry Lyndon*. Is it possible MI6 was using the production as a way to keep tabs on what MI5 was up to in Ireland during this time? And if so, did the threats against the production possibly originate with someone connected to MI5? Or was Kubrick assisting MI6, which had jurisdiction in the ROI?

But this assumes MI5 was the driving force behind Operation Clockwork Orange, and the broader campaign of destabilization across the UK and Northern Ireland, which may not have been the case. Stephen Dorrill and Robin Ramsey, writing in *Smear!*, probably the most balanced account of this era, saw the situation as far more complex. Incidentally, Dorril and Ramsey are also the longtime editors of the UK-based parapolitical journal *Lobster*. The same

---

378 Anthony, A. (2009, November 1). Observer profile: John le Carré: A man of great intelligence. The Guardian. https://www.theguardian.com/theobserver/2009/nov/01/profile-john-le-carre
379 D'Alessandro w/ Ulivieri, 245.
380 Paul Foot, *Who Framed Colin Wallace?*, 41.

publication Tony Frewin, one of Kubrick's longtime assistants, contributed several articles on the JFK assassination to.

The major figure Dorril and Ramsay fingered behind the plotting was a former MI6 officer and MP called G.K. Young. They speculate that MI6, or more likely a cabal within the organization, was directing the psywar campaign. Later efforts to implicate MI5, such as those by ex-MI5 officer Peter Wright in his *Spycatcher* book, were part of this disinformation campaign.[381]

If some faction of MI6 was promoting these efforts, it makes Kubrick's role even harder to discern. Production didn't start again until February 1974. By this time, it moved back to the UK. Kubrick is known for the meticulous pre-production he did for his films. And yet, little attention has been paid to the abandonment of Ireland and shift to the UK in a matter of months. This had never been the plan and reportedly forced Kubrick to reconceive the film during the lull.[382]

This was unfolding as he was coming to a decision to withdraw *A Clockwork Orange* from the UK. It's worth noting that Kubrick himself believed the threats he received during this time were over *A Clockwork Orange* and not *Barry Lyndon*.[383] Which doesn't make a lot of sense if they were coming from the IRA. *Orange* was banned in the Republic of Ireland in 1973 before it hit cinemas.[384] Why would they be concerned over a film that was never released in the ROI? Unless they found audience reactions to it around London as curious as I do...

Conversely, if it was some other party, what did they say to convince Kubrick to move his production within striking distance of a near war zone? Kubrick is known to have a fear of being kidnapped, which was an ongoing concern in both the ROI and Northern Ireland during The Troubles. At a minimum, this seems an uncharacteristically risky move on Kubrick's part.

These developments fueled Kubrick's desire to keep *A Clockwork Orange* banned in the UK for the rest of his life. When EMI requested that Warner intervene and allow them to screen the film during the late 1970s, Kubrick used the confidentiality agreement he'd negotiated with Warner in 1973 to put the kibosh on these designs. Kubrick clung to this agreement for the rest of his life.[385] In fairness, Kubrick and his family received a considerable amount of threats over the film, including several ticking parcels left by the mail service. The sensational accounts of violence linked to the film by the British tabloids didn't help matters either.[386] But was this full court press totally coincidental, or was there a hidden hand?

---

[381] Stephen Dorril & Robin Ramsay, *Smear! Wilson & the Secret State*, 328-330.

[382] LoBrutto, 386.

[383] Baxter, 289-290.

[384] Baxter, 286.

[385] James Fenwick, *Stanley Kubrick Produces*, 175.

[386] Robert P. Kolker and Nathan Abrams, *Kubrick: An Odyssey*, 322.

It's interesting to note the encounters Kubrick had with the British government during this time. After *A Clockwork Orange* was cleared for release by British censors, Reginald Maudling—Edward Heath's Home Secretary—ordered a private screening to further review the picture.[387] During this time, Maulding was involved with GEN 42, a secret cabinet committee monitoring some of the worst abuses in Northern Ireland.[388]

The election of Harold Wilson, Heath's successor, was even more concerning. Denis Healey, co-founder of the International Institute for Strategic Studies, was poised to become Wilson's Chancellor of the Exchequer. One policy put forward by Healey was an annual wealth tax that would include foreign residents residing in the UK over nine years.[389]

Kubrick, in other words.

With his personal and corporate taxes set to increase substantially, Kubrick threatened to leave the country. As he had brought in over $30 million to the UK film industry at a time when it was moribund, this was no idle threat. Further, he was instrumental in encouraging filmmakers like Steven Spielberg and George Lucas to film in the UK. A lot of money was on the line, to put it mildly. Kubrick made his position clear to Geoffrey Howe, the Conservative shadow chancellor in 1977, as well.[390] Kubrick was engaged in a complex game of economic chicken with the UK government during the most domestically turbulent period the nation experienced in the Cold War.

Kubrick blinked, opting to remain in the UK.[391] But with few exceptions, Kubrick's disdain for Labour was solidified. He maintained a friendship with onetime party head Michael Foot,[392] who was considered to be on Labour's left wing. But Foot had a reputation for his pragmatism, and more importantly, was Healey's primary rival for Labour's leadership during the early 1980s. But on the whole, Kubrick remained staunchly anti-Labour, fearing financial ruin from taxation if the party ever returned to power.[393]

Taken in the context of the political intrigues playing out in the UK, it seems evident far more was going on during the production of *Lyndon* than what has been acknowledged. A clue can perhaps be discerned via reactions to a 1990 film called *Hidden Agenda*. The movie was directed by the politically-charged British filmmaker Ken Loach and was largely based upon

---

[387] Alexander Walker, *Stanley Kubrick Directs: A Visual Analysis*, 236.

[388] Martin Dillon, *Trigger Men*, 12-13.

[389] James Fenwick, *Stanley Kubrick Produces*, 174; Robert P. Kolker and Nathan Abrams, *Kubrick: An Odyssey*, 360-361.

[390] James Fenwick, *Stanley Kubrick Produces*, 174-175; Robert P. Kolker and Nathan Abrams, *Kubrick: An Odyssey*, 360-361.

[391] Robert P. Kolker and Nathan Abrams, *Kubrick: An Odyssey*, 361.

[392] Robert P. Kolker and Nathan Abrams, *Kubrick: An Odyssey*, 477.

[393] Robert P. Kolker and Nathan Abrams, *Kubrick: An Odyssey*, 492-493. After Margaret Thatcher became Prime Minister in 1979, the Tories remained in power until 1997. When Labour finally returned to power, Kubrick was less threatened by Tony Blair's centrist policies.

Colin Wallace's account of Operation Clockwork Orange. The film generally received positive reviews, but one particular critic took serious issue with it.

His name was Alexander Walker. Hailing from Belfast, where the Kincora Boys Home was located, Walker was a staunch Unionist. Over the years, he earned a reputation for moralizing. Walker famously attacked the films of Ken Russell, David Cronenberg and Takashi Miike for their violent and sexually charged content.

As for *Hidden Agenda*, Walker took issue purely along political lines. He viciously attacked Loach and the film's screenwriter during its Cannes press conference. A polite way of describing his outburst would be to say he denounced the film as IRA propaganda. When Loach tried to defend his film, he was shouted down by Walker's fellow British film critics. The controversy Walker unleashed that day still surrounds the film.[394]

Why is Walker's criticism relevant? Because, as was noted at the onset of this thing, he was a longtime friend of Kubrick's. Walker wrote one of the earliest Kubrick bio's during the early 1970s and was one of Kubrick's unofficial writing partners. Emilio notes he was a regular presence during the writing of *The Shining* and *Full Metal Jacket*.[395] The trust Kubrick placed in Walker despite his well known loathing of the press is curious. For whatever reason, Walker managed to maintain Kubrick's trust for decades. Perhaps this is partly what inspired his vehement reaction to Loach's film. Maybe it was a little too close to the truth and risked implicating his friend?

One final mystery surrounding Kubrick's sojourn in Ireland is the Kennedy factor. They're easily the most famous Irish-American family in the world while the ROI was long regarded as a sensitive situation in foreign policy circles. The strong anti-British sentiment in the ROI led to the nation taking an official stance of neutrality during WWII while the IRA and other nationalist circles played footsies with the Nazis.[396] In the postwar years, several notorious "former" Nazis, most notably Otto Skorzeny, relocated to the ROI and remained a fixture there until the mid-1960s.[397]

Skorzeny was a guerilla warfare specialist and considered a pioneer of special operations forces. In the postwar years, Skorzeny partially supported himself by training military forces

---

[394] Carroll, B. (2003, October 1). Hidden Agenda. Senses of Cinema. https://www.sensesofcinema.com/2003/cteq/hidden_agenda/

[395] D'Alessandro w/ Ulivieri, 119, 172.

[396] Sanders, A. (2014, May 30). "senator Edward Kennedy and the Ulster Troubles: Irish and Irish-American politics, 1965-2009" Historical journal of massachusetts (2011). Academia.edu. https://www.academia.edu/4877175/_Senator_Edward_Kennedy_and_the_Ulster_Troubles_Irish_and_Irish_American_Politics_1965_2009_Historical_Journal_of_Massachusetts_2011_. For more on Nazi Germany's cultivation of Ireland, see H.P. Albarelli Jr., *Coup in Dallas: The Decisive Investigation Into Who Killed JFK* (New York: Skyhorse Publishing, 2021), especially 300-318

[397] Crutchley, P. (2014, December 30). How did hitler's scar-faced henchman become an Irish farmer? BBC News. https://www.bbc.com/news/uk-northern-ireland-30571335 . For more on this subject, see H.P. Albarelli Jr., *Coup in Dallas: The Decisive Investigation Into Who Killed JFK*, 296-306, 318-325, etc.

and trafficking arms.[398] Thus, it's interesting his time in Ireland roughly coincided with "Operation Harvest" (1956-1962), the last major IRA campaign in Northern Ireland before the Troubles. When Skorzeny first arrived in Ireland during 1957, he was greeted by members of the Irish government, including future prime minister Charles Haughey. Haughey later played a crucial role in the above-mentioned Arms Crisis of 1970.[399]

Soon after taking office, JFK appointed his good friend, Florida businessman Grant Stockdale, as US Ambassador to Ireland. Stockdale routinely brushed elbows with Skorzeny at various Irish state functions during this time. The former Nazi was closely scrutinized by intelligence officials in the diplomatic mission during Stockdale's tenure.[400]

Stockdale served in Ireland until July 1962. He fell from the 13th floor of Miami's DuPont Building and died on December 2, 1963, less than two weeks after JFK was assassinated. Edward "Ted" Kennedy, the long serving US Senator and younger brother of JFK, flew to Ireland six months after his brother was assassinated. Three weeks after returning to the United States, on June 19, 1964, he was in a plane crash that claimed the life of pilot Edward Zimny near Lawrence, MA.[401]

This was just the beginning of Ted Kennedy's engagement with Ireland. While little remarked upon, Kennedy emerged as one of the most vocal critics of British policy in Northern Ireland as well as the IRA by the early 1970s. Arguably no American would play a greater role in the peace process and ending the Troubles than Kennedy. In 2009, Kennedy was made an honorary Knight of the British Empire for his efforts.

But that was later. In 1971, the British were rather perturbed by Kennedy inserting himself into the debate over Northern Ireland. During that year, Kennedy described it as "Britain's Vietnam" and called for international intervention. British officials feared he would use the US House of Representatives to demand the UN intervene in Northern Ireland with peacekeepers. Kennedy's stance moderated somewhat the following year when he began to discuss the situation with Catholic Northern Ireland political leader John Hume, one of the architects of the 1968 protests. This, combined with an alleged IRA bomb plot targeting the family Caroline Kennedy (JFK's daughter) was then staying with in Northern Ireland, led the US congressman to take a firm stance against the paramilitary.[402] Some even went so far as

---

[398] For more on Skorzeny's contributions to modern day SOFs. and his role in training and arming them, see Ralph P. Ganis, *The Skorzeny Papers: Evidence for the Plot to Kill JFK* (New York: Hot Books, 2018).

[399] Crutchley, P. (2014, December 30). How did hitler's scar-faced henchman become an Irish farmer? BBC News. https://www.bbc.com/news/uk-northern-ireland-30571335; H.P. Albarelli Jr., *Coup in Dallas*, 300.

[400] H.P. Albarelli Jr., *Coup in Dallas*, 325-328.

[401] H.P. Albarelli Jr., *Coup in Dallas*, 333.

[402] Sanders, A. (2014a, May 30). "senator Edward Kennedy and the Ulster Troubles: Irish and Irish-American politics, 1965-2009" Historical journal of massachusetts (2011). Academia.edu. https://www.academia.edu/4877175/_Senator_Edward_Kennedy_and_the_Ulster_Troubles_Irish_an

to accuse Ted Kennedy of capitulation to the British by the time of Jimmy Carter's 1977 peace initiative.[403]

Kubrick entered Ireland in the midst of Ted Kennedy's political evolution on the Irish question. Whether Kubrick's time there contributed to Kennedy's stance on Northern Ireland has likely been forever lost to the sands of time.

One final point to consider is Warner Brothers reaction. As I noted in the introduction, Warner appears to have leverage over Kubrick post-*Lyndon*. *The Shining* may be the only post-*Spartacus* picture Kubrick was pressured into making by a studio. Superficially, this can be explained by *Lyndon*'s poor box office returns. But if there was another agenda at play, wouldn't Kubrick be given some leeway by Warner?

But this assumes the studio was aware of a covert agenda behind the filming. It's possible they were in the dark, or perturbed over Kubrick's decision to ban *Orange* in the UK. Or perhaps the Republican administrations of Nixon and Ford brought pressure against the studio to crack down on Kubrick.[404]

Another, and perhaps the most plausible possibility, is that Kubrick went "rogue" in regards to *Lyndon*. By the Christmas break, he'd blown through the original $2.5 million budget while only filming 10 percent of the picture.[405] When filming recommenced in 1974, Kubrick had reconceived the movie and burned through an additional $9 million to bring it to competition. I can't help but wonder that, after his experiences in Ireland, Kubrick felt "entitled" to make a passion project out of his original conception of the film. Support for this notion can be found in the revelation that Kubrick didn't even inform Warner of the move to England until production had fully set up camp there. This move alone is estimated to have added $4 million to the budget and an additional 40 days of shooting.[406]

Kubrick pitched *Lyndon* to Warner as a romantic epic along the lines of *Gone With the Wind*, but there's very little to no romance in the movie. The courtship between Barry (Ryan O'Neal) and Lady Lyndon (Marisa Berenson) takes place largely off screen. While Kubrick is fairly faithful to the William Thackeray novel upon which his film is based, this is one of the major plot points deemphasized. Predictably, Kubrick dwells on the Seven Years War during

---

d_Irish_American_Politics_1965_2009_Historical_Journal_of_Massachusetts_2011_.

403 McManus , S. (2011, August 24). How the Horsemen galloped the wrong way. Irish Echo Newspaper. https://www.irishecho.com/2011/8/how-the-horsemen-galloped-the-wrong-way. Kennedy was one of four Irish-American Congressmen dubbed the "Four Horsemen" who were embraced by the UK and ROI for their more moderate stance.

404 As I recount in *The Art*, Kennedy supporters within the political establishment were at the forefront of efforts to destabilize the Nixon administration. There is compelling evidence, for instance, that the Pentagon Papers were originally compiled by Kennedy backers in the State Department to aid RFK's 1968 presidential campaign.

405 Baxter, *Stanley Kubrick: A Biography*, 287.

406 Robert P. Kolker and Nathan Abrams, *Kubrick: An Odyssey*, 344.

the film's first half, but the second is a moody rumination on Barry's rise and fall. He becomes a spy and gambler followed by efforts to secure a legacy for his son. Tragedy inevitably ensues. What the viewer is left with is a big budget character study.

One can't help but feel Kubrick felt a certain kinship with Barry. Both were social climbers in circles they never felt truly accepted in: Barry as an Irishman among the British aristocracy, Kubrick a Jew among America's old guard WASP elite. Like Barry, Kubrick supported himself as a gambler at times. Both left their homeland for a foreign country. And perhaps Barry's conscription into espionage was something Kubrick could relate too.

Barry begins the film as love struck and earnest to the point of naivety. He's betrayed by his own family, leading to misadventures in Ireland before a career of soldiering in the Seven Years War. Eventually, he is enlisted as a spy. This enables him to break free from the Prussian army he's Shanghaied into and eventually enter the ranks of the British aristocracy.

In managing this, Barry becomes quite a roguish figure. But, everyone in the film, and especially the aristocracy, is corrupt to the core. Despite his at times reprehensible behavior (especially in regards to Lady Lyndon), Barry is a doting father (which ultimately leads to his son's tragic death) and still capable of basic human decency when it matters. He's spurred to confess to an Irish gambler that he's been dispatched to spy upon him and throws his shot during the final duel with Lord Bullington (Leon Vitali), his sniveling stepson.[407] Bullington's pistol misfired during the opening round, but Barry couldn't bring himself to press the advantage. Bullington has no such honor, and wounds Barry in the leg with his next shot. Barry loses the limb and is finally driven from the aristocracy.

One is left with the sense that this was an autobiographical picture for Kubrick, and easily his most personal until *Eyes Wide Shut*. It was not the film Warner was expecting. Realizing he would not be given the chance to make his *Napoleon* picture, Kubrick potentially used the chaos in Ireland to make something nearly as close to his heart. Perhaps even more so. Napoleon was the man Kubrick aspired to be, but Redmond Barry was closer to who he was.

When all is said and done, *Barry Lyndon* stands as the most mysterious production Kubrick ever worked on. Which is probably why it's been almost entirely ignored by Cryptokubrologists with the exception of the goddamned NASA cameras.

---

[407] Bullington's character is another change Kubrick made. In the novel, Bullington is a much more sympathetic figure having served in the American Revolution for the British while his stepfather's lavish lifestyle bleeds the family dry. In Kubrick's hands, he becomes the embodiment of the pampered and privileged progeny of the upper classes.

Chapter Four:

Saturn Returns

Eyes Wide Shut

Both *Eyes Wide Shut* and the production behind it are the stuff of legend. The shoot went on for 400 days, which is still the lengthiest ever recorded. It witnessed two stars, Harvey Keitel and Jennifer Jason Leigh, being replaced in the midst of production. And Kubrick himself famously died during the final stages of editing.

Given all these factors, it's hardly surprising the film has inspired so much speculation and conspiracy theorizing over the years. So before diving into the film proper, I want to briefly address several popular misconceptions about it. The first is that the version released in theaters on July 16, 1999, was more or less Kubrick's final cut, with a few minor additions made after the director's death.

In reality, it was only the first cut. Kubrick was known for editing his films right up to the last moment. In the case of *The Shining*, he even did attention edits after the film was released theatrically in the US. As such, Kubrick surely would have continued tinkering with the film for as long as possible. Further, few have denied changes were made to the soundtrack and to the content displayed during the masked ball after the director's death. Specifically, some clumsy CGI was used to impose figures over the more explicit moments so as to avoid an NC-17. Kubrick was contractually obligated to turn the film in with an R rating, so changes would have inevitably occurred to this sequence.

Upon his death, his longtime assistant, Leon Vitali, took over the small editing team Kubrick was working with. Additional input came from Christiane, Kubrick's wife; and Jan Harlan, his brother-in-law and longtime producing partner. Based on the notes Kubrick left, now displayed at the Stanley Kubrick Archive, it does seem that many of the changes left were minor and that Vitali followed Kubrick's instructions to the letter as much as possible. But Kubrick indicated the edits could become more elaborate based on the MPAA's reaction to the masked ball. This was the centerpiece of the film and the most tampered with sequence after Kubrick's death. No one knew for sure what Kubrick would have done in regards to the censors. Such is the official narrative, anyway. We'll return to the significance of posthumous tampering to this sequence in a bit.[408]

Another misconception is the choosing of the July 16, 1999 release date. This is a major plank of the "Kubrick filmed the Moon Landing" conspiracy theories. As the narrative goes, Kubrick had it put in his contract that *Eyes Wide Shut* had to be released on that date to mark the 30th anniversary of the moon landing, or lack thereof. And it is true, Kubrick was contractually obligated to have *Eyes* ready by that date. But, there's more to the story.

---

[408] Alexander, K. J. (2019, July 30). Debunking the myths around eyes wide shut, Stanley Kubrick's final film. AnOther. https://www.anothermag.com/design-living/11844/debunking-the-myths-of-eyes-wide-shut-stanley-kubricks-final-film. For an in-depth breakdown of the postproduction, see Robert P. Kolker and Nathan Abrams, *Eyes Wide Shut: Stanley Kubrick and the Making of His Final Film*, 113-132.

For starters, Kubrick had not brought a film in on time in decades. Kubrick was notorious for underestimating the length of film. Virtually everything he directed dragged on well beyond the initial schedule. So, Kubrick placing a firm debate on when he would finish filming anything is rather implausible to begin with. He knew as well as anyone that once production began on his films, complications would inevitably emerge.

As for *Eyes Wide Shut*, he began filming in late 1996. The tentative plan was to wrap shooting early the next year and have the film ready for release by late 1997, or more likely, 1998. This schedule was quickly scrapped in early 1997 when it became evident that shooting would drag on for an extended period of time. Kubrick did not settle on the July 16th date until September 1998, after principal photography was completed. And even then, it was not solely Kubrick's decision. Both Kubrick and Warner Brothers did extensive research on when would be the best weekend to drop the film for the best box office debut. July 16th was the date they jointly agreed to in September 1998.[409]

By all accounts, Kubrick genuinely believed he would be finished filming *Eyes* well before 1999. He had preproduction on *A.I.* running simultaneously and his archives indicate that he planned to begin filming that picture, with Steven Spielberg as the director, by '99.[410] In other words, there is absolutely nothing to indicate some Machiavellian plan, on Kubrick's part, to time *Eyes'* release to the 30th anniversary of the Apollo landing. Like pretty much everything connected to the moon landing claims, these allegations don't hold up to even precursory scrutiny.

One final misconception I want to address is Harvey Keitel's departure from the film. For years, this was chalked up to a scheduling conflict, as was Jennifer Jason Leigh's departure, but there have been rumors for years that there was more to Keitel's leaving. Then, in 2016, Keitel came out and acknowledged that Kubrick had in fact fired him. Keitel offered no additional details, but noted that he felt "disrespected" by Kubrick on the set. This has usually been taken as a reference to Kubrick's tendency to shoot fifty or more takes of a particular scene. Actor Gary Oldman suggested as much, claiming that Keitel quit after Kubrick filmed him walking through a door 68 times.[411]

Emilio D'Alessandro, Kubrick's longtime driver, is one of the few to offer details concerning Keitel's time on the set. He notes that the veteran character actor arrived shortly after filming began in November 1996. Kubrick put Keitel through five days of rehearsals before shooting what appears to be the only sequence with Keitel. Extensive rehearsals prior to

---

[409] Robert P. Kolker and Nathan Abrams, *Eyes Wide Shut: Stanley Kubrick and the Making of His Final Film*, 85-86, 111, 129, 132.
[410] Alison Castle, "Stanley Kubrick's A.I.," in *The Stanley Kubrick Archives* ed. by Alison Castle, 661; Robert P. Kolker and Nathan Abrams, *Eyes Wide Shut*, 38.
[411] Prigge, M. (2022, November 25). Harvey Keitel opened up about getting fired by Stanley Kubrick. UPROXX. https://uproxx.com/movies/harvey-keitel-fired-eyes-wide-shut-stanley-kubrick/

filming were Kubrick's norm and it was well-known. D'Alessandro describes Keitel as sullen during this time and speaking less and less each day.

After filming Keitel's first scene, production moved to another location. On the first day there, Keitel was to do a scene with Tom Cruise and an unnamed actress. Something went wrong and Keitel left the production that same day. What's more, production never set foot in that location again. This is quite peculiar, consider the meticulous preparation Kubrick did for locations. D'Alessandro describes Kubrick as totally silent that day when he was driving him home. It may have been the only drive Emilio ever made with Kubrick when the director said nothing. The next day, production resumed as if nothing had happened.[412]

One of the most salacious rumors to make the rounds dates back to 1998, shortly after the film wrapped. According to the likes of Howard Stern and *The Daily News*, Keitel was fired after a sex scene with Nicole Kidman got out of hand. Keitel, the consummate method actor, was too in-character while simulating masturbation and ejaculated. And onto Nicole Kidman's hair no less. As a result, Cruise and Kidman reportedly threatened to abandon the film if Kubrick did not fire Keitel.[413]

There are some issues here. The big one is that the proponents of this rumor allege that Keitel's scenes were mostly completed and that they had to be reshot from scratch. But, there are numerous reports that Keitel was only with the production for a matter of weeks. Also, Sidney Pollack, who replaced Keitel, was brought in pretty early in the game. Conversely, Marie Richardson, only joined the production after principal photographer wrapped. These were for reshoots, which Jennifer Jason Leigh was genuinely unavailable for.[414]

Another issue relates to *The Bad Lieutenant* and *There's Something About Mary.* The former star's Keitel and features him in what was then one of the few instances of masturbation in a mainstream movie. Elsewhere, *Something About Mary* (1998) was hugely popular during this era, with the semen in the hair gag becoming a pop culture staple. I suspect a gossip columnist fused these two strands for a film that generated any number of outrageous rumors during its production.

The one thing that gives me pause in dismissing these allegations outright are sketches by Chris Baker, alias Fangorn, made for the film that turned up the Stanley Kubrick archive. Several are quite sexually explicit, and are related to Alice (Nicole Kidman)'s fantasies. One involves her on a horse with the Navy man. She leans forward so that he can penetrate her from behind, atop the horse. Another shows her naked, and surrounded by a group of men. These images were quite surreal and much more graphic than what ended up as the dream sequence involving Alice and the Naval officer.[415] "Realism" is often offered up as to why

---

[412] Emilo D'Alessandro with Filippo Ulivieri, *Stanley Kubrick and Me*, 299-300.
[413] Braunstein, P. (1998, December 29). Mouths wide open - the Village Voice. Village Voice. https://www.villagevoice.com/mouths-wide-open/
[414] Robert P. Kolker and Nathan Abrams, *Eyes Wide Shut*, 111.

Kubrick opted to go in that direction rather than with Fangorn's original conception, but given how strange and surrealistic the film is, this isn't a very compelling explanation. Much like Keitel's firing, why Kubrick abandoned this more graphic approach remains a mystery. And it should be emphasized that I've found nothing to indicate Keitel's firing played a role in this decision.

With the misconceptions out of the way, let's start getting into the film in earnest. A common criticism levied at Kubrick is the impersonality of his films. I would reject that claim on the whole, but especially in regards to *Eyes Wide Shut*. There is no question this was a deeply personal project for Kubrick. The apartment inhabited by Tom Cruise and Nicole Kidman is modeled upon the one the Kubricks had in NYC during the 1960s. The artwork on the walls is mainly by Christiana and Katherina Kubrick.[416] Both his wife and adopted daughter also have cameos in the film, along with Katherina's real life son and longtime assistant/driver Emilo D'Alessandro.[417]

The Somerton manor where the masked ball takes place is located at Glen Cove, Long Island. The Kubricks briefly lived near there during the 1960s.[418] Bizarrely, the first meeting between Kubrick and Christiane occurred at a masked ball. As Christiana describes it, she was performing and Kubrick was the only one in attendance not wearing a costume.[419]

Finally, the New York City of *Eyes Wide Shut* is not the NYC of the late 1990s, a common criticism of the film when it was released. It's much closer to the NYC of Kubrick's youth. But beyond that, it's the most overtly surrealistic film Kubrick had made since the 1950s. This is a reflection of the artistic circles Kubrick was running in during that time when he was married to Ruth Sobotka. Indeed, I would argue the film is a tribute to both NYC and its artistic avant-garde during this era. It may also be a tribute to Sobotka, who was also an accomplished ballet dancer. She performed on numerous occasions with the New York Ballet company, most notably in a production of *The Nutcracker*. *The Nutcracker* is referenced in *Eyes*. In this context, *Eyes* is very much a return to first principles for Kubrick on any number of levels.

Weighing heavily over the film's visual style is director Max Ophuls, a filmmaker cited by Kubrick as an influence for much of his life. Ophuls directed two cinematic adaptations of Arthur Schnitzler's plays. The author's *Traumnovelle* is what *Eyes* is based upon. Kubrick probably discovered Ophuls in 1950s NYC among Sobotka's artistic circles.[420]

---

[415] Robert P. Kolker and Nathan Abrams, *Eyes Wide Shut*, 84.
[416] Robert P. Kolker and Nathan Abrams, *Eyes Wide Shut*, 80.
[417] Robert P. Kolker and Nathan Abrams, *Eyes Wide Shut*, 69.
[418] Robert P. Kolker and Nathan Abrams, *Eyes Wide Shut*, 171; LoBrutto, *Stanley Kubrick: A Biography* , 321; Baxter, *Stanley Kubrick: A Biography*, 229.
[419] Robert P. Kolker and Nathan Abrams, *Eyes Wide Shut*, 24.
[420] Robert P. Kolker and Nathan Abrams, *Eyes Wide Shut*, 19-21, 24.

This may even have been when Kubrick first conceived of what eventually became *Eyes*. Some have suggested Sobotka is who introduced Kubrick to Arthur Schnitzler. There is an ongoing debate as to when Kubrick first read the novel. If Michael Herr is to be believed, Kubrick initially read *Traumnovelle* during the late 1950s and was immediately enchanted. Kirk Douglas claims he brought the novel to Kubrick's attention during that same time, but James B. Harris insists Kubrick had read the novel prior to their meeting in 1955. It's possible Kubrick may have first encountered Schnitzler and *Traumnovelle* via his father's library growing up.[421] All in all, Kubrick was familiar with the book by 1959 at the latest.

And that gets into the equally murky debate of when Kubrick decided to adapt the novel. He bought the right to it during the early 1970s and officially began the process then. It was even briefly slated to be his follow-up to *A Clockwork Orange*, but was soon abandoned.[422] Nonetheless, Kubrick informed Michael Herr that he had purchased every copy of the book he could get his hands on, ensuring that it was little known by the 1980s.[423] But Kubrick probably began the process of adapting it even before acquiring the rights.

James Fenwick found descriptions of a trio of films Kubrick worked on during the late 1950s that he dubbed the "marriage trilogy." All three of these projects bear some similarities to what became *Eyes Wide Shut*. [424] Terry Southern, who co-wrote *Dr. Strangelove* with Kubrick, dedicated his 1970 book *Blue Movie* to the director. The plot revolves around a major Hollywood director trying to make a big budget porno film. This was based upon some of the work he did for Kubrick during the late 1960s relating to the director's efforts to adapt Schnitzler.[425]

It's also interesting to note how Kubrick's thinking on adapting the novel evolved over the years. Remarkably, he originally envisioned it as a comedy. Kubrick stuck with the concept of *Traumnovelle* as a comedy for years. At one point, he saw it as a starring vehicle for Woody Allen during the 1970s.[426] Later, he envisioned Steve Martin in the lead role after screening *The Jerk*.[427] When he decided to do it as a serious movie is unknown, but the comedy version was still being discussed as late as the early 1980s. At that point, Terry Southern was brought in to work on the script.[428] This was a project Kubrick lived with for decades, toying with a variety of ways to bring it to the screen.

---

[421] Robert P. Kolker and Nathan Abrams, *Eyes Wide Shut*, 14.

[422] Baxter, 260; James Fenwick, *Stanley Kubrick Produces*, 194.

[423] Michael Herr, *Kubrick*, 7.

[424] James Fenwick, *Stanley Kubrick Produces*, 74-77.

[425] James Fenwick, *Stanley Kubrick Produces*, 194; Kolker and Adams, *Eyes Wide Shut*, 28.

[426] Kolker and Adams, *Eyes Wide Shut*, 32. Even more intriguing is that Kubrick was considering setting the film in Dublin when he envisioned it as a vehicle for Allen. He was even considering a return to Ireland for the shoot.

[427] Kolker and Adams, *Eyes Wide Shut*, 34; Michael Herr, *Kubrick*, 8-9.

[428] Kolker and Adams, *Eyes Wide Shut*, 34-36.

Obviously, this movie was very important to Kubrick. To answer why this is, I need to first address one of the most enigmatic characters in *Eyes*: the Naval officer Nicole Kidman fantasizes about. This is almost universally interpreted as a reference to Scientology, but I think this is an overly simplistic take. Let's go back to *A Clockwork Orange*. The brainwashing procedure in the film was probably inspired by a real program called Project Pelican. And who ran Pelican?

The Navy.

And if I'm correct about Andrija Puharich, he began his service to the national security state with the Navy. As has been discussed, The Nine (Puharich's time traveling, inter-dimensional extraterrestrial beings) were heavily promoted by *Star Trek* creator Gene Roddenberry, a Navy man. And if I am correct, *Outer Limits* creator Leslie Stevens, son of Admiral Leslie C. Stevens, was also a part of these circles.

If Kubrick followed the Manson saga, and I strongly believe that he did,[429] he was surely aware of Scientology's influence on Manson. He could have even encountered Mae Brussell's allegation that Nathaniel Dight, a Navy man, was in contact with The Family. The reader will recall that Kubrick read Paul Krassner's *The Realist* regularly until at least *2001*. Krassner first popularized Brussell's research and later explored her allegations regarding Dight in *The Realist*. Krassner also considered Scientology founder L. Ron Hubbard's status as a Naval intelligence (ONI) officer during this time.[430]

Hubbard possibly served in NYC with Morse Allen just as the US entered WWII. At the time, both men were detailed to the Office of Naval intelligence.[431] Allen later ran the day to day operations of BLUEBIRD and later ARTICHOKE during the late 1940s and 1950s. Pelican was incorporated into Bluebird during this period.

It's quite curious and little remarked upon that by the late 1960s there appear to be two UFO-centric cargo cults, of The Nine and Scientology, active in elite circles, especially Hollywood, and both connected to the Navy. Let us not forget famed sci-fi author Robert A. Heinlein, whose *Stranger in a Strange Land* novel laid the blueprint for any number of counterculture cults from the 1960s onwards.[432] Heinlein also worked with the ONI during WWII[433] and had known Hubbard for years.

---

[429] As was noted in an earlier chapter, Kubrick was a friend of Roman Polanski's.

[430] Krassner recounts his time investigating Manson with Brussell in his autobiography. See , *Confessions of a Raving, Unconfined Nut*, 236-239, etc.

[431] For a brief description of Allen's time with the ONI, see John Marks, *The Search for the "Manchurian Candidate"*, 26. Allen served in the Navy from 1940-45. See Allen-Morse. ALLEN-MORSE | The United States Navy Memorial. (n.d.). https://navylog.navymemorial.org/allen-morse.

[432] The most well known instance of this is the Church of All World, a neo-pagan outfit still active today. Despite extensive evolution over the years, many of CAW's rituals are still steeped in *Stranger in a Strange Land*. Incidentally, was also cited by Charles Manson as an influence. For more on this subject, see Carole M. Cusack, *Invented Religion: Imagination, Fiction and Faith* (Burlington, VT:

I feel strongly Kubrick was aware of these connections. Virtually every major sci-fi writer of the "Golden Age"—i.e. Heinlein, Isaac Asimov, L. Sprague De Camp, John W. Campbell—had a connection to the US Navy from WWII.[434] The one glaring exception was Kubrick's *2001* co-writer, the British Arthur C. Clarke, but Clarke got his start in the pages of Campbell's legendary *Astounding* and corresponded with virtually all of these figures for years. As such, Kubrick potentially had some very pointed reasons for making the object of Nicole Kidman's desire a Navy man. And it went well beyond Scientology. In the initial drafts of the script, Kidman's fantasies did not involve the Naval officer. Instead, Kubrick had this changed early in the writing process.[435]

The decision to cast Scientologist Tom Cruise and his wife in the film probably played into this. Keep in mind, Kubrick cast Cruise prior too Vivian joining Scientology. He was eyeing Cruise for this part as far back as 1993 and always planned on using a married Hollywood couple for the film.[436] Further, Kubrick supposedly never discovered that Vivian had joined the church. The official narrative holds that the family did not find out until after the director's passing. it was obvious at Kubrick's funeral when Vivian attended with her Scientologist "handler" and complained of back pain that had been caused "10, 000 years ago." It's common for the church to assign a minder to prominent members they wish to keep an eye on. Cruise had his own handler during the filming of *Eyes*, personal assistant Michael Doven. Kubrick ended up casting Doven in the film as an extra because of how often he was on the set.[437]

I'm not entirely convinced of Kubrick's ignorance concerning his daughter's conversation. The reader will recall he had no less a figure than Jack Nicholson keeping an eye on her. Nicholson has been a Hollywood fixture for decades. He surely would have had some inclination of the circles she was traveling in.

The Masked Ball (Background)

Ashgate Publishing, 2010), 53-82, etc.

433 ONI asked Heinlein to assemble a group to brainstorm "unconventional responses" to Japanese kamikaze attacks. Other members of this group included L. Jerome Stanton, Fletcher Pratt, George O. Smith, John W. Campbell and L. Sprague De Camp. All of these men were science fiction writers who had experienced various degrees of success. See Alec Nevala-Lee, *Astonishing: John W. Campbell, Isaac Asimov, Robert A. Heinlein, L. Ron Hubbard, and the Golden Age of Science Fiction* (New York: Dey St., 2018), 201-203.

434 While never formally in the Navy, Asimov worked at the Philadelphia Naval Yard with Heinlein during WWII. See Alec Nevala-Lee, *Astonishing: John W. Campbell, Isaac Asimov, Robert A. Heinlein, L. Ron Hubbard, and the Golden Age of Science Fiction.*

435 Kolker and Adams, *Eyes Wide Shut*, 52.

436 Kolker and Adams, *Eyes Wide Shut*, 67-68.

437 Kolker and Adams, *Kubrick: An Odyssey*, 569-570, 581.

Eyes Wide Shut's masked ball, often erroneously referred to as an orgy, is the film's centerpiece. This was a sequence that obsessed Kubrick throughout the writing process and all the way through production. He invested more time in it than anything else in the film. The sequence was choreographed by Yolande Snaith, who specialized in contemporary dance. She auditioned hundreds of models to find those with the body type Kubrick was looking for. The director was especially influenced by the nude sketches of artist Helmut Newton. He insisted that no women with breast implants be used. Both the men and women selected were chosen for their classically proportioned and athletic features. There was a preference for female models with figures similar to Nicole Kidman.[438]

The sequence was carefully plotted out over a period of five to six months before filming began. Kubrick held rigorous rehearsals for days with the participants before shooting began on September 28, 1997. Many configurations of the ritual were rehearsed, with changes still being made once shooting began. Filming usually began at five or six in the evening and continued until 2 a.m. Production on this sequence didn't wrap until November 1.[439]

And this was just the shooting phase. Kubrick agonized over the sequence for years during the writing process and continued to tinker with it throughout the editing. Obviously, there's a lot to unpack here. We'll start with the location.

In the film, the manor where the masked ball unfolds is called Somerton. Kubrick researched several real life locations for inspiration. One that influenced his conception of Somerton was San Simeon, the castle William Randolph Hearst family constructed for his mistress. It was famously the inspiration for Xanadu in Orson Welles' *Citizen Kane*, a film Kubrick greatly admired. Kubrick had some familiarity with San Simeon, having previously used it as the location of Crassus' villa in *Spartacus*.[440]

Three separate locations were used for this sequence, including Highclere Castle in Hampshire, Elveden Hall in Norfolk, Mentmore Tower in Buckinghamshire. The interiors of Somerton were largely shot at the first two locations while the final one only provided the exterior shots.[441] But it's the last one everyone fixates on because it used to be a Rothschild residence. This has led to further speculation that one of the principal inspirations for the orgy sequence was the famous Surrealist Ball thrown by Marie-Hélène de Rothschild in December 1972 at her Ferrières Château.[442] It's an interesting theory. While surrealism is present in virtually all of Kubrick's films, it's at the forefront in *Eyes*.

---

[438] Kolker and Adams, *Eyes Wide Shut*, 70-72.

[439] Kolker and Adams, *Eyes Wide Shut*, 103.

[440] Kolker and Adams, *Eyes Wide Shut*, 80.

[441] Kolker and Adams, *Eyes Wide Shut*, 80; Rodney Hill, "Eyes Wide Shut" in *The Stanley Kubrick Archives* ed. by Alison Castle, 616-617.

[442] One of the guests at the ball was future *Barry Lyndon* star Marisa Berenson. See Schneider, M. (2018, July 23). Glimpses of the extravagant Surrealist Ball of 1972. DangerousMinds. https://dangerousminds.net/comments/glimpses_of_the_extravagant_surrealist_ball_of_1972.

But the regalia displayed at the orgy, while aiding to the film's surrealist nature, comes from much older traditions. This is not a surrealist ball. It's a Saturnine Ball, which will be explored further. For now, I want to emphasize the actual location of the fictitious manor. As a road sign reveals, it's located near Glen Cove on Long Island. This very, very exclusive area of Long Island, referred to as the Gold Coast back in the day. This place has been a staple of pop culture for some time. It provided the backdrop to Fitzgerald's jazz-era classic *The Great Gatsby* and was later used as the location for much of Hitchcock's *North by Northwest*. It's also interesting that Glen Cove, Maine, is where Puharich's Round Table Foundation was based during The Nine séances.

As was noted in an earlier chapter, Kubrick briefly lived in Long Island during the mid-1960s. And that raises the question of whether he was aware of the curious parties being held further down the coast in the Hamptons.

These parties became the center of controversy in 1980 after Melonie Haller was found unconscious and bloody on a commuter train to Manhattan. Haller, a minor actress, claimed that not only was she beaten and raped at one of the Hamptons' manors, but that the ordeal was filmed. The house was owned by the alleged perpetrator, Roy Radin, a show business promoter and wannabe producer. His residence, located in Southampton, was dubbed Ocean Castle and bears some resemblance to Somerton.

It further came to light that Radin was part of a broader milieu in Southampton, according to journalist Anthony Haden-Guest. His source, described as the godfather of the scene, was dubbed the “Roman Senator” due to his aristocratic bearing. Per the Senator, he had spent many happy years in England. There, he frequently attended certain townhouses and country estates where the so-called *le vice anglais* was practiced with patriot fervor.

The Roman Senator was so taken that he decided to bring these practices back to the Cousins of Southampton. After some resistance, the Roman Senator dedicated a sunny afternoon and two cat-o'-nine tails to what was described as "raising the consciousness of a willing volunteer." Said volunteer was apparently tied to a tree at the time. Henceforth, the spot was dubbed the "Whipping Tree" and became a staple of the scene.[443]

Many years later, Haden-Guest revealed the name of his source. The Roman Senator was a mysterious private detective named Thomas Corbally. The shamus was long rumored to have served with the OSS during WWII, but this seems unlikely. There's no doubt he did some time in military intelligence, however. Corbally also had ample mob connections dating back to his childhood in New Jersey.[444]

---

[443] Anthony Haden-Guest, "Melonie Haller's Lost Weekend," *New York Magazine*, May 12, 1980, 44-47, https://books.google.com/books?id=cOUCAAAAMBAJ&pg=PA44&lpg=PA44&dq=melonie+haller+roy+radin&source=bl&ots=IRKZbAgCUH&sig=g-x8KCEv2PNRQ2nOpNN7CDgYLIc&hl=en&ei=e5a3S5vgPIKgsgODqJnpDA&sa=X&oi=book_result&ct=result&resnum=3&ved=0CAsQ6AEwAg#v=onepage&q=melonie%20haller%20roy%20radin&f=false.

During the early 1960s, the detective made the scene in London. There, he became embroiled in the Profumo Affair, a scandal that brought down the government of Harold Macmillan in 1963. Profumo revolved around a love triangle involving a Soviet GRU officer moonlighting as a military attaché; John Profumo, then serving in Macmillan's cabinet as Secretary of State for War, and a 19-year-old model named Christine Keeler.[445]

As the scandal unfolded, it was revealed that Keeler was one of several girls run by society osteopath named Stephen Ward for exclusive friends in the British aristocracy. Corbally befriended Ward, likely at the behest of his mentor and longtime employer, attorney Roy Cohn. You see, it's long been rumored that John F. Kennedy, shortly after winning the presidency, but before assuming office, was serviced by Ward's ring. With allegations flying that Ward was a Soviet agent, such associations would be devastating to JFK.

After being spurned by McCarthy in favor of Cohn during the 1950s, Robert F. Kennedy nursed a vendetta against Donald Trump's future attorney and political mentor for years. When RFK became attorney general, Cohn was on his short list, along with Jimmy Hoffa.[446] With the attorney general of the United States trying to destroy him, JFK's possible links to Profumo must have seemed like manna from heaven for Cohn. I explored these intrigues at length in *A Special Relationship: Trump, Epstein and the Secret History of the Anglo-American Establishment* for anyone looking for more details.

Also in that work, I noted some of the peculiarities of Ward's circles. For years, he was a fixture in the orgy scene of the aristocracy. S & M was big, but I found accounts with magical trappings Ward participated in. Actor/comedian Michael Bentine went so far as to accuse Ward of running a modern Hell-Fire Club,[447] though there is nothing to corroborate this. Bentine was a patient of Ward's at one point and an original member of *The Goons* with Peter Sellers. As for the *Dr. Strangelove* star, he was a social friend of Ward's.[448]

---

444 Haden-Guest has provided one of the only in-depth accounts of Corbally's background. See Haden-Guest, A. (2015b, July 18). The Wildest Hamptons Bondage Party. The Daily Beast. https://www.thedailybeast.com/the-wildest-hamptons-bondage-party. Another came from Buzzfeed: Javers, E. (2017, September 7). This private investigator was the original most interesting man in the world. BuzzFeed News. https://www.buzzfeednews.com/article/eamonjavers/this-private-investigator-was-the-original-most-interesting.

445 Profumo and Corbally's role in the scandal has been explored in such works as Phillip Knightley & Caroline Kennedy, *An Affair of State: The Profumo Case and the Framing of Stephen Ward* (New York: Atheneum, 1987); Anthony Summers and Stephen Dorril, *The Secret Worlds of Stephen Ward: Sex, Scandal and Deadly Secrets in the Profumo Scandal* (New York: Open Road, 2013); and Douglas Thompson, *Stephen Ward: Scapegoat* (London: John Blake, 2014). The co-author of the first book, Caroline Kennedy, was JFK's youngest daughter and potentially exposed to an IRA bomb plot. This was addressed earlier in this work.

446 See Burton Hersh, *Bobby and J. Edgar: The Historic Face-Off Between the Kennedys and J. Edgar Hoover That Transformed America* (New York: Carroll & Graf Publishers, 2007), 388-400, etc.

447 Michael Bentine, *Doors of the Mind: An Exhilarating Exploration of the Paranormal* (London: Panther Books, 1984), 134-151.

448 Douglas Thompson, *Stephen Ward: Scapegoat*, 75, 130, 146-147.

This makes Corbally's description of the whipping he administered in Southampton as a form of consciousness raising all the more intriguing. Italian Traditionalist and mage Julius Evola, crippled from the waist down after World War II, indicates in his writings that S & M, and especially whippings, could be used as a form of sex magic for consciousness raising.[449]

At this point, I need to emphasize that I've found no concrete evidence of occultism being practiced at the Hamptons parties. The same can not be said of the scene Corbally participated in England. And Peter Levenda, not always the most trustworthy source, claims in the third book of his *Sinister Forces* trilogy that Roy Radin approached the denizens of the Magical Childe about filming their rituals.[450] As Levenda was a fixture of that scene, we can probably take him at his word in this case.

Would Kubrick have been aware of any of this? He lived in Long Island, but possibly before Corbally brought his techniques to the US. However, the Melonie Haller scandal became a major media sensation circa 1980. Given the Hollywood connections and the close proximity to his former residence, I suspect Kubrick would have followed these developments. Especially given his long standing interest in porn. In this context, it's worth noting that the scenes involving Nicole Kidman's character and the Naval officer were filmed in grainy footage akin to what would be used for a blackmail tape.

Further, if I'm correct and Kubrick had links to the Kennedy administration, he may have been privy to insider knowledge concerning JFK's role in Profumo. In that regard, it's also worth noting Kubrick was working in the UK on *Dr. Strangelove* during the timeframe the scandal was beginning to blow up in the press. Even academic Kubrick scholars have acknowledged the likelihood that Profumo influenced *Dr. Strangelove*.[451] And of course, star Peter Sellers at least knew Ward socially.

This makes an anecdote recounted by Frederic Raphael, Kubrick's co-writer on *Eyes* screenplay, in *Eyes Wide Open* especially tantalizing. Kubrick requested Raphael to concoct a background for Zeigler and the denizens of Somerton. Raphael responded by faxing Kubrick what purported to be an extract of a highly classified FBI document.

Therein, a network dubbed "The Free" was outlined. They were a wealthy clique that "admired JFK's impudent defiance of public morality." They became disillusioned with the

---

449 See, for instance, Julius Evola, *Eros and the Mysteries of Love: The Metaphysics of Sex* (Rochester, VT: Inner Traditions International, 1991), 88-89. Interestingly, Evola's occult journey in the WWI-era Dadaist movement is effectively the precursor to Surrealism. For more on Dada's influence on Evola, see Kevin Coogan, *Dreamer of the Day: Francis Parker Yockey and the Postwar Fascist International* (New York: Autonomedia, 1999), 292-293, etc.

450 Peter Levenda, *Sinister Forces: A Grimoire of American Political Witchcraft Book Three: The Manson Secret* (Walterville, OR: Trine Day, 2006), 225. The Magical Childe bookstore was the heart of NYC's occult scene during the 1970s. For more on this scene, see Michael G. Lloyd, *Bull of Heaven: The Mythic Life of Eddie Buczynski and the Rise of the New York Pagan Scene* (Hubbardston, MA: Asphodel Press, 2012).

451 George Case, *Calling Dr. Strangelove*, 81.

Democratic Party after it was overtaken by "hicks" following JFK's assassination. The group was nearly exposed when a prostitute recounted the group's activities during an interview for an Arkansas TV station. Fortunately, she was "taken care of."

Authority for dealing with leaks was vested in a subgroup within The Free known as "The Plumbers." This group was somewhat akin to Plato's Nocturnal Council, a law unto themselves. The FBI encountered rumors of Plumber involvement in the deaths of Frannie de Zoete and Leslie van der Groot. The former was said to have died at a Palm Beach hotel while the latter drowned in a car belonging to a senator.[452]

These are clear references to tragedies involving the Kennedy family. The latter is a blatant dig at Ted Kennedy and his role in the death of Mary Jo Kopechne. This occurred in 1969, when Kennedy drove a car off a bridge while Kopechne was his passenger, resulting in her death. It's long been rumored Teddy was intoxicated at the time. Many believe Kopechne was still alive in the car when Kennedy fled. He waited a full 24 hours to report the incident. This tragedy is commonly referred to as the "Chappaquiddick incident" after the river in which the events unfolded.

As for "Frannie de Zoete" and Palm Beach, this is referring to David Anthony Kennedy, one of RFK's sons. David was found dead in a Palm Beach hotel room in 1984. Allegedly, he died of a drug overdose. What's more, the Kennedy family long maintained a compound at Palm Beach. Inevitably, there were a lot of rumors surrounding his death, including that he was given a hotshot by dealers he had burned and that members of the Kennedy family tampered with the crime scene before police arrived. The hotel his body was found at, the Brazilian Court, was closed and sold to new ownership just a week after Kennedy's death, and it didn't reopen until a year later.[453] And no, the new ownership wasn't Donald Trump, though he acquired nearby Mar-A-Lago in 1985, the same year the Brazilian Court reopened.

But to return to the Kennedys, Palm Beach has not been kind to them. William Kennedy Smith, a nephew of JFK and RFK, was tried and acquitted of rape charges there in 1991, and in 2019, Saoirse Kennedy Hill, RFK's granddaughter, also died of a drug overdose there. Obviously, Hills' death was not a factor on the script, but I suspect the Palm Beach location was selected to hint at the scandal involving both Doug Kennedy and Smith.

Kubrick phoned the scribe not long after Raphael faxed these pages to him. And Kubrick was greatly concerned, demanding to know where he got the material from. In Raphael's retelling, Kubrick was convinced the FBI document was real and even accused the scribe of

---

[452] Frederick Raphael, *Eyes Wide Open*, 146-148.

[453] Aydlette, L. (2019, August 21). History: Which Kennedy family member overdosed in a Palm Beach Hotel?. The Palm Beach Post. https://www.palmbeachpost.com/story/news/courts/2019/08/21/history-which-kennedy-family-member-overdosed-in-palm-beach-hotel/112145702/. Among the Kennedy family members present in Palm Beach at the time of David's death was Caroline, JFK's star-crossed youngest daughter whom we keep encountering.

hacking into the FBI's database. The conversation Raphael recounts between Kubrick and himself on this matter is especially striking about midway through, which is worth repeating here:

S.K.: Freddie, I need you to tell me honestly where you got this stuff. This is potentially—

F.R.: Stanley, totally honestly, I got it where I get everything: my head.

S.K.: You telling me you made this up?

FR.: But only because it's true. You asked for it, I did it. I enjoyed it, as a matter of fact.

S.K.: It has no basis in fact?

F.R.: Stanley, I made it up, okay?

S.K.: How did you do that?

F.R.: Making things up's what I do for a living. It's pretty well all I do. I write fiction. I make things up. I look at the world and...I make things up on the strength of what I see and hear, I guess. I do not mend fuses or water-ski or have a pension scheme. I made it up. It was fun; much more fun than...

S.K.: Okay as long as we're not...on potentially dangerous ground here. It's pretty convincing, you know that?

F.R.: Nice of you to say so. Think of it as an example of what I do when I'm free to play by myself. An apple for the teacher.

S.K.: And it didn't come from anywhere that might...you know... embarrassing?

F.R.: Look, it came out of my head, fully formed. How embarrassing is that? I made the whole damn thing up. It was not a problem.[454]

Needless to say, there's a lot to unpack here. As was noted above, Kubrick began working on what became *Eyes* for many years prior to hiring Raphael. By this point in time, Kubrick had a stable of writers and he had brought many of them in on *Eyes* at various points. Candia McWilliam, Diana Johnson, Michael Herr, Terry Southern, Anthony Burgess and John le Carre, alias David Cornwell, were all approached. Kubrick really wanted Cornwell to be his principal writing partner on *Eyes*, but the former MI6 man preferred to merely advise on the script.[455]

Why Kubrick decided to approach Raphael at such a late date to hammer out the final script is a bit of mystery. The scribe had won an Oscar for *Darling* and was nominated for another with *Two For the Road*. But that was in 1966 and '67, respectively. Raphael's star had fallen

---

[454] Frederick Raphael, *Eyes Wide Open*, 148-149.
[455] Kolker and Adams, *Eyes Wide Shut*, 36-37, 42.

considerably since then, primarily working on television. Still, Raphael nominally fit the bill for what Kubrick looked for in a writing partner. He was intelligent and more a novelist than a screenwriter. Kubrick disdained professional screenwriters, preferring the storytelling ability of novelists. And several of Raphael's most celebrated works dealt with couples in distress. What's more, his more recent efforts such as *The King's Whore* had veered into the realm of erotic thriller.

However, Kubrick preferred working with people he already had some kind of relationship with at this point in his life. He was not opposed to bringing in fresh blood, but typically people that came with a recommendation from someone in his inner circle. Kubrick had met Raphael once previously, in 1972, and Kubrick was apparently a fan of Raphael's 1971 novel *Who Were You With Last Night*, which some have argued was an updating of Schnitzler's *Traumnovelle*.[456] However, Raphael indicates that the first time he read *Traumnovelle* was when Kubrick sent him a copy in 1994. Kubrick does not seem to have acknowledged their 1972 encounter either, where Raphael tried to interest Kubrick in making a film based on the classical figure of Electra. Curiously, during this encounter, Kubrick, production designer Ken Adams, Raphael, and their wives and others, apparently played a proto-version of "never have I ever" with matchsticks.[457]

Raphael is an interesting figure in his own right. He was born in Chicago, but spent much of his life in the UK. His father worked for the Shell Oil Company and he attended St. John's College, Cambridge. In other words, he surely rubbed elbows with the British gentry a time or two.

To return to Raphael's faux FBI document, let's begin breaking down Kubrick's reaction. As I've argued, I strongly believe Kubrick had established ties with the Kennedy White House, beginning with his relationship with Kirk Douglas, and that continued till at least *2001*. Then there's the specter of Roy Radin and the Southampton scene presided over by Thomas Corbally, a key player in Profumo. Again, JFK may have been involved in Stephen Ward's ring.

Suffice to say, Raphael's inclusion of the Kennedy family in this hypothetical network known as The Free appears quite pointed. Especially in light of the Epstein revelations. Further, as I recount in *A Special Relationship*, many of the families implicated in Epstein's ring previously turned up in Profumo. The Kennedys were among those that transcended the generations. RFK Jr., for instance, flew on Epstein's private airplane a time or two.[458]

Even more bizarre is the fact that Kubrick himself toyed with incorporating elements of the Ted Kennedy/Mary Jo Kopechne into his adaptation as far back as 1989. The death of a

---

[456] Baxter, *Stanley Kubrick: A Biography*, 262-263.

[457] Frederick Raphael, *Eyes Wide Open*, 13-14.

[458] See, for instance, Blanco, A. (2024, January 7). RFK Jr reacts to unsealed Epstein Court docs: "I like what's happening." The Independent. https://www.the-independent.com/news/world/americas/us-politics/rfk-jr-epstein-list-names-unsealed-b2474620.html.

woman at the hands of a powerful man under suspicious circumstances later became a central plot point in *Eyes*. This is one of the few subplots largely missing from *Traumnovelle*. I've seen no indications that Kubrick ever discussed the Chappaquiddick incident with Raphael. Still, this is a notorious event and would have been an obvious one for Raphael to consider in relation to the parapolitical aspects of *Eyes*. It's also interesting to note that the Heidi Fleiss scandal influenced Kubrick's conception of the Somerton sect.[459] Fleiss, the so-called Hollywood madam, was aided by Thomas Corbally, who provided her with money for legal defense.[460]

So, what was going on here? Was this Raphael's subtle way of letting Kubrick know that he was aware of the source material he was using beyond Schnitzler? Or, was this a subtle hint at how far Kubrick could go with real life inspirations? Raphael made a point of invoking mysterious deaths surrounding the Kennedy family. Whatever the case, he got Kubrick's attention.

Masked Ball Symbolism

By the by, Kubrick stays faithful to both the Schnitzler novel and even the 1969 Austrian adaptation of *Traumnovelle*. Essentially, all the elements from the novel and the earlier adaptation make it into the film, with only minor changes typically concerned with updating the material for the 1990s. The one glaring exception is the masked ball.

In the novel and earlier film, the group behind the orgy is a kind of private swingers' club. There's no question they're aristocrats. The chevalier outfits they have beneath their priest robes are a clear indication of this, but while they may be a secret society, there are few indications of them being a full blown cult. In Kubrick's hands, they're transformed into an elite cult with rituals inspired by some of the oldest traditions. Before delving into that, I want to briefly address the genesis of this sequence.

There was no part in the original script Kubrick had Raphael work on more than the masked ball. Kubrick demanded numerous drafts from the writer. He presented the difficulty in developing the scene to Raphael as deriving from the lack of instruction in *Traumnovelle*. He fretted to his scribe, "What happens out there in that house? Arthur doesn't tell us a lot." For once, Raphael was in agreement, describing Schnitzler's account as a kind of "blue musical."[461]

---

[459] James Fenwick, *Stanley Kubrick Produces*, 195-196; Robert P. Kolker and Nathan Abrams, *Kubrick: An Odyssey*, 484, 529..

[460] Javers, E. (2017, September 7). This private investigator was the original most interesting man in the world. BuzzFeed News. https://www.buzzfeednews.com/article/eamonjavers/this-private-investigator-was-the-original-most-interesting.

[461] Frederick Raphael, *Eyes Wide Open*, 99.

Both Kubrick and Raphael did their own research for this sequence, supposedly to fill in the gaps. Initially, Raphael wanted the Bill Harford (Tom Cruise) character to be a closet Jew who is exposed as such at the orgy. In this early version, the revelers would wear costumes akin to SS uniforms. Kubrick summarily rejected this approach.[462] It was at this point that Raphael hit the books. He consulted Richard Sennett's *Flesh and Stone* and possibly Georgina Masson's *Courtesans of the Italian Renaissance*, though it's uncertain if Raphael actually read the latter book in full or took quotations from it found in the former.[463]

Regardless, Raphael's version was explicitly Catholic. It appears to have been strongly influenced by an orgy thrown by the Duke of Valentino on the Halloween of 1501. The spectacle unfolded at the Vatican, with the Pope himself supposedly attending. Following suite, Raphael has the guests at the ball mostly dressed in priest robes, often those of a cardinal. Some are described in Papal Guard uniforms. One figure is made to look like the Pope. An early part of the action takes place in a side chapel, with a faux communion involving a large plate of ice cream made to look like a naked woman that priests distribute to the guests.[464]

Kubrick made additional suggestions to Raphael for his research. He sent him erotic art from the likes of Egon Schiele, Gustav Klimt and the after-mentioned Helmut Newton. He also suggested that Raphael research Roman orgies. These artists, most especially Schiele, greatly influenced Kubrick's later composition of the film.[465]

For his part, Kubrick immersed himself in the culture of fin-de-siecle Vienna and Europe's broader secret sexual history. As far back as 1959, he had discussed Schnitzler's work with his grandson, Peter, and had further discussions with him during the 1970s. This was when Kubrick toyed with doing *Traumnovelle* as his follow up to *A Clockwork Orange*. During the late 1980s and early 1990s, he consulted with J.P. Stern, an authority on German literature who had published books on Kafka, Nietzsche and Schnitzler during this same timeframe.[466]

Kubrick later contacted folklorist Gershon Legman. Between 1948 and 1951, he edited the groundbreaking *Neurotica* magazine that was so crucial in promoting the early Beat movement. Several years later, Legman relocated permanently to France, where he collected rare erotica for the rest of his life. He is described as an authority on the secret sexual history of Europe. Legman was especially taken with dirty jokes, of which he published several volumes of.[467]

---

[462] Kolker and Adams, *Eyes Wide Shut*, 54-55.

[463] Frederick Raphael, *Eyes Wide Open*, 100-101

[464] Kolker and Adams, *Eyes Wide Shut*, 55; Frederick Raphael, *Eyes Wide Open*, 100-101.

[465] Kolker and Adams, *Eyes Wide Shut*, 55.

[466] Kolker and Adams, *Eyes Wide Shut*, 66.

[467] Kolker and Adams, *Eyes Wide Shut*, 36.

Legman put Kubrick in contact with his friend, the New York-based Dr. Clifford J. Scheiner. He was a collector of, and dealer in, erotica. Like Legman, he possessed a vast knowledge of Europe's hidden sexual history. He was also a medical doctor who seemingly became Kubrick's only real physician after his father passed. Kubrick was described as trusting Scheiner "in a way he didn't trust most doctors."[468] Anthony Frewin thanked a "Dr. Cliff Scheiner" in his *The Assassination of John F. Kennedy* book.[469] This is surely the same person, indicating Kubrick's de facto doctor had an interest in the JFK assassination.

Legman is an endlessly intriguing figure. He managed to acquire contributions from the likes of Allen Ginsberg and Marshall McLuhan for *Neurotica*. For a brief period of time, he worked as a bibliographer and book scout for the Kinsey Institute, though he later broke with Kinsey. Despite his obsession with erotica, he railed against violence in American culture. He was actually one of the first social critics to take aim at the comic book industry, arguing that it was harmful to children in the pre-code days.[470]

Kubrick owned every issue of *Neurotica*, which he acquired during the magazine's original run (1948-1951).[471] He followed Legman's work well before they were introduced during the 1980s. Paul Krassner was also a friend of Legman's and republished his articles in *The Realist* beginning in the early 1960s.[472] This would have been during the period Kubrick is known to have been a regular reader of *The Realist*. Further, the man who put Kubrick in contact with Legman, Tony Frewin, was introduced to *The Realist* by Kubrick during the filming of *2001*.[473] The reader will recall Frewin was a JFK assassination buff and contributor to the parapolitical journal *Lobster*.

Legman was a fierce critic of the CIA, going so far as to denounce 1960s counterculture as a fraud perpetrated by the spy agency.[474] In the latter years of his life, he suspected journalists who trekked to his isolated French home of being undercover FBI or CIA agents.[475] Legman was also an early foe of L. Ron Hubbard and Scientology, publishing a parody of the nascent movement in *Neurotica* during 1950. Krassner later reprinted it in *The Realist* circa 1963.[476]

---

[468] Kolker and Adams, *Eyes Wide Shut*, 66-67.

[469] Anthony Frewin, *The Assassination of John F. Kennedy: An Annotated Film, TV, and Videography, 1963-1992.*, xv.

[470] For a full-length exploration of Legman's life, see Susan G. Davis, *Dirty Jokes and Bawdy Songs: The Uncensored Life of Gershon Legman* (Urbana, IL: University of Illinois Press, 2019).

[471] Kolker and Adams, *Eyes Wide Shut*, 36; Abrams, *Stanley Kubrick: New York Jewish Intellectual*, 5-6.

[472] Susan G. Davis, *Dirty Jokes and Bawdy Songs: The Uncensored Life of Gershon Legman*, 2, 185.

[473] Kolker and Adams, *Eyes Wide Shut*, 36; Mick Broderick, *Reconstructing Strangelove*, 6-7.

[474] Susan G. Davis, *Dirty Jokes and Bawdy Songs: The Uncensored Life of Gershon Legman*, 170. While such a claim is fairly common now, Legman made his argument in 1967 against the backdrop of the Summer of Love.

[475] Susan G. Davis, *Dirty Jokes and Bawdy Songs*, 188.

[476] Goodyear, D. (2008, August 12). Scientology spoof. The New Yorker. https://www.newyorker.com/culture/dana-goodyear/scientology-spoof.

Dr. Scheiner is a character in his own right. From 1976 until the mid-1990s, he worked in the ER at NYC's Kings County Hospital Center. After being stripped of his duties towards the end of 1995, he was formally fired by the hospital in 1996. Supposedly, this was over disciplinary issues. Several instances were cited: lack of basic medical knowledge, repeated displays of rudeness, refusal to or delay in evaluating or treating patients in violation of the Consolidated Omnibus Budget Reconciliation Act of 1985 ("COBRA"), and insubordination.[477]

My suspicion is that Scheiner questioned the medical orthodoxy, but I have no evidence of this. But given Kubrick's suspicion of the medical profession, this would be the most logical explanation for the trust he placed in Scheiner as an MD. The doctor later brought a lawsuit against his former employers, alleging that they had violated his first and fourteenth amendment rights. As of 2011, the lawsuit still dragged on. Scheiner continued to practice medicine at other locations throughout this time while continuing to study erotic art.

So much for Kubrick's research into eroticism. What is of far greater interest to us here is his metaphysical research. An obvious influence is Carl Jung, whom Kubrick was quite taken with. Psychoanalysis always underpinned Kubrick's films, but especially in regards to Jung.[478] Kubrick's use of color is probably influenced by Jung's alchemical writings. Another work Kubrick was fascinated by for much of his life and which greatly influenced *Eyes* is James George Frazer's *The Golden Bough*.[479] I suspect the decision to move the timeframe of the film to Christmas, rather than during Carnival (Mardi Gras in the US, the setting in *Traumnovelle*) was greatly inspired by this work. We'll unpack that further down.

One of the most intriguing works Kubrick used for his research is a somewhat rare book called *Cult and Occult* by Peter Brookesmith. Orthodox Kubrick scholars know not what to make of this. In *Eyes Wide Shut: Stanley Kubrick and the Making of His Final Film*, authors Robert P. Kolker and Nathan Abrams note with puzzlement two passages Kubrick underlined in this work. The first goes: "regarding sexual activity as an authentic sacrament: 'the outward and visible sign of an inward and spiritual grace.' Such a sacramental use of sexual intercourse can supposedly be employed as a means of acquiring occult power and, at its highest, lead to the ultimate goal of the mystic: union with the divine." The other passage they note states: "The emperor Barbarossa held young boys against his stomach and genitals to transfer their energy." Predictably, Kolker and Abrams treat these anointments with mockery, chalking them up to Kubrick's flair for the unusual.[480]

In fact, they're crucial to understanding what is being depicted at the masked ball. But before getting to that, I want to address what is *not* being depicted: a Satanic rite, though it's often

---

[477] Scheiner v. New York City Health and Hospitals, 152 F. Supp. 2d 487 (US District Court for the Southern District of New York, 2001), https://law.justia.com/cases/federal/district-courts/FSupp2/152/487/2482868/ (accessed February 24, 2024).

[478] Baxter, *Stanley Kubrick: A Biography*, 14.

[479] Michael Herr, *Kubrick*, 9-10.

[480] Kolker and Adams, *Eyes Wide Shut*, 66.

described as such. Before unpacking this, I want to emphasize: There *are* documented cases of elite Satanic cults. Probably the oldest known instance with real credibility involves the circles around Joan of Arc's companion, Gilles de Rais (1405?-1440) during the final years of his life.[481] Catherine de Medici, of the prominent Italian noble family who became the Queen, and later Queen Mother, of France, may have been active in a Satanic cult during the sixteenth century. We're on firmer footing with the so-called "Affair of the Poisons," which unfolded in France between 1677 and 1682.[482] Finally, there was a well documented Satanic "craze" in France during the 1880s and 1890s. Huysmans' *La-Bas* is a thinly fictionalized account of these circles.[483]

That being said, a few disclaimers need to be set. First, documented evidence of actual Satanic cults largely center around France or country's with a similar cultural heritage. Secondly, in every credible case I've encountered, there is a Catholic presence, typically involving a priest as a participant, and finally, the prerequisites for the centerpiece of Satanic ritualism, the Black Mass, are dependent upon Christianity.

Specifically, sacraments such as holy water must be blessed by an ordained priest. The mass itself is performed on consecrated ground, which is why churches are normally used in a credible Black Mass. And finally, the ceremony *must* be performed by an ordained priest. An ordained priest can bless holy water, consecrate ground and properly perform the functions of a Black Mass. At its core, the Black Mass is a mockery or inversion of a conventional mass. I.e., the mass is said backwards, the priest copulates with a woman, typically on the altar, etc.[484]

This is why I firmly believe that historic Satanism is a kind of Christian heresy, or more precisely, the left-hand version of Catholicism. Like the left hand variety of tantric Buddhism, it is principally concerned with overturning social taboos. It is the transgressive form of Catholicism.

---

[481] "Simon," *Papal Magic: Occult Practices Within the Catholic Church* (New York: Harper, 2007), 10. De Rais was likely one of history's most prolific serial killers as well. While periodic attempts have been made to argue his innocence, most historians accept his guilt while acknowledging the extent of his crimes may have been exaggerated. He may have also inspired the Bluebird fairy tale. Georges Bataille authored one of the most compelling accounts of De Rais based upon the original court transcripts: Georges Bataille with Richard Robinson (trans.) *The Trial of Gilles de Rais* (Los Angeles, Amok Books, 2004).

[482] Simon," *Papal Magic: Occult Practices Within the Catholic Church*, 33-39.36 People were executed as part of the scandal in the court of Louis XIV. A circle of aristocrats were suspected of participating in Black Masses in which infants were sacrificed. While few dispute the historical basis of these claims, the scale has been questioned. The most balanced account of the affair is Anne Somerset, *The Affair of the Poisons: Murder, Infanticide and Satanism at the Court of Louis XIV* (London: Phoenix, 2003).

[483] See Robert Ziegler, *Satanism, Magic and Mysticism in Fin-de-siecle France* (New York: Palgrave Macmillan, 2012); and Tobias Churton, *Occult Paris: The Lost Magic of the Belle Époque* (Rochester, VT: Inner Traditions, 2016).

[484] Peter Levenda, *Sinister Forces: A Grimoire of American Political Witchcraft Book I: The Nine*, 287, etc.

And this is most assuredly *not* what Kubrick is showing in *Eyes Wide Shut*. Frankly, if this is what he was going for, then he need only stick closer to *Traumnovelle*. There, it is strongly suggested the cult depicted is potentially Satanic. The events of that work unfold against the backdrop of Carnival. The participants dress in priest robes, especially those used by monks. The women are dressed in the robes of nuns. This costuming was also used in the 1969 film. There are indications that Kubrick may have considered going in this direction. He invested quite a considerable amount of time researching the robes of monks and nuns from the Middle Ages through the Renaissance for *Eyes Wide Shut*, but none of this made it into the film.

Really, the only element in the masked ball consistent with a Black Mass is the use of backwards priests chants that overlay the ceremony, but an earlier version of the soundtrack made clear Kubrick was working from a broader palette. In the US theatrical version, when Tom Cruise was wandering through the mansion, a scripture from the Bhagavad Gita is recited over the soundtrack. Its translation goes: "To protect the righteous, to annihilate the wicked, and to reestablish the principles of dharma I appear on this earth, age after age." This recitation was later removed for the international release and the DVD after protests from the American Hindus Against Defamation complained of its use.[485] Regardless, the original use of this passage from the Bhagavad Gita provides us with further insight into what Kubrick was going for.

Another crucial clue comes in the form of the film's most iconic features: the Venetian masks. There is no basis in the novella for them. While the participants in *Traumnovelle*'s orgy wear masks, they're never described and one is left with the impression that they are conventional Carnival masks. The Venetian masks are widely associated with Venice's legendary Carnival, but the wearing of them traditionally began on December 26th. This is Saint Stephen's Day, which also marks the beginning of the Feast of Fools in some calendars. Later, the masks were allowed from October 5th till Christmas, thus enabling Venetians to wear them for a good portion of the year.

When Kubrick decided to use the Venetian masks is unknown, but once the decision was made, he was all in. Previously, Kubrick may have used the Zanni Venetian mask as an inspiration for the one worn by Alex in *A Clockwork Orange*. Kubrick was possibly influenced by their use in Edgar Allen Poe's classic *The Cask of Amontillado*. Not only do Venetian masks appear in this work, but there are some rather pointed references to Freemasonry. This could be another sly literary reference on the director's part.

Regardless, Kubrick wanted the real McCoy. His longtime driver, Emilo D'Alessandro, was Italian, and Kubrick enlisted members of his family to travel to Venice and painstakingly photograph the masks there for selection. Kubrick purchased hundreds of masks from Venice and had them shipped to the UK. There, his costume designer added additional tweaks.[486]

---

[485] Rodney Hill, "Eyes Wide Shut" in *The Stanley Kubrick Archives* ed. by Alison Castle, 624-625.

Why is this important?

The Republic of Venice, obviously. From the late Middle Ages till at least the fifteenth century, Venice was easily the most powerful city-state in Europe and a major player in international affairs. And it would remain a significant power through the seventeenth century. This made the 20-30 noble houses who ruled Venice during this time among the most powerful aristocracies in the world and certainly among the richest.

What's more, throughout this timeframe, Venice was the principal rival to the papacy. Indeed, Venice and Roman were essentially vying for supremacy in Western Europe during the Republic's heyday. This antagonism was baked in from the beginning. And that's because Venice is a true Roman city --i.e., its republic was founded by the Eastern Roman Empire, more commonly known as the Byzantine Empire, in 697. Even after it officially broke with Byzantium during the following century, it maintained close ties with the Eastern Romans until the fall of Constantinople. Its prominence as a trading nation was largely a result from the access to the Silk Route the empire provided it with.

There was already a substantial Greek and Eastern European population in Venice prior to Constantinople's fall to the Ottomans. In the aftermath, Venice was a popular refuge for everyone from nobles to soldiers. Well before this, efforts to import the spiritual traditions of the Eastern Empire were underway. And these traditions went beyond conventional Eastern Orthodoxy.

This is a very complex subject that I can only touch on briefly here. Suffice to say, mystical strands such as Gnosticism and Neoplatonism never really went away in the Eastern Empire, but continued, and often openly, till the fall of Constantinople. During the final years of the Empire, the legendary Orthodox cleric Plethon attempted a full scale pagan revival in Italy. Many of his notions gained traction among the Venetians, as well as other Republics such as those in Ferrara and Florence. This laid the foundation for some of the most occulted works of the Renaissance.[487]

It was during this time one of the earliest known and most mysterious Tarot decks appeared. It is commonly known as the Sola-Busca and has been found in the possession of not just some of the most prominent noble houses in Italy, but across Europe.[488] Dating from the late fifteenth century, it is probably the most compelling evidence for some type of ancient astral magic surviving into the modern era.

---

[486] D'Alessandro with Ulivieri, *Stanley Kubrick and Me*, 309-310; Kolker and Adams, *Eyes Wide Shut*, 73-74.

[487] Peter Mark Adams, *The Game of Saturn: Decoding the Sola-Busca Tarocchi* (London: Bibliothèque Rouge/Scarlet Imprint, 2017), 129-132, etc. It is more precisely, a "tarocchi," but Tarot will be used here for simplicities' sake

[488] Peter Mark Adams, *The Game of Saturn: Decoding the Sola-Busca Tarocchi*, 249. Traces of the deck have been found in London and Paris most notably.

I had the pleasure of interviewing Peter Mark Adams, the author of *The Game of Saturn*, in 2021. I consider that work to be absolutely pivotal. It's one of the few scholarly arguments for an elite cult of Saturn surviving into the Renaissance. As you may have gathered, the Sola-Busca tarot is at the heart of Adams' argument.

During the interview, I asked Peter about *Eyes Wide Shut*. After comparing it to the *Traumnovelle* book and film, he described Kubrick's cult as one with "strong Saturnine associations." And this was not something that came from the earlier book and movie. While Adams took issue with Kubrick's depiction, it was on the grounds that the historic cults of Saturn were "far less glamorous" than what is shown in the film. To Adams, this also posed an interesting question in regards to why Kubrick would do this.

Even more surprising to Adams is that Kubrick got the ritual presented at the mask ball "so right." Peter further elaborated, noting: "If you were going to conduct a Saturnine style ritual, that is the way you would go about it. The colors used, the style of music employed, the Antinomian physical, or physicality of it, and I can't imagine what the source of that was because it certainly isn't in the original novel or the film that was made of the novel in 1969. So, somehow he synthesized the notion of magical ritual in a very, very powerful way. And that leads me to think that there must have been a source giving them that information or a direct exposure to that type of environment for that to be possible. I mean, you can't get that much that right without it."[489]

It's taken me a few years to fully grok what Peter was getting at. But, I think I'm finally ready to unpack this.

A major tip of the hat occurs during the film's opening frames. In this famous sequence, Nicole Kidman struts into the screen and begins disrobing before the opening title. For our purposes here, what is important about this shot are the two pillars between which Kidman stands, and the mirror off to the side. Most see this as a reference to Freemasonry, with the pillars representing Boaz and Jachin. But I believe Kubrick is actually hinting at what Boaz and Jachin are symbolic of: Castor and Pollex, also known as the Dioscuri, or simply Gemini.

Throughout the ancient world, the Milky Way was widely regarded as the repository of souls. Those set to incarnate descended from there and those returning ascended there. In many traditions adopted by the West from Mesopotamia, there were said to be two gateways. They could only be accessed during the solstices.[490] Souls ascending through the Gate of Capricorn in the South. During the Age of Pisces, this was in Sagittarius. But, it was ruled over by Saturn, the cosmic demiurge.

---

[489] Peter Mark Adams, interviewed by Steven W. Snider, *The Farm Podcast*, Podbeam, originally published December 16, 2021. Note: This interview is now only available on *The Farm Podcast Mach II*'s Patreon, https://www.patreon.com/thefarmpodcastII.

[490] Giorgio De Santillana & Hertha von Dechend, *Hamlet's Mill: An Essay Investigating the Origins of Human Knowledge and It's Transmission Through Myth* (Boston: Nonpareil Book, 1977), 244-249; Peter Mark Adams, *The Game of Saturn*, 42-45.

Conversely, souls descending into the physical realm did so in the north, via the Gate of Cancer. And in the Piscesian age, this gateway resided in Gemini. What's more, the Gate of Cancer was the ultimate crossroads. It was said to be where the Zodiac and the Milky Way intersected with one another. As the Zodiac can be seen as the great keeper of time while the Milky Way was commonly viewed as eternity, this where the rubber met the road, so to speak. It was at this crossroads where one becomes imprisoned in time. This gateway was ruled over by the moon. Hence, the notion of "drawing down the moon" in neo-paganism.[491]

In my estimation, this opening scene, of the two pillars, is a clear reference to the Gate of Cancer. This image is repeated again at Zeigler's Christmas Party, when the audience is first introduced to the cheerful robber baron and his wife.

But to return to the first appearance of the pillars: It's equally important to note what Kubrick frames within them: an explicitly sexual image of a naked woman and a mirror. The latter plays into the ancient tradition of theurgy, or literally meaning "god work." At its core, theurgy is the practice by which an incarnated individual can either project his consciousness upwards through the Gate of Capricorn to explore the celestial realms. Or, conversely, he can draw down something from the celestial realms via the Gate of Cancer to merge with his consciousness.[492] A common method for achieving either is the practice of scrying, which is normally achieved via a mirror or a reflective object. The darker the better. Essentially, the practitioner puts themselves in a trance by gazing into the mirror.[493]

It is my firm opinion that *2001* and *Eyes Wide Shut* are companion pieces and it's probable that Kubrick viewed them as such. And this has nothing to do with the moon landing hoax allegations.

What links these two films is the art of theurgy. *2001* is a treatise on the power of scrying. The character of Moonwatcher (Dan Richter) conceives humanity's first weapon and uses it to achieve dominion over the first humanoids. He gains the knowledge of arms by gazing into the black monolith that appears before him. The film's celebrated stargate sequence begins with the astronaut Bowman (Keir Dullea) gazing into the monolith. When the gateway opens, he's presented with a conjunction of planets, centered around Jupiter.

---

[491] Peter Mark Adams, *The Game of Saturn*, 47-49, etc; Giorgio De Santillana & Hertha von Dechend, *Hamlet's Mill: An Essay Investigating the Origins of Human Knowledge and Its Transmission Through Myth*, 242.

[492] Peter Mark Adams, *The Game of Saturn*, 49, etc. For more on the importance of theurgy in late Antiquity, see Algis Uzdavinys, *Philosophy and Theurgy in Late Antiquity* (Briar Knoll, OH: Angelico Press, 2010).

[493] The use of mirrors in theurgic practices has existed since Antiquity. See Iamblichus, *On the Mysteries* trans. Emma C. Clarke, John M. Dillon, and Jackson P. Hershbell (Atlanta: Society of Biblical Literature, 2003), 111, for a critical account of their use. In the modern era, scrying with black mirrors was popularized by the Elizabethan philosopher and magician John Dee. See Jason Louv, *John Dee and the Empire of Angels: Enochian Magick and the Occult Roots of the Modern World* (Rochester, VT: Inner Traditions, 2018), 72-77, 170-172, etc.

But, in the novel and the original conception, this was supposed to be a Great Conjunction of Jupiter and Saturn. However, for the purpose of ascension—which is what Bowman is doing, escaping the prison of time—he takes the Gate of Capricorn in the south. This would go through the constellation of Sagittarius, which Jupiter rules over. Thus, what ends up on screen is very close to what the ancient theurgists claimed to experience during the ascensions. And had Kubrick gotten his way, it would have been spot on.

The director made the decision to change the space ship Discovery's destination from Jupiter to Saturn. Supposedly, he thought Saturn looked more visually striking. But the special effects team was not able to develop a believable replication of Saturn's rings in time, necessitating the change back to Jupiter.[494] But there may have been another reason beyond Saturn's aesthetic qualities, as shall be addressed further down.

As outlandish as this may seem, the notion of the soul making a journey through the cosmos was a fairly common notion in late Antiquity. Above the cosmos was a creator god, perhaps more accurately described as a universal intelligence that all things in the heavens and earth derived from. The practice of theurgy enabled mortal souls to traverse the heavens and return to this source.[495] In these celestial journeys, both the gods and human souls made use of vessels. In Egypt, the gods were depicted in "solar barque," which the theurgists seem to have viewed as not entirely material.[496] Human souls were encased in "pneumatic vehicles."[497]

Despite years of rigorous research for scientific justifications of everything on screen, Kubrick opted to scrap virtually all of the dialogue and tell a story through images and music.[498] What emerges is one of the most spiritually significant films of the twentieth century. While it's rarely described as such, viewing the film was a religious experience for many viewers who witnessed it as its initial release.[499] Kubrick consciously abandoned the hard scientific approach he took early in the film's production for what he described to Arthur C. Clarke as "magical enchantment."[500]

What ends up on screen owes as much to metaphysics as science. Kubrick's fascination with mythology is well known and works such Homer's *The Odyssey* (which *2001*'s storyline roughly confirms to) in addition to Joseph Campbell's *The Hero With a Thousand Faces* have been acknowledged in the film's development.[501] In recent years, orthodox Kubrick scholar

---

[494] Michael Benson, *Space Odyssey*, 136-138, 144.

[495] See, for instance, See Iamblichus, *On the Mysteries*, 317, etc.

[496] See Iamblichus, *On the Mysteries*, 293-297.

[497] See Iamblichus, *On the Mysteries*, 91. For an in-depth discussion of this topic, see Michael Griffith, " Proclus on Place as the Luminous Vehicle of the Soul", *Dionysius*, vol. 30, 2012, 161-186, https://www.academia.edu/4480794 (accessed February 26, 2024).

[498] Nathan Abrams, *Stanley Kubrick: New York Jewish Intellectual*, 120-121.

[499] See, for instance, Joe R. Frinzi, *Kubrick's Monolith*, 124-147, etc.

[500] Flippo Ulivieri, *2001 Between Kubrick and Clarke*, 98-99.

[501] Michael Benson, *Space Odyssey*,72-73.

Nathan Abrams has made a sound case for the kabbalah contributing to *2001*'s spirituality. Zen Buddhism, which Kubrick had studied since the late 1950s, was also a factor.[502]

Gnosticism and Neoplatonism have been described as the world's first ancient astronaut religions. Based on what is depicted in *2001*, Kubrick seems to have embraced such a position. Put simply, Clarke saw the monolith as an alien "teaching machine." Kubrick presents it as a magical instrument. The former may have inspired giggles from the audience. The latter induced a state of awe. One can scarcely imagine a better fictional depiction of the theurgic ascension than what unfolds during the star gate sequence. The decision to tell the film's narrative largely through visuals skillfully mimics this process.

Kubrick's interest in psychedelic mushrooms may have been inspired by these traditions. In 1964, English poet Robert Graves mused that the sacrament used by initiates in the Eleusinian Mysteries was *Amanita muscaria*.[503] Andrija Puharich's 1959 work *The Sacred Mushroom* proposed mushrooms in Ancient Greece and other major cultures even earlier. But Plato was known as an enthusiastic supporter of the Eleusinian Mysteries. Kubrick could have theorized that the fantastical soul journeys the theurgists claimed to experience were partly induced by techniques learned at Eleusinian.

But, to return to *Eyes Wide Shut*. In this opening image, the mirror is off to the side. Front and center is a nude woman. This is Kubrick's way of telling us that *Eyes* is partially a treatise on theurgy, but using sex magic rather than mirrors. Hence, the reason the mirror is off to the side. A sacred marriage, or *Hieros gamos* as it was known to the ancients, uses sex for a mystic union with the divine. This when some deity inhabited one or both participants during a ritualized sex act. This function was often performed by sacred prostitutes in Antiquity. These were temple prostitutes with ritual training. There is no question Kubrick was aware of such notions. The book *Cult & Occult* found in his *Eyes* research materials has multiple sections dedicated to such topics.

Eight pointed stars are featured prominently throughout Zeigler's mansion, both during the opening Christmas party, and later, during the final confrontation with Tom Cruise in his billiards room. The star is quite striking. A standard Christmas star is normally five points. However, the Star of Bethlehem, the alleged inspiration for the Christmas star, is normally depicted with 8 points. This derives from the star the three Magi followed to witness the birth of Christ.

But long before this association, the eight pointed star was connected to the goddess Inanna, as she was known to the Sumerians, and Ishtar to the Babylonians. The inclusion of the Magi has long been viewed as a reference to Babylonian paganism. The Ishtar association is what Kubrick conspiracy theorists point too. She was also known as Aphrodite to the Greeks and

---

[502] Nathan Abrams, *Stanley Kubrick: New York Jewish Intellectual*, 121-128, etc.

[503] Terence McKenna, *Food of the Gods: The Search for the Original Tree of Knowledge* (New York: Bantam Books, 1992), 133.

Venus to the Romans. She was both a goddess of war and fertility, both being quite appropriate to *Eyes.* It's not a bad notion and probably has some merit. After all, the earliest known sacred prostitutes were connected to Inanna in Sumer. However, I see another, more compelling explanation.

The bronze female statues holding lamps displayed throughout Somerton have also been likened to the goddess. Lamps have long been connected to Ishtar worship. As Venus, she was closely associated with the morning light, or dawn, by the Romans.

But rather than Ishtar, they may be another theurgic reference. The object being held up by the woman in the statues may not be a lamp. It could represent a konos, later known in Latin as a turbo. This derived from the notion of "Hekate's Top," a spherical form of iunx. Basically, it looked like a kind of spinning top. Its bowl-like interior is designed to capture the precipitate of the moon in liquid. The center can be used for a burnt offering, especially incense. It was said to mimic the spiral path of the ascending and descending deities.[504] This is echoed by Red Cloak, the master of the procession at the masked bowl. He's equipped with a staff and a thurible, which may be a later form of the turbo. In the Sola-Busca tarot, magicians engaged in drawing down the moon are shown using a staff and turbo as ritual implements. The red garb is illustrative as well, for in classic theurgic workings, an emphasis was placed on wardrobe being consonant with the objective of the rite. The red attire is indicative of a serpent-dragon deity and draconian energy.[505]

Obviously, the serpent is loaded with symbolism. But, when depicted as an ouroboros, it becomes closely associated with Saturn as a symbol of time. And it has special significance when connected with the gates of the sun. In *The Game of Saturn*, Peter Mark Adams writes: "[T]he Devil, a figure conventionally depicted by Capricorn, but who is, nevertheless, the most ancient deity, Ammon-Saturn. The dragon depicted on the card is therefore an aspect or reflex of the hypercosmic demiurge refracted through the seventh planetary sphere of Saturn. As such, he guards the southern gate of the sun, assigned to the ascent of the souls in the constellation of Capricorn. To invoke such an entity would require the mage to engage in the most extreme ritual process, one that radically altered awareness and exfoliated a field congruent with that of the inward flowing power of the god."[506]

In this case, the mage is not attempting to ascend to this entity, as would be the case with the Gate of Capricorn. Rather, he is drawing the entity down to him through the Gate of Cancer. The ritualistic orgy is a means of generating occult energy and enticing the deity with earthly delights. This is why Kubrick's decision to set the film during Saturnalia is so crucial. To fully grasp this, we need to go back to the origins of the festival.

---

504 Peter Mark Adams, *The Game of Saturn*, 162-164; Algis Uzdavinys, *Philosophy and Theurgy in Late Antiquity*, 453.
505 Peter Mark Adams, *The Game of Saturn*, 150, 162.
506 Peter Mark Adams, *The Game of Saturn*, 191.

When at war, the Romans practiced a rite known as *evocatio* that was intended to subvert the wrath of another peoples' gods by ritually incorporating them into the Roman pantheon. And in no wars was this ritual taken to its darkest extremes quite like the ones involving Carthage. The rites of Saturn were expanded as an *evocatio* for Ba'al Hammon, the monstrous patron god of Carthage, whom Saturn was identified with. This involved one of the only recorded instances in which the Romans performed human sacrifices. Livy recounts that, in the aftermath of these rituals, the people cried out day and night "Saturnalia" and from there the day was declared a holiday into perpetuity.[507]

In *The Golden Bough*, a work Kubrick was intimately familiar with, James George Frazer argued at length that human sacrifice was practiced during the early forms of Saturnalia. Specifically, he argues that a divine consort of an Ishtar stand-in was the original sacrificial victim. In effect, someone would be chosen to perform the role of Ishtar's divine consort, ending in their death, but prior to this, they were given license to break all taboos. This later developed into the notion of the King of Saturnalia, and the Lord of Misrule.[508]

This is the function Bill Harford (Tom Cruise) is chosen to play. He's invited to Zeigler (Sydney Pollack)'s Christmas parties year after year, though he's not entirely sure why. Then, by a seemingly chance encounter with his friend Nick Nightingale (Todd Field), he's put on the path to the Masked Ball. A key part of Saturnalia is the reversal of roles, with slaves becoming masters. While Harford is hardly a slave, he is little more than hired help to people like Zeigler. But, he's given the opportunity to enter their exclusive circles. Numerous opportunities for him to commit infidelity appear. It's widely believed the Milich character (Rade Šerbedžija) is connected to the cult. It's not a stretch that Marion (Marie Richardson) is as well. Her father clearly enjoyed the kind of wealth Zeigler does.

Even the prostitute (Vinessa Shaw) Harford encounters at random may not be so random. It's often remarked how unrealistic it is for a woman that attractive to be working as a common prostitute. But, what if she's also working for the cult? A possible clue is provided by the character's name, Domino. Domino is also the name of one of the Venetian masks Harford later encounters at the ball. Further, Domino's apartment features several ritualistic masks on the wall. The later revelation that she has AIDs ensures Harford will not continue to make inquiries about her.

While it may seem a reach, this interpretation has to be taken in the context of the other major change Kubrick made to *Traumnovelle*: the addition of the Zeigler character. No such figure is present in Schnitzler's novella or the film adaptation. In adding this character, the opening party becomes more significant. In the novella, the party doesn't appear directly, only being discussed in the aftermath. This sequence, along with the bookend sequence at the end when Harford and Zeigler discuss the Masked Ball, are the only two additions that

---

507 Peter Mark Adams, *The Game of Saturn*, 64-65.

508 James George Frazer, *The Golden Bough: A Study in Magic* Abridged 2nd & 3rd ed.(London: Oxford University Press, 1994), 630-634, etc.

have no basis in the book. And they dramatically change the context of what happens at the ball.

Zeigler lends *Eyes Wide Shut* an element of *Young Goodman Brown*. In Hawthorne's legendary short story, the title character attends a witch's sabbath in which he discovers all the town's people are part of the coven. Further, his wife is poised to be initiated. Whereas in *Traumnovelle*, with the exception of the Nightingale character, the events that transpire are at a distance to the protagonist's life. What I mean by that is Nightingale is the only one at the ball in *Traumnovelle* Fridolin (Harford in the movie) knows. The woman who saves Fridolin's life may be an aristocrat, but it's left uncertain, as well as why she would do so in the first place.

But in *Eyes Wide Shut*, it is revealed in the final scene with Zeigler that both he and Mandy (Julienne Davis), the prostitute Harford revives at the Christmas party, were at the ball. It's strongly implied Zeigler's wife was also in attendance, along with Nightingale. Throw in Milich's all but certain links, and Harford is left surrounded by members of Zeigler's circle throughout that night. Kubrick even goes further, implying Alice's dream after Harford's return from the ball may not be a dream. The possibility lingers that she was there. It makes one of the final lines Harford utters to her at the toy store, "And no dream is just a dream?," all the more ominous. That line is taken directly from the novella and Schnitzler takes elements from the ball and puts them in Albertine (Alice in the movie)'s dream, as does Kubrick.

But in *Traumnovelle*, Albertine's dream comes off as more of a premonition or vision of her husband's activities. In Kubrick's hands, the distinct possibility that she was there is strongly implied. The waters are further muddied by the ambiguity as to where his mask came from when it appears in their bed. In the book, it's fairly clear Albertine found it after her husband misplaced it. But this is not so clear in the film. Kubrick adds to the ambiguity by entirely omitting the conversation they have after Harford tells Alice what has happened to him.

In this context, I don't think the possibility that Domino or Marion are part of the cult can be dismissed. This isn't to say that they definitely are, but I firmly believe Kubrick wanted the audience to wonder. This is one of the things that makes his version so unsettling: Harford may have been surrounded by the cult for much of his professional life and is totally unaware of it. Who is and is not connected to Zeigler is one of the film's central mysteries.

This also leaves the distinct possibility, as I mentioned earlier, that Harford is being steered by the cult, beginning with Zeigler's Christmas party, to embark upon some kind of bizarre ritual drama. Perhaps all of the things that happen to Harford on the night of the ball are initially engineered by the cult, and perhaps they are simply the unintended consequences of ritual drama playing out. Or perhaps a combination of both. Kubrick delights in the ambiguity here as to what is intentional and what is synchronistic.

Fortunately for Harford, he does not make a good Lord of Misrule. His inability to give in to temptation may be the ultimate reason why he escapes these encounters alive. And with that, I think I've said enough on the Masked Ball.

Is it truly possible that Kubrick was aware of a Saturn cult? I'm certainly not the first one to suggest such. Rather, Saturnine musings are among the most popular of Cryptokubrologists. But their argument is typically based on the black cube symbolism attributed to Saturn. Black cubes, obelisks, and stones are now commonly associated with Saturn, but how far back it goes is debatable. Some have traced it to the pre-Islamic mythology around the Kaaba, but this is far from certain.[509] With the rise of the Internet, the black cube mythos went viral. Pop culture touchstones such as the *Hellraiser* puzzle cube, the Borg ships of the *Star Trek* franchise and *2001*'s monolith are promoted as evidence of an elite cult of Saturn.

This is one of the more intriguing theories Cryptokubrology has put forward. We've already explored the potential overlap between Kubrick, Leslie Stevens and the *Star Trek* franchise. it's not beyond the realm of extreme possibility that these circles pushed black cube symbolism of Saturn. But ultimately, there is no evidence of this.

The same cannot be said in regards to Kubrick's knowledge of a Saturnine cult.

The Fraternitas Saturni, more commonly known as the Brotherhood of Saturn, was formed during 1926 in Germany. It had several prominent members during the Weimar Republic, most notably Albin Grau, a production designer on F.W. Murnau's 1922 classic *Nosferatu*. Some of the group's later symbolism appears in that film.[510]

The Fraternitas Saturni still exists to this day and have practiced elaborate sex magick rituals for decades. Kubrick would have been aware of this outfit from *Cult and the Occult*, which has an entire section dedicated to them.[511] Many of the topics I've just discussed, such as the use of sex magick for possession by a deity, are dealt with at length in this work. I would argue not only is it possible Kubrick was using a Saturnine cult as the basis for Zeigler's group,

---

[509] See, for instance, Arthur Moros, *The Cult of the Black Cube: A Saturnian Grimoire* 2nd ed. (Germany: Theion Publishing, 2021), 112-113.

[510] See Stephen E. Flowers, *The Fraternitas Saturni: History, Doctrine, and Rituals of the Magical Order of the Brotherhood of Saturn* (Rochester, VT: Inner Traditions, 2018). The Fraternitas Saturni grew out of another German magical order known as the Ordo Templi Orientis (OTO). This group was famously taken over by legendary English magician Aleister Crowley around the time of World War I. Crowley brought his system of Thelema, which also involved sex magick, into the OTO. The Fraternitas Saturni maintained correspondences with the OTO until WWII and briefly renewed the contact after the war. The reader will recall that Kubrick was in Pasadena during the early 1940s at the height of rocket scientist Jack Parsons' infamy. Parsons was also an acolyte of Crowley and a member of the OTO. Kubrick could have first become aware of the OTO during this time. It's also interesting to note that L. Ron Hubbard, who stole Parsons' wife, long claimed the Office of Naval Intelligence dispatched the future cult leader to Pasadena to keep tabs on Parsons. See George Pendle, *Strange Angel: The Otherworldly Life of Rocket Scientist John Whiteside Parsons*, 273-274, etc.

[511] Peter Brookesmith (ed.), *Cult and the Occult* (London: Guild Publishing, 1985), 147.

it is the most likely inspiration based on his research material. Given what has just been discussed about theurgy, the Fraternitas Saturni's use of astrology in its sexual rituals would have been especially intriguing to the director. And totally in keeping with the film's use of the winter solstice timeframe.

Don't misunderstand me: the Fraternitas Saturni was only a partial inspiration. Kubrick probably used the cult as a foundation upon which he added additional Saturnine mythos taken from Frazer and the like. The importance of Saturnalia in *The Golden Bough* cannot be overstated and Kubrick surely used Frazer's musings in his conception of a cult of Saturn. But the important takeaway is that Kubrick would have been aware of a historic cult of Saturn among Weimer's upper crust by the time he made *Eyes Wide Shut*.

Nor is the Fraternitas Saturni the only secret order to influence the conception of the Somerton sect. I've already noted the Masonic symbolism present in the two columns. Some have gone so far as to view Eyes Wide Shut as an allegory for the 33 degrees of the Scottish Rite of Freemasonry.[512] While that's a stretch, there's no doubt Kubrick employed Masonic symbolism in this and other films. Elsewhere, the college students that hurl homophobic taunts at Bill Harford can be identified as Yalies via their sweatshirts. Yale is the home of Skull and Bones, the notorious fraternity much speculated upon by conspiracy theorists. For years it's been rumored that initiates were placed naked in a coffin where they confessed their sexual history to older members.[513] This bears some similarity to Harford being commanded to strip before the Somerton sect before being redeemed.

Sir Francis Dashwood's Hell-fire Club seems another obvious inspiration.[514] The "Order of the Friars of St. Francis of Wycombe" (as it was formally known) began taking shape around the late 1740s. The group was inspired by Rabelais' Abbey of Thelema in *Gargantua and Pantagruel*. Thelema, meaning "Do as thou wilt," was later appropriated by Aleister Crowley for his own occult theology. The famous Hell-fire Club caves at Wycombe featured a statue of the Egyptian deity Harpocrates, whom Crowley later embraced as the Avatar of the Age of Horus, the "crowned and conquering child." But if Crowley was partly inspired by Dashwood's Hell-fire Club, it was primarily for its notoriety. There's little evidence of actual ceremonial magick being practiced by the group, though it has long been accused of Black Masses.[515]

---

[512] "M," "33 Degrees of Eyes Wide Shut," 33 Degrees of Eyes Wide Shut, originally published November 21, 2020 (accessed March 4, 2024), https://33degreesofeyeswideshut.wordpress.com/.
[513] Don Oldenburg, " Tippy-Top Secret," *The Washington Post*, April, 2004, https://www.washingtonpost.com/archive/lifestyle/2004/04/04/tippy-top-secret/09d44db5-3de4-4960-8f64-0e1ef57d6c95/. Note: While the coffin story is widely regarded as fact, it's never been confirmed. And if true, probably went out of practice decades ago.
[514] Much of what is written on the historic Hell-fire clubs is sensational rubbish. Geoffrey Ashe, *The Hell-fire Clubs: A History of Anti-Morality* 4th ed. (Gloucestershire: Sutton Publishing, 2003), is one of the few credible accounts.
[515] Geoffrey Ashe, *The Hell-fire Clubs: A History of Anti-Morality*, 124-131, etc.

The reality of Dashwood's Hell-fire Club was closer to the elite swingers club presented in *Traumnovelle*. The membership was of the aristocracy and monied classes. Dashwood and others had ties to the ruling Whig party. It is here *Eyes*'s debut to Dashwood is most evident. The reader will also recall that Peter Sellers' friend Michael Bentine accused Stephen Ward, the central figure in the Profumo scandal, of running a modern day Hell-fire Club. While there's no evidence of this, Kubrick surely would have been fascinated by such allegations if he was aware of them.

A not-so-obvious influence is experimental filmmaker Maya Deren. Peter Mark Adams has theorized that traces of the rites of Ammon-Saturn, the Carthaginian deity "adopted" by the Romans, passed to the Americas during the trans-Atlantic slave trade via folk practices. Specifically, the recurring presence of spirit possession in Vodun and related practices has very ancient origins in North Africa.[516] Possession is at the heart of the theoretical Saturnine tradition as well.

As for Maya Deren, in 1953 she published a book called *Divine Horsemen: Living Gods in Haiti*. It was the result of several years of research conducted on Vodou in Haiti. The book was edited by Joseph Campbell, whose *Hero With a Thousand Faces* influenced the mythical aspects of *2001*. To this day, *Horsemen* is still considered one of the most scholarly accounts of Vodun. She also extensively filmed the Haitian rituals. Some of this footage was eventually released as the 1977 documentary *Divine Horsemen: Living Gods in Haiti* posthumously.

Deren's research serves as the basis for the Vodun section in *Cults and the Occult*.[517] She's mentioned by name while her experiences of being possessed as part of the rituals are addressed. Kubrick surely knew who Deren was well before acquiring this book. She lived in Greenwich Village at the same time as he did and she was part of the filmmaking circles he was on the periphery of then.[518] It's possible he interacted with her socially on occasion. And surely, her mention in *Cults and the Occult* would have drawn his attention if he was not already familiar with her Vodun research.

Finally, *The Story of O* inevitably contributed to the Somerton sect. The "classic" work of sado-masochistic erotica was akin to the *Fifty Shades of Grey* of the Cold War era. It was written by French journalist Anne Desclos under the pen name of Pauline Reage and published by Olympia Press in 1954. Kubrick was well aware of the publisher. They famously issued *Lolita* after more reputable publishers passed. Olympia also released *Candy*, which Terry Southern co-authored, and various novels by William S. Burroughs. A friend suggested that Kubrick attempt to adapt *The Story of O* during the late 1950s, but nothing came of it.[519]

---

[516] Peter Mark Adams, *The Game of Saturn*, 12-123, etc.

[517] Peter Brookesmith (ed.), *Cult and the Occult*, 148-151.

[518] Robert P. Kolker and Nathan Abrams, *Kubrick: An Odyssey*, 73.

[519] Robert P. Kolker and Nathan Abrams, *Kubrick: An Odyssey*, 199.

Still, portions of *Eyes* seem to have been influenced by it. "O," the novel's protagonist, enters an erotic netherworld where women are groomed as sexual slaves in isolated chateaus for an exclusive secret society. Sado-masochism is a major part of their training. One of the senior figures in the sect is an English aristocrat named "Sir Stephen." One can't help but think of the circles Thomas Corbally and Stephen Ward intersected in. One of the most striking plot points of *O* is the owl mask the protagonist is made to wear as a sign of her submission towards the end of the book. Some of the other women are also assigned masks.

O's owl mask was inspired by surrealist artist Leonor Fini, a contemporary of Max Ernst, André Breton and George Balanchine, and lover of Desclos. Fini's costumes were legendary, as were her erotic paintings, frequently inspired by the Marquis de Sade. Her work was regularly displayed at the Museum of Modern Art, a favorite haunt of Kubrick's, during the 1930s.[520] The secretive world hinted at by Fini's surrealist balls and *The Story O* clearly influenced Kubrick's development of the Somerton sect. Kubrick may have had knowledge of life imitating art in this regard. The sado-masochism documented in *Secrets of Playboy* that became commonplace during the 1970s could have been lifted directly from *The Story of O.*

It's worth noting that Russian surrealist and occultist Maria de Naglowska's Brotherhood of the Golden Arrow has been cited as the real life inspiration for the secret society in *The Story of O.* The group was founded in Paris during 1929. It practiced an extreme form of sex magick heavy on sado-masochism. Two figures we've noted during this work, surrealist artist Man Ray and Italian Traditionalist and occultist Julius Evola, reputed members, as was Jean Paulhan, a longtime lover of Anne Desclos who wrote the intro to *O.*[521]

I've seen nothing to indicate Kubrick was aware of this obscure sect, but the black robes used by the Somerton sect as well as the sexual poses used are in keeping with what little is known of the Brotherhood's rituals. While never confirmed, some accounts hold that sexual intercourse was performed at the end of meetings and observed by Naglowska's followers[522]

---

[520] Daniel McDermon, " Sex, Surrealism and de Sade: The Forgotten Female Artist Leonor Fini," *The New York Times*, November 6, 2018 (accessed March 4, 2024), https://www.nytimes.com/2018/11/06/arts/design/leonor-fini-artist.html.

[521] Cynthia Varaday, "The First Lady of Satan and the Brotherhood of the Golden Arrow," *Medium*, November 25, 2019 (accessed March 4, 2024), https://cynthiavarady.medium.com/maria-de-naglowska-the-first-lady-of-satan-b9bdee6bf66a; Stephen E. Flowers and Crystal Dawn Flowers, *Carnal Alchemy: Sado-Magical Techniques for Pleasure, Pain, and Self-Transformation* (Rochester, VT: Inner Traditions, 2013), 52. There's no question that Evola knew Naglowska and that they influenced one another. Evola briefly discusses Naglowska in *The Metaphysics of Sex* (261-263). Confirmation for Man Ray and Paulhan and other celebrated figures linked to Naglowska (i.e. Andre Breton, Antonin Artaud, Georges Bataille, etc) remain elusive. But there's no question Naglowska influenced the surrealist scene. Two of her best known supporters are surrealist author Ernest Gengenbach and painter Camille Bryen. One of the best studies of Naglowska was written by another surrealist, Sarane Alexandrian. See Donald Traxler, "Introduction: The Reconciliation of Light and Dark Forces in Maria De Naglowska with Donald Traxler (trans.), *The Light of Sex: Initiation, Magic, and Sacrament* (Rochester, VT: Inner raditions, 2011), 1-2, 116n1.

Maria De Naglowska with Donald Traxler (trans.), *The Light of Sex: Initiation, Magic, and*

not unlike what occurs at the masked ball. There are also some similarities between what is shown in this sequence and Naglowska's "Water Dance" ritual,[523] which may explain why Kubrick hired a specialist in modern dance to choreograph the ball. While Naglowska remains obscure to this day, she had a small but dedicated following in France. Gershon Legman lived there for decades, and given his interests, it's not beyond the realm of possibility he heard of Naglowska.

What should be clear is that there were some quite esoteric and darkly erotic doctrines making the rounds in the surrealist and Dadaist avant-garde that Kubrick cut his teeth in. From Man Ray to Maya Deren to *The Story of O*, there is no shortage of occultic doctrines Kubrick could have been exposed to, especially during his marriage to Ruth Sobtoka. Given that *Eyes Wide Shut* is very much a tribute to this scene, it's not hard to believe the Somerton sect also came out of this milieu. I reiterate a point I made at the beginning of this work: Kubrick's films cannot be understood without taking into account the influence of the Dadaist and surrealist movements that touched him early in life.

Sacrament, 43n.

[523] Maria De Naglowska with Donald Traxler (trans.), *The Light of Sex*, 84-97.

Conclusion:

Open Your Eyes

Eyes Wide Open

Why is *Eyes Wide Shut* so personal to Kubrick?

Because it is a reflection on his life, and possibly even a confession. At the heart of the film is the relations fathers have with their daughters.

Harford has a young daughter. Later, he has the daughter of a just-deceased patient literally throw herself at him, and practically on her father's death bed. Following this, Hartfort encounters the owner of a costume shop who appears to pimp his teenage daughter (Leelee Sobieski) out to wealthy businessmen. And in this case, said costume shop proprietor even looks eerily like a younger Kubrick.

Virtually all of the women depicted in the film are prostitutes, in one form or another, and all are seemingly under the domination of men. This is another striking change from *Traumnovelle*. In the source material, the women are mostly aristocrats, especially at the ball.

As Kubrick only had daughters, it's impossible not to read into this as a reflection on his children. Kubrick obviously identifies with the Tom Cruise character. As with *Barry Lyndon*, which rivals *Eyes* as Kubrick's most personal film, the protagonist is a social climber who finds himself in over his head among the aristocracy. Make no mistake, the world of Victor Ziegler is every bit an aristocracy as what Redmond Barry confronts. As for Cruise's Bill Harford character, I think Kubrick perceives him as himself in 1950s New York as his career is taking off. The surreal night Harford spends wandering New York is a reflection on the paths open to Kubrick. It's very much like *A Christmas Carol* in this sense, and likely one of the reasons Kubrick set in during the holiday season.

Milich has the exact costume on hand Harford needs for the Masked Ball. This has been widely interpreted as evidence that Milich is tied to the cult in some way. I see no reason to quibble with this particular take. It's also implied, via the Japanese businessmen, that Milich entered these circles by pimping out his daughter. But even in making this sacrifice, he is still on the fringe.

Even before then, Harford had an awkward situation with Marion. Upon her fathers' death, she confesses her love to Harford and states that she wants to leave her fiancé for him. This is especially bizarre, because it's later revealed her fiancé looks strikingly similar to Cruise, and the actor who plays him, Thomas Gibson, was even a friend of Cruise's in real life.[524] I think this is a comment on how women are passed around, so to speak, in these circles, and specifically, it represents Kubrick's own concerns about his daughters after his death.

It's interesting to note that Jennifer Jason Leigh originally played this part, but her scenes were re-filmed with Marie Richardson after she wasn't able to find another opening in her

---

[524] Robert P. Kolker and Nathan Abrams, *Eyes Wide Shut*, 69.

schedule. The reshoots happened after Kubrick's relationship with his daughter Vivian had gone into a tailspin. I can't help but wonder if this was a factor in Kubrick's decision to reshoot this scene. We have the pathetic spectacle of Richardson throwing herself at Cruise, a Scientologist. This scene is one reason why I don't buy Kubrick's ignorance of Vivian's conversion.

Even more unsettling are the subtle hints that the Richardson character is wired for a certain type of man. And that brings us to Alice Harford. Alice who fantasies about her Navy man in a peculiar Wonderland. And shown in grainy footage, like what we would expect from a hidden camera filming a couple without their awareness. Like what Roman Polanski has been accused of doing.

For reasons such as this, it has been widely speculated that Alice is a mind control victim, and that she may even be her husband's handler. This obviously gets into very speculative and controversial territory. But if *A Clockwork Orange* is any indication, this is a subject that intrigued Kubrick.

What's more, the research of Andrija Puharich may have been put towards such ends. In *A Secret Order*, H.P. Albarelli describes a project under the auspices of ARTICHOKE that "involved the training of small cadres of women for work as Agency and Military couriers, as well as young girls and teenagers for mostly unknown objectives apparently related to the CIA's interest in hypnosis, sleight-of-hand, and telekinesis." This program supposedly ran from 1953-1963. One example given of its operational use involved the process of narco-hypnosis on women being used as couriers.[525]

This tracks with research I've done over the years on this subject. Richard Case Nagell, an Army and CIA intelligence officer and Dick Russell's source for *The Man Who Knew Too Much*, claimed he was hypnotized for "compartmentalization of information" while working as a courier.[526] Candy Jones, a famous alleged mind control victim from the 1960s, also described this process.[527]

Further, I uncovered a declassified FBI document from 1949 that was from an early meeting of a group that later became known as the Artichoke Committee, but this harkened back to the Bluebird days. The document explicitly states that two major interests of Bluebird was the ability to deconstruct and reconstruct an individual's personality; and to implant screen or false memories.[528]

---

[525] H.P. Albarelli Jr., *A Secret Order*, 42-43.

[526] Dick Russell, *The Man Who Knew Too Much* (New York: Carroll & Graf, 1992), 380

[527] Walter Bowart, *Operation Mind Control* (New York: Fontana, 1978), 115, etc.

[528] United States Department of Justice Federal Bureau of Investigation, "Biological Warfare," D.M. Ladd, DocID: 34386951, Washington, Federal Bureau of Investigation, 1949, https://drive.google.com/file/d/1MeOxLwRaYpzVbAdti8gkVNRdModl5k6b/view

I can't help but think of one of DC's more notorious madams: Heidi Rikan. Heidi was a former high class prostitute for various Mafioso who eventually ended running a call girl ring out of the Watergate at the time of burglary. In the decades since the Watergate scandal broke, much evidence has emerged that Heidi's operation was the real target of the burglary. Especially since Heidi was being supplied with equipment through a cut out by James McCord, one of the infamous Plumbers.[529]

McCord was a CIA veteran, one who had worked out of its Office of Security for years. And there, he was close to figures like Morse Allen, who ran ARTICHOKE's day to day operations.[530] The reader will recall that it was Morse Allen who patronized Andrija Puharich's work with ARTICHOKE. And here, in Watergate, is one of Allen's former underlings working indirectly with Heidi. Nor was McChord the only ARTICHOKE figure linked to Watergate. General Paul Gaynor, the longtime director of ARTICHOKE, was in contact via a cut-out with McCord during his Plumber days.[531] And it's even more curious, when you consider that Heidi was born in Nazi Germany, and experienced horrendous sexual abuse from her father, who served in the German Navy during the war, and that Heidi became a prostitute for the mob after spending a year in the US Army before being abruptly discharged.[532]

Hugh Hefner and the Playboy mansion also come to mind. As the 2022 docu-series *Secrets of Playboy* makes clear, Hef was running an Epstein-like blackmail operation out of the mansion and various resorts. All of these facilities were loaded with cameras and audio equipment. Additional sources have come forward collaborating these claims since the series originally aired.[533] Further, many former Bunnies have acknowledged a process of "grooming" often involving drugs and sexual humiliation.

Kubrick knew many people active in the Playboy scene over the years, including Roman Polanski and Jack Nicholson. Fellow director John Huston was also a regular guest. Huston, a one time close friend of suspected Black Dahlia murderer George Hodel, maintained a residency in Ireland for years. During the 1972-1973 period (which partly overlapped with Kubrick's time in Ireland), Playboy Bunny Paige Young was Huston's guest there. Young went on to commit suicide in 1974. Close friends have maintained her suicide was driven by the abuse she suffered in the Playboy milieu, especially from Hefner and Huston.[534] Paige's time in the Republic of Ireland also overlapped with the Kincora scandal in Northern Ireland.

---

[529] See Phil Stanford, *White House Call Girl: The Real Watergate Story* (Port Townsend, WA: Feral House, 2013), especially 101-105.

[530] H.P. Albarelli Jr., *A Terrible Mistake*, 88, etc.

[531] Jim Hougan, *Secret Agenda: Watergate, Deep Throat and the CIA* (New York: Random House, 1984), 22, 227-230. The cut-out was McCord's friend, Lee Pennington. A former FBI agent and senior member of the American Legion, Pennington was active in the American Security Council for years.

[532] Phil Stanford, *White House Call Girl*, 21-24.

[533] See, for instance Holmes, H. (2024, January 19). Crystal Hefner exposes blackmail and black mold at the Playboy Mansion. The Daily Beast. https://www.thedailybeast.com/crystal-hefners-book-exposes-blackmail-black-mold-at-playboy-mansion.

[534] Parry, R. (2014, December 4). Exclusive: Passed around by Bill Cosby, Hugh Hefner and dozens of

And let us not forget about Profumo. Kubrick was in the UK when the scandal was unfolding. Peter Sellers knew Ward and traveled in many of the same circles. Thomas Corbally later brought the S & M stylings he learned in the UK to Long Island. Kubrick makes a point of placing Somerton near Glen Cove, an area he had previously lived in. Kubrick's friend, Jack Nicholson may have known Corbally through Heidi Fleiss.[535] Some have claimed servicing Nicholson was such an honor for Fleiss that she regularly gave him girls for free.[536] Inevitably, Hugh Hefner also procured girls from Fleiss.

As was noted previously, even orthodox Kubrick scholars have ruminated on Kubrick's likely interest in Profumo. James Fenwick cited the Heidi Fleiss scandal as part of the climate political/social *Eyes Wide Shut* was conceived in.[537] The intersection between sex and power politics was something that long fascinated Kubrick. Through both his research and his social circles, it is possible he would have been aware of Corbally.

The same can also be said of Hefner and the Playboy empire. Kubrick's fascination with porn may have been partly driven by the dark side of the industry. Beginning around 1980, *Deep Throat* (1972) star Linda Lovelace accused Chuck Traynor, her one-time agent and husband, of coercing her into prostitution and porn via a combination of physical and sexual abuse mixed with hypnosis.[538] Whether you call it grooming or brainwashing, both are applicable to Lovelace's claims. Lovelace also made the scene at the Playboy mansion, where she supposedly performed bestiality at one point.[539]

I would be remiss for not addressing the faith of Ray Radin, the owner of the Southampton mansion where Melonie Haller was assaulted. He made headlines again in May 1983, when he disappeared while working on what became the 1983 Francis Ford Coppola film *The*

Hollywood honchos - this is the Playboy playmate of the month who felt so used and abused by the most powerful leading men she took a gun and shot herself in the head. Daily Mail Online. https://www.dailymail.co.uk/news/article-2857873/Passed-Bill-Cosby-Hugh-Hefner-dozens-Hollywood-honchos-Playboy-Playmate-Month-felt-used-abused-powerful-leading-men-took-gun-shot-head.html.

[535] Spargo, C. (2016, June 2). Johnny Depp, star wars creator George Lucas and Jack Nicholson among names found in Hollywood madam Heidi Fleiss' infamous Black book. Daily Mail Online. https://www.dailymail.co.uk/news/article-3620128/Johnny-Depp-Star-Wars-creator-George-Lucas-Jack-Nicholson-names-Hollywood-Madam-Heidi-Fleiss-infamous-black-book.html.

[536] Staff, O. (2022, March 21). Madam to the stars: The steamy life of Heidi Fleiss. OK Magazine. https://okmagazine.com/p/madam-to-the-stars-the-steamy-life-of-heidi-fleiss-hollywoods-ceo-of-sex/.

[537] James Fenwick, *Stanley Kubrick Produces*, 195-196.

[538] Briggs , J. B. (2002, April 25). Linda's Life. National Review Online. https://web.archive.org/web/20070329001130/http://www.nationalreview.com/comment/comment-briggs042502.asp.

[539] Torres, L. (2022, February 14). Hugh Hefner's ex-girlfriend says she once walked in on the Playboy founder engaging in sex acts with their dog. Business Insider. https://www.businessinsider.com/secrets-of-playboy-hugh-hefner-bestiality-sex-acts-2022-2.

Cotton Club. Several weeks later, his body turned up. Once foul play was confirmed, the press dubbed Radin's demise the "*Cotton Club*" murder.

At the time of his death, Radin was putting together financing for the film with legendary producer Robert Evans. The two men had been put in contact with one another by Karen Greenberger, a woman tied to the Medellin cartel. She reputedly put up part of the early funding for the film. Evans was a person of interest in the murder for a time.[540]

I bring up this incident because Evans was a longtime friend of Jack Nicholson's[541] and another of Heidi Fleiss' customers.[542] He also had a relationship with Polanski, but it fell apart during the filming of *Chinatown*, which Nicholson starred in while Polanski directed and Evans produced.[543] In other words, this was the same social circle of actors and filmmakers who intersected with figures from George Hodel's family, Charles Manson and his Family, and the ever-present Thomas Corbally. The same circles Kubrick lingered on the periphery of. Surely the *Cotton Club* murder would have interested him for this reason alone.

And let us not forget Kubrick's longtime friendship with pioneering A.I. researcher Marvin Minsky, who was later implicated in Jeffrey Epstein's ring.[544] Or the accusations of pedophilia that briefly delayed Arthur C. Clarke's knighthood during the late 1990s.[545] Finally, there's the Kincora scandal, which he was in close proximity to during the filming of *Barry Lyndon*, and the specter of James B. Harris, his early production partner. Harris carried on an affair with an underage Sue Lyon that does not appear to have been entirely consensual. Combine this with revelations concerning associates like Roman Polanski, and one can begin to understand Kubrick's obsession with his family's safety, especially his daughters. In order to spare his family, Kubrick not only relocated to an isolated manor in the UK, but possibly chose to look the other way for years. Like the Bill Harford protagonist, he retreated into an illusion of family bliss in the hope of keeping the darkness at bay. But if Vivian is any indication, it was only temporary.

Eyes wide shut indeed.

The Minotaur

---

[540] Despite the celebrity intrigue of the *Cotton Club* murder, it has only inspired one full length account, Steve Wick, *Bad Company: Drugs, Hollywood and the Cotton Club Murder* (New York: St. Martin's Paperbacks, 1990).

[541] See Patrick McGilligan, *Jack's Life*.

[542] Tyrnauer, M. (1994, September 1). Evans Gate: Vanity fair. Vanity Fair | The Complete Archive. https://archive.vanityfair.com/article/share/8be43690-ca2f-4d81-a2e5-5256b81f5154.

[543] See San Wasson, *The Big Goodbye: Chinatown and the Last Years of Hollywood* (New York: Flatiron Books, 2020).

[544] Jasun Horsley, *Kubrickon*, 80.

[545] Michael Benson, *Space Odyssey*, 442.

I opened this work partly questioning where the money came from. And as we reach the conclusion, I now return to this question. The financial independence Kubrick secured during the 1960s was probably related to the intelligence work that underpinned his filmmaking career. I suspect he continued to engage with elements of the Anglo-American intelligence community for years to come, but less so via psywar after the 1970s.

Often overlooked is the epic amount of research Kubrick did for his films, especially the science fiction centric-ones. This would have provided ideal cover for what is known as "future projections." In intelligence analysis, this is a huge field. For instance, the Pentagon has an entire think tank, the Office of Net Assessment, whose sole purpose is to predict future trends.

Kubrick worked on *A.I.* for over two decades, having started it at some point during the late 1970s.[546] In researching *A.I.*, Kubrick not only heavily investigated the field of artificial intelligence and robotics for years, but also future political and environmental trends. Through the decades he worked on the film, he routinely consulted with leading scientists in related fields to craft a depiction of the future every bit as accurate as what *2001* managed.[547] Kubrick compiled troves of data for this project alone. And this doesn't even cover the endless research into war he conducted throughout his life. At a minimum, the data Kubrick gathered in these fields would have rivaled what many think tanks and intelligence services had. Kubrick was by all accounts a brilliant man and surely would have made a stellar intelligence analyst for future trends. Is this possibly how he supplemented his income, or came up with the money to acquire so many materials for his films? It would certainly go a long way towards explaining his cash flow.

Was this Kubrick's reward after the turbulent 1960s and 1970s? While it may make many conventional Kubrick scholars uncomfortable to contemplate the director in any kind of intelligence work, analytical endeavors may be an easier sell. But it seems clear to me Kubrick's relationship with the Kennedy administration and the family itself warrants far greater scrutiny. It's remarkable that there's so little written about Kubrick's reaction to the JFK assassination during *Dr. Strangelove*, and it's equally suspect no Kubrick academics have questioned Anthony Frewin's engagement with the JFK parapolitical crowd. Surely Kubrick was aware of Frewin's activities in that regard. But if he was, no one has ever bothered to comment upon it.

While some academics have attempted to explore Kubrick's time in Ireland in terms of broader geopolitical currents, the proverbial surface has only been scratched. Especially in light of the controversy surrounding *A Clockwork Orange* and Kubrick's dispute with the British government over his taxes. Kubrick appears to be on the periphery of pivotal events in both the United States and United Kingdom during the 1960s and 1970s, respectively. He

---

[546] Baxter, *Stanley Kubrick: A Biography*, 302-304,

[547] Alison Castle, "Stanley Kubrick's A.I.," in *The Stanley Kubrick Archives* ed. by Alison Castle, 654.

may have never been as close to the action again, but there are indications he maintained secrets until his death.

Recall an incident I mentioned earlier in this work recounted by Emilo D'Alessandro, Kubrick's longtime driver and assistant. Emilo shared an anecdote following Kubrick's death where he discovered a group of people rummaging through Kubrick's papers, filing cabinets and computer. They even searched Kubrick's Rolls Royce. When D'Alessandro demanded they get Christiane's permission to go through her husband's private affairs, he was met with a snort.[548]

How many other filmmakers have had their papers and computer searched in such a fashion after death? This is the kind of reaction one would expect to the death of someone possessing state secrets. What did they think Kubrick had that warranted such a response?

As much as I want to dismiss the sensational claims of Kubrick possessing child pornography, I can't. Especially in light of Kubrick's adaptation of *Lolita*. Kubrick reimagined what is in essence a rivalry between two pedophiles for the "affections" of a 12 year old girl into a tragic love story. Some of this can be explained by the production codes still in effect during the early 1960s. It would have been impossible to get approval from the censors if Lolita remained 12 for instance, necessitating her age being raised to 14.

But that can't explain the changes Kubrick made to the Humbert Humbert (James Mason) character. In the Nabokov novel, Humbert is prone to violent behavior towards his first wife and Lolita while he outright murders her mother. Kubrick removes practically all traces of Humbert's violent side save for half-hearted musings on murdering Charlotte Haze (Shelly Winters). Charlotte ends up dying in a tragic accident. In the Kubrick film, she rendered a caricature of a pompous WASP suburban mother. The audience shares in Humbert's contempt for her. And rather than dominating Lolita as he does in the book, Humbert is mesmerized by her in the film. This is symbolized by the famous sequence of him painting her feet. Their illicit road trip, rather than an ongoing violation of the Mann Act, is reduced to a "harmless romp."[549]

In the end, Humbert reveals that he truly loves Lolita rather than being an irredeemable sexual predator. The story becomes, in Kubrick's words, a "tragic romance" and one of the great love stories. Kubrick was driven to adapt *Lolita* only after he saw its potential as a love story. Apparently his conception was strongly influenced by a review of the Nabokov novel that appeared in *Encounter* by Lionel Trilling.[550] Both the writer and publication have intelligence links. *Encounter* was co-sponsored by the CIA and MI6 through the Congress of Cultural Freedom, another CIA/MI6 front. In the early days, *Encounter*'s propaganda functions were part of the Psychological Strategy Board's broader initiative. In practical terms, this meant certain writers were emphasized as part of the West's cultural war with

---

[548] Emilo D'Alessandro with Fillippo Ulivieri, *Stanley Kubrick and Me*, 333.
[549] Nathan Abrams, *Stanley Kubrick: New York Jewish Intellectual*, 88.
[550] Nathan Abrams, *Stanley Kubrick: New York Jewish Intellectual*, 72.

the Soviets. Nabokov was one of them, along with the likes of Bertrand Russell, Arnold Toynbee, Jorge Luis Borges.[551] Tilling was at the forefront of the conservative intellectual wing of the Congress for Cultural Freedom.[552]

For these reasons, Kubrick's adaptation of *Lolita* may fall within the culture wars with the Soviet Union. As an expat Russian, Nabokov's literary legacy and his ability to thrive in the democratic West had great propaganda value to the intelligence services. A successful Hollywood adaptation of such a controversial novel would be another feather in the West's culture war cap. The reader will recall that the de Rochemont brothers, Kubrick's early patrons, collaborated with the CIA in adapting Orwell's *Animal Farm* for just such a purpose.

But even that can't explain why Kubrick identifies so strongly with Clare Quilty (Peter Sellers). The prominence of the character in Kubrick's *Lolita* is another dramatic departure from the book. Nabokov's Quilty is a shadowy figure referenced in only a handful of pages until the fatal confrontation with Humbert. Kubrick makes Humbert's killing of Quilty the film's opening and explores the ways the writer stalks Humbert throughout the film. Quilty has been compared to the Minotaur who has lured Humbert into his labyrinth.[553] This is especially fitting in lieu of the Minotaur/labyrinth symbolism so prevalent in *The Shining*, which we'll get to in just a moment.

Nabokov's Quilty already shared a lot of similarities with Kubrick. The writer placed his origins in New Jersey and his education at Columbia University. His hobbies included photography, pets and fast cars. His occupation is playwright and TV writer. Kubrick was from the Bronx, audited classes at Columbia and loved photography and pets. He also worked in TV for a time and owned many fast cars despite his fear of high speeds. Kubrick was a passionate ping pong enthusiast and boxing fan, a characteristic Quilty has in the film. Quilty's female companion has a Village Beat look and vaguely resembles Toba Metz and Ruth Sobotka, Kubrick's first two wives. Some have even speculated Sellers was impersonating Kubrick at times while playing Quilty.[554]

Quilty becomes the repository of Humbert's darkness, the shadow that his civilized veneer keeps at bay. Humbert is redeemed in the end not just because he realizes that he truly loves Lolita, but also because he recognizes the abuse he has inflicted upon her. While still blaming Quilty, he acknowledges that the writer "took advantage of a sinner." He is able to see the darkness in himself through Quilty and acts to destroy it.

One can only wonder how much of the duel between Humbert and Quilty represents Kubrick's own struggle within himself during this time. Kubrick was a father three times over when *Lolita* wrapped. During the filming, his production partner began a relationship with

---

[551] Frances Stonor Saunders, *Who Paid the Piper?*, 165-189, etc.

[552] Frances Stonor Saunders, *Who Paid the Piper?*, 157-158.

[553] Nathan Abrams, *Stanley Kubrick: New York Jewish Intellectual*, 90.

[554] Nathan Abrams, *Stanley Kubrick: New York Jewish Intellectual*, 90-91.

Lyon that was exploitative, to put it mildly. Did these experiences change Kubrick and influence the redemption Humbert has in the film?

One of the most intriguing aspects of *Lolita* is the title character's final break with Quilty. When Humbert encounters Lolita four years later, she reveals that she left Humbert for Quilty after he enticed her with the prospect of working in Hollywood. But the movies Quilty intends to feature her in are "art films," clearly a reference to pornography, and involving a minor no less. This plot point is taken directly from the novel and eerily mirrors later accusations against Kubrick. Which raises more unsettling implications in regards to the director's identification with Quilty.

Kubrick arguably made one other film dealing with pedophilia: *The Shining*. While this interpretation remains highly controversial, a strong case can be made that Jack Torrance (Jack Nicholson)'s abuse of his son Danny (Danny Lloyd) goes beyond the physical, as it is presented in the King novel. Proponents of this theory point to the film's disturbing use of bear symbolism. Danny is shown with bears throughout the film: a framed picture of two of them hangs over his bed at the beginning of the film. Later, after Danny passes out, he comes to with his trousers around his ankles while laying on top of a stuffed bear. Towards the end of the film, Danny's mother Wendy (Shelly Duval) encounters two male figures engaged in oral sex in one of the Overlook's rooms. The man performing the act is dressed in a bear costume. Some have interpreted this peculiar scene as Wendy's realization that Jack is sexually abusing their son.[555]

This casts an unsettling light on Danny's imaginary friend, Tony. Danny describes Tony as "the little boy who lives in my mouth." Danny inserts a finger into his mouth while speaking as Tony early in the film. This certainly explains the mysterious bear scene, which has long mystified viewers. There's also an early scene of Jack reading a *Playgirl* magazine (as opposed to *Playboy*, meaning he is looking at male models) featuring a headline that proclaims: "Incest: Why parents sleep with their children."[556] Coupled with an unsettling scene midway through in which Jack is almost forcing Danny to sit on his lap, certain conclusions seem unavoidable.

In this context, the horrors of Stanley Kubrick's *The Shining* reveal themselves as the trauma of a child being sexually abused by a parent. The ghosts can be seen as manifestations of this abuse. This is especially true of room 237. The female phantom that inhabits it is literally the embodiment of Danny's abuse. It attempts to choke the life out of the child. When Jack confronts it, he is first seduced before realizing what he is confronting. His mental collapse hastens after this moment, implying that his psyche is shattered after recognizing himself as an abuser. He was likely unaware of his crimes before then, entering into a trance-like state

---

[555] Russell, C. (2022, May 7). What does the bear mean in Stanley Kubrick Film “The shining”? Far Out Magazine. https://faroutmagazine.co.uk/what-does-the-bear-mean-in-the-shining/.
[556] Russell, C. (2022, May 7). What does the bear mean in Stanley Kubrick Film “The shining”? Far Out Magazine. https://faroutmagazine.co.uk/what-does-the-bear-mean-in-the-shining/.

to indulge in his perversities. One can draw parallels to David Lynch's *Twin Peaks* series, which I believe was heavily influenced by *The Shining*. At the heart of both works are the ongoing traumas experienced by a child that has been sexually abused by a parent.

As I noted in the introduction, Kubrick identifies with Jack Torrance and Nicholson may be imitating Kubrick in his performance. This parallels Sellers' interpretation of Quilty. But what ends up onscreen is quite different. Quilty, despite his perversities, is a highly romanticized figure. He's the most interesting character in the film. Everyone in the picture is obsessed with him in one fashion or another. He is magnetic. Jack Torrance, by contrast, is a pathetic figure at the onset of *The Shining* and becomes all the more so as it progresses. He's a total failure as a father: a drunken abuser who can barely hold a job down. Where Quilty is cosmopolitan and witty, Jack is a hick and a bigot with pretensions of sophistication. Quilty is a successful writer whose talents we never doubt. Conversely, we suspect getting Jack's novel published would be an even greater struggle than he has writing it.

Do Quilty and Jack Torrance (to say nothing of Milich and Marion's father) represent something Kubrick feared in himself? Does the evolution of Quilty to Jack represent how he came to perceive this side of himself and where it could have led to in his family?

Bizarrely, the reason Vivian Kubrick cited for declining to score *Eyes Wide Shut* (she had previously scored *Full Metal Jacket*) was that "the script could awaken some bad memories of satanic ritual abuse she had experienced in a former incarnation."[557] At this point I need to emphasize that I have found absolutely **nothing** to indicate that Kubrick abused his daughters, sexually or otherwise. Nor has anything in this investigation led me to entertain the possibility. By all accounts, Kubrick was fiercely protective of his daughters. During the filming of *Barry Lyndon*, Vivian developed a crush on star Ryan O'Neal, who played into it by engaging in mildly flirtatious behavior with the 12 year old girl. When Kubrick found out, he was outraged and had words with O'Neal that led to a permanent rift in their relationship.[558]

But at the heart of Kubrick's fascination with *Traumnovelle* was the question of whether having "improper" fantasies was the same as acting upon them. Is Bill/Fridolin's attempted infidelities equivalent to Alice/Albertine's fantasies? Kubrick rose to prominence in an era when there was a certain "romanticism" surrounding older men having affairs with teenage girls. This was especially true in the music industry, where blind eyes and winks were directed at rock stars seducing teenage groupies. Kubrick was on the periphery of this scene. Friends like Roman Polanski[559] and James Harris were knee deep in it. Is this a sign that Kubrick fantasized about such things and it troubled him?

Was this the minotaur at the heart of the labyrinth that forever haunted Kubrick?

---

[557] Robert P. Kolker and Nathan Abrams, *Kubrick: An Odyssey*, 569.

[558] Robert P. Kolker and Nathan Abrams, *Kubrick: An Odyssey*, 339.

[559] Kubrick seems to have remained in contact with Polanski until his death. Se Kolker and Abrams, *Kubrick: An Odyssey*, 526.

These are not the type of questions orthodox Kubrick scholars have been willing to ask. One of the best, Nathan Abrams, has noted that while Kubrick is one of the most-written about filmmakers to ever live, very little of it concerns his actual life.[560] Virtually all accounts of Kubrick are concerned exclusively with his films.

This is nowhere more true than among Cryptokubrologists. I was aware of this state of affairs long before I started this book. But even then, it was shocking to see how little actual research Cryptokubrologists have done on their subject. Most seem to give *Room 237* a viewing or two, then begin weaving elaborate narratives over the symbolism in Kubrick's films. This is an approach that's doomed from the beginning. Kubrick is one of the most oblique filmmakers of his era. Without understanding Kubrick the man, it's impossible to put the proper historical, social or cultural context to his films. To say nothing of the personal. Not that that has ever stopped Cryptokubrologists.

And so, to complete the circle, I return to my opening plea. This is not in any way, shape, or form, the final word on the parapolitical aspects of Stanley Kubrick's life. It is hopefully an opening salvo that will generate the kind of archival research into the director's life that he so justly deserves. My hope is that I have made the case for serious scholars with the means to do so to search for the answers to the questions raised here in the Stanley Kubrick Archives and among his remaining family and collaborators.

I truly hope that I have succeeded. No public figure has had a greater influence on my life and career than Mr. Kubrick. As such, this has been the most rewarding project I've ever undertaken, beginning with the lectures this book grew out of up to its completion. After years of admiring Kubrick the filmmaker, I feel as though I've finally started to get a sense of the man behind the pictures. Hopefully those of you who have made it this far will be inspired to get to know Mr. Kubrick better as well.

Or, at least consider something other than Kubrick hoaxing the moon landing...

---

[560] Nathan Abrams, *Stanley Kubrick: New York Jewish Intellectual*, 1.

Printed in Great Britain
by Amazon

43929788R00084